THE MODES
AND MORALS
OF PSYCHOTHERAPY

THE MODES
AND MORALS
OF PSYCHOTHERAPY

Second Edition

Perry London

Harvard University
Graduate School of Education

⬤HEMISPHERE PUBLISHING CORPORATION, Washington
A subsidiary of Harper & Row, Publishers, Inc.

Cambridge   Philadelphia   San Francisco   Washington
London   Mexico City   São Paulo   Singapore   Sydney

THE MODES AND MORALS OF PSYCHOTHERAPY, Second Edition

The first edition of this book was published under the title
The Modes and Morals of Psychotherapy by Holt, Rinehart and Winston, Inc.

This book is in *The Series in Clinical and Community Psychology,* edited by
Charles D. Spielberger and Irwin G. Sarason.

567890 *BRBR* 8987

The principal editorial advisor was Vincent J. Adesso; the sponsoring editors were
Kathleen Roach and F. P. Begell; the editors were Christine R. Flint and Bettie Loux
Donley; the production supervisor was Miriam Gonzalez; the typesetter was Peggy M.
Rote. This book was set in Press Roman by Hemisphere Publishing Corporation.
Braun-Brumfield, Inc. was printer and binder.

Library of Congress Cataloging in Publication Data

London, Perry.
    The modes and morals of psychotherapy.
    (The series in clinical and community psychology)

    Bibliography: p.
    Includes index.
    1. Psychotherapy—Moral and ethical aspects.
I. Title. [DNLM: 1. Ethics. 2. Morals. 3. Psychotherapy.
WM 420 L847m]
RC480.5.L593 1985   174'.2   84-29769
ISBN 0-89116-290-9 (hard cover)
ISBN 0-89116-350-6 (soft cover)
ISSN 0146-0846

This book is dedicated with love to
my lifelong mentor,
RABBI DOCTOR ISRAEL MOWSHOWITZ
Office of the Governor of New York.

Contents

IV
HUMAN COMPLEXITY AND INTEGRATIVE THERAPY

Preface

Books are weapons in the wars among ideas. The first edition of this book, in 1964, was seen as such a weapon, and it (and I) were conscripted as reluctant "irregulars" in the psychotherapy civil wars then being fought. Behavior therapies had not yet found a place in the Establishment, and older competitors were loathe to give them one.

Those conflicts, still alive, have since become less boisterous and more subtle, while psychotherapy of every kind has prospered and proliferated. The two main arguments of the first edition, accordingly, are still in place: psychotherapy is a moralistic as well as scientific enterprise, and its many variations require cataloging, with technique the best foundation for doing this.

These themes, more accepted than they used to be, are not much acted on within "the trade." Students are little more alerted to the moral aspects of their work than they ever were. Nor are they always better schooled in the scientific issues of psychotherapy or trained more broadly today than in the past. The field is still too rife with politics. Because of this, competing methods, some of them excellent, find little hospitality in one another's academic parlors or their clinics. This robs students and practitioners of the knowledge that has increased immensely since the first edition of this book and of the perspective that might come from having it. It may rob the public of the best results that could accrue from psychotherapy.

What's new, these 20 years, does not affect fundamental themes I wrote about in 1964. Seeing them only in the context of those times, however, makes them look antiquated to new students of psychotherapy. This new edition was necessary, therefore, to cover what has happened since: Scholarship and scientific study have done much to resolve conflict and validate the major modes of psychotherapy; spinoffs of familiar therapies have moved the field toward synthesis, integration, and ecumenism, on one hand (Cognitive Behavior Therapies), and toward antinomian religions and recreation on the other (TM, Arica, *est*); and professionalism has grown widespread and diffuse beyond the power of any single group to limit or control the craft. Including these changes in the present text made it necessary to rewrite the entire work. The book is the same as it was in object and design. The words are mostly new.

Part I is an overview. It reports how psychotherapy is often forced to be a moral agency, illustrated by cases and situations where moral dilemmas abound. It tells how therapy's expansion from narrow medical treatment to broad and often ill-defined counsel created confusion; how the study of technique rather than theory is the best way to sort it out; and how most forms of psychotherapy can be strung conceptually on a continuum of techniques intended to give patients insight or move them to healing action. Finally, it sets a historical context of the social and psychological ambience in which psychotherapy developed and became part of a scientific "Establishment" from which the eccentricities of experiential therapies, until very recently, caused their exclusion.

Part II deals with insight therapies, their major techniques, scientific status, and moral problems. Part III does the same, at greater length, for behavior therapies—concentrating on exposure treatments of anxiety as the earliest, most argued, and best proved, and on operant methods—the "purest" behavioral methods theoretically, the most significant socially and, in some views, the most doubtful morally.

Part IV speaks to the "second generation" of behavior therapies and the intellectual and practical forces that gave rise to cognitive behavioral treatments. The important integrative and ecumenical implications of second generation approaches, only now beginning to be taken seriously by the profession, are also briefly discussed. These movements toward integration combine insight and action modes, but all stop short of social integration. Like earlier therapies, they leave individuals to make their own way in society. For this reason, the Integrity Therapy of O. H. Mowrer is treated at length, as the best developed of a treatment genre that aims to integrate individual, society, and morality.

Part V returns to the broad themes of the book. Chapter 13 concerns professionalism and the scientific status of psychotherapy, now well-supported by rigorous research. Chapter 14 speaks to the moral implications of psychotherapists as, necessarily, manipulators of behavior. Where moral issues are involved, they take the roles of secular priests who arbitrate the moral dilemmas of secular people. This is an uncomfortable function, but it is unavoidable, I submit, and can be best pursued by studying what science may have to say of human nature and its moral limits.

The work is longer than the first edition; there is more to say. Its positions are, I hope, clearer, more sharply stated, and better illustrated than they were. It is still meant alike for a general and a scholarly audience. The form is only slightly changed; the "commentary" section has been omitted, and reference to other work is cited parenthetically by date and author in the text. A summarizing "Argument" is given at the opening of each part. For the rest, the Preface to the first edition stands now as it did a generation back.

Finally, I would like to acknowledge those dear friends, colleagues, patrons, and relatives around the world who helped with this book in many ways. For clerical, editorial, or logistical aids, I am grateful to Elizabeth Alberti, Pauline Cooper, and Debra S. London, all of Jerusalem; Marie Bertocci, David Capell, Howard Dippell, Michael Fishman, Dr. David Gordis, Dr. Felice Gordis, Lisa Gordis, Sheila Lammas, and Joel Mogy, all of Los Angeles; Dr. Kathleen Jordan, AT&T Bell Laboratories, New Jersey; T. George Harris, Joel Gurin, and the staff of *American Health*, New York; Helen Stone, Paris; and Edward Keating, Sarasota, Florida, and the Keating Family Foundation. I am in special editorial debt to Dr. Zev Klein, Dean of the Overseas College, Hebrew University of Jerusalem; Dr. Morris Parloff, then Chief, Psychosocial Treatments Research Branch, National Institutes of Mental Health; David Shipler, Israel Bureau Chief of the New York Times; and Dr. Barry Wolfe, Assistant Chief, Psychosocial Treatments Research Branch, National Institutes of Mental Health. Their careful critiques of the whole manuscript produced hundreds of improvements in it. Fred P. Begell of Hemisphere Publishing Corporation was great support through endless drafts and revisions. Finally, my loving thanks to Beverly London, my wife, tough critic, tender coach, and tireless support.

Perry London

February 1984
Jerusalem

Preface to the First Edition

At the cost of militancy and persistence over many years, the craft of psycho-therapy has gained a position of eminence in our society. Its professors and prac-titioners, once contemptuously regarded as eccentrics mumbling arcane obsceni-ties at the fringe of medicine, have advanced from relative obscurity to chairs of eminence and couches of opulence in the finest universities and neighborhoods in the Western World. America, with its mixed traditions of hospitality toward all kinds of ideological novelty and of personal self-seeking, has been the kindli-est of hosts to this endeavor.

But there are reasons to think that psychotherapy has gained more of social respectability than of intellectual integrity. A detailed examination of the surfeit of schools and theories, of practices and practitioners that compete with each other conceptually and economically, shows vagaries which, taken all at once, make unclear what it is that psychotherapists do, or to whom, or why.

If these remarks are critical, they are not meant to be hostile or destructive, but are mainly intended to imply that psychotherapy requires more careful analysis and articulation than it sometimes gets, for it can be best used only when it is most understood.

This book essays to systematize and make explicit some issues and ideas that are critically important to every aspect of psychotherapy but are often only im-plicit in its practice. The burden of its argument involves two main dimensions of discourse.

First is its contention that psychotherapy is a *moralistic* as well as a *scientific* undertaking to such an extent that it cannot be properly understood as the latter unless it is also thoroughly evaluated as the former. Therapists use their technical skills and scientific opinions as the basis for studying and treating their patients, but it is in terms of moral concerns that they decide the ultimate goals and objectives of their treatment. In fact, our society only sanctions the practice of psychotherapy and the existence of therapeutic guilds because of a tacit assumption that the moral order to which therapists address their skills is one that ultimately benefits the social order through its treatment of the needs of individuals. The ambiguities of value inherent in a democratic society make it easy to overlook this fact, just as the ambiguities of the therapeutic process make it easy to overlook the implications of therapy's outcome, but therapists may compromise their integrity by doing so and patients may sacrifice full value of the experience by letting them.

The second major argument of this book is that while the morals of psychotherapy have not been attended to enough, the modes of therapy have multiplied at such a pace that it becomes impossible to attend to them enough if they must be examined one by one. The winds of change in psychotherapy have reached gale force, for better or for worse, and new positions, schemes, and remedies come up so fast, especially among the Action modes, that some of the material in this book is already dated as it goes to press. The very speed and quantity of developments make it vital to design some systematic conceptual scheme in which all kinds of psychotherapies, including many yet to be discovered, can be comprehended, interpreted, and evaluated. The best basis for such a system, it is argued, is the dimension of therapeutic technique, where schools may be positioned according to the normal activities of their expositors. Some thoroughness of understanding of each school is lost thereby, but much is gained, I hope, by way of clarity and perspective.

A word on form: This work is addressed both to a general and to a scholarly audience, and its organization has been designed with the intent of satisfying the specialized needs of the latter without excessively trying the patience and indulgence of the former. For this reason, the body of the work contains no technical references, and footnotes are kept to a minimum, permitting the main arguments to be studied without too many distractions. The Commentary, which contains parenthetical information and arguments, opinions of different authorities, and occasional gossip, also contains complete citations of the many works that were used in the preparation of this one. An index of names is also provided.

Many dozens of students and colleagues were kind enough to criticize part or all of this book while in preparation. Their comments often resulted in alterations of the text that salvaged many parts from falsehoods, errors, and incivilities. For this I am especially grateful to Professors Joseph Becker, Charles Leonhard, and Donald R. Peterson, all of the University of Illinois; Professors Albert Bandura, Kenneth Mark Colby, and Albert Hastorf, and to Mr. Byron Klorfine, Mr. Paul Verden, and Mrs. Suzanne H. Troffer, all of Stanford University; Professors James H. Bryan and Lowell Storms of the University of California at

Los Angeles; Dr. Norman Matlin and Mr. Erik Wensberg, both of Columbia University; Dr. David Rosenhan, of Educational Testing Service.

This work was undertaken at the suggestion of Professor O. H. Mowrer of the University of Illinois and the insistence of Mr. Erik Wensberg, founding Editor of the Columbia University *Forum*. The work of writing it was encouraged and supported by Professors Lloyd G. Humphreys and Donald R. Peterson, respectively Head of the Department of Psychology and Director of Clinical Psychology Training at the University of Illinois.

I am also grateful to Miss Carol Kupers of U.C.L.A. for many hours of congenial help in clerical crises.

Finally, I am indebted to Vivian London for a multitude of editorial and personal aids, of both kinds too many, varied, great, and private to be decently detailed.

Dedicated to the beloved memory of
my father
MAX LONDON (1895-1963)
who urged and inspired me to write books
and
to the memory of
my student
BYRON KLORFINE (1940-1964)
for whose critical approval this book was meant

Los Angeles, California   P.L.
February 1964

I

SCIENCE, MORALS, AND PSYCHOTHERAPY

THE ARGUMENT

Psychotherapy is a moral force, and psychotherapists, in turn, are moral agents as well as healing technicians. Moral problems affect how therapists see their client's needs, set goals of treatment, and work in sessions. The fact is inherent in the enterprise. A century before Freud launched modern psychotherapy, Phillipe Pinel had named his psychiatric methods "moral treatment." A century after, psychotherapy methods are still not "medical" in the common sense. In some ways, they can never be.

It is not all the same for everything psychotherapists do. For much of what they treat, an unvoiced general moral consensus tells them to ease suffering with little care for how the sufferer will live when healed. It needs so much work to learn how to do so, and so much damage comes from faulty craftsmanship, that psychotherapy training, accordingly, has been preoccupied with craft and with its technical results, not with the moral values that inspire it nor the moral quality of its products.

But these are important parts of psychotherapy and always were. Most of its discourse has always concerned the vital social negotiations of people's lives. And the treatment itself was always mainly done by social intercourse. The social life of human beings is the chief arena of their moral concerns. Also, treatment may depend directly on a moral posture of the participants toward how the patient's life is being lived and how it should be lived. Psychotherapy is necessarily, therefore, moral treatment.

If this was true even in therapy's early unpopular years, when only deep neurosis seemed to merit this esoteric medicine, it is now more often seen, as "the acids of modernity" vary the complaints that people bring to psychotherapists, sophisticate their tolerance of their deviant or secret selves, increase their aspirations for well-being, and aggravate the pain of doubting that their lives are meaningful. All mental suffering qualifies today as ground for mental healing.

Nowhere is this more evident than at the margin of problems and of patients where no paralysis, no phobia, no obsession, and no defect of skills disturbs the sufferer, but rather a gap in practice or in peace of mind that separates that person from the rest. There, deviance is the disorder, not just a symptom of it. By definition, where deviance is called disorder, no troubled life is ever lived alone, and our individual splashes in the sea of circumstance sends ripples that overlap each other's tides. There, one person's cure may put another at risk of suffering. Deviance without dysfunction is the touchstone of moral discourse for psychotherapy. For it, this craft is nothing if not moral. For other problems, it is true in less degree. In any case, there are no palpable guidelines for its morality.

The moral agency of psychotherapy did not arise by chance. It is rooted, like the many theories and techniques of therapy, in a scientific thesis—functional autonomy, which says that neurosis is a product of behavior and of mind, not body. Experience found merit in this view. With time, the natural breadth of this taxonomy broadened further to include boundless definitions of disorder by whomever wished, and in whatever terms they fancied relevant. As the boundaries widened for saying what needs treatment, they widened also for deciding what treatment is and what outcomes should be seen as good. Thus therapies multiplied, while theory, method, goals, and moral bearing grew confused, confounded, and diffuse.

To sort and clarify them, technique has most to teach. It is most important to working therapists, most palpable to clients, most concrete, conspicuous and measurable to scientists, and most capable of description to everyone. Cataloged by their techniques, two psychotherapeutic trends or emphases dominate the whole profession academically, economically, and in the stature they command at sources of wealth and power. One stream, here called Insight therapy to reflect the aim and method of its techniques, is represented chiefly by Psychoanalysis and its variants, along with Rogerians, Humanistic-Existential psychotherapy, Gestalt treatment, and many others. The other stream is here called Action therapy to reflect its operations. Most of its subdivisions are called collectively Behavior Therapy, but they vary as much as do Insight therapies, though commonly with shorter histories.

A long polemic between schools in either camp debates what psychotherapy should treat and how the treatment should proceed. Insight therapists have looked most to the meaning of symptoms in people's mental life; they teach them how to explore their minds, to value inner experience, to find those meanings and to be responsible for them. Action therapists have aimed to bring direct relief of symptoms, much as physicians do for many ills. Each approach has yielded some knowledge of behavior, some help with mental troubles, and some scientific enigmas and moral contradictions. Studying their extremes and their virtues, faults, and riddles makes clear why some intellectual offspring of both camps today seek more eclectic and ecumenical techniques and theories for their treatment armories. It also shows the moral quandaries that inhere in all of psychotherapy and which must be seen to understand this enterprise.

1

The Morals of Psychotherapy

Insofar as they are concerned with the diagnosis and treatment of illness, modern psychotherapists have grown up in the tradition of medicine. But the nature of the ailments they deal with and the way they treat them set them apart from physicians and in some ways make them function like clergymen. They deal with sickness of the soul, as it were, which cannot be cultured in a laboratory, seen through a microscope, or cured by injection. Their methods have little of the concreteness or obvious empiricism of the physician's—they carry no needle, prescribe no pill, wrap no bandages. They cure by talking and listening. The infections they expose and destroy are not bacterial nor viral—they are ideas and memories, painful emotions and untoward acts that debilitate people and prevent their functioning well and happily.

Our common understanding of the physician's duty is to relieve people of suffering regardless of their moral condition. Dedicated physicians have always treated the good and bad alike, ministering to their physical needs as best they could.

They have done so for reasons that are technically and theoretically sound. For their technical work, physicians rarely need to look to the moral attributes of their patients, for these generally do not bear on the diagnosis to be made or on how to combat illness. In theory, they are committed to saving and enhancing the patient's life and physical well-being. Duty says: "Treat them all and treat them as they come." It may be the noblest tradition of medicine.

Psychotherapists have been nobly moved to adapt this idea to their craft. In so doing, they think the mental therapist is not a moralist, should not speak to the morals, religion, business, or politics of patients, and has no right, in course of practice, to make value judgments of them, to preach at them, or to promote to them some "good" way of life. Therapy's purpose is to relieve their suffering, their anxiety, their guilt, their mental aberrations, their helpless actions, their neuroses or psychoses, not to change their lives along some moral lines or toward some ideology.

This argument has much to favor. It has helped scholars to study objectively the causes of mental troubles and the kinds of people who suffer from them. It has helped therapists, free of metaphysical concerns, to develop a repertory of techniques that can often be used much as physicians use their store of pills and skills. It has been largely responsible for creating a helping art that has proved useful and that also has legitimate claims to being a scientific discipline.

No one can overstate the value of freedom from morals and metaphysics to the conduct of scientific research, to the choosing of hypotheses, and to the objective treatment of data. But psychotherapists in actual practice rarely do research. They are clinicians. And much of the material with which they deal, as clinicians, is neither intelligible nor usable without thought to some system of values. The fact embarrasses us who would like to be impartial scientists and unbiased helpers. But it is a fact which, for many reasons, may be painfully important to psychotherapists. Moral considerations may largely dictate how they define their clients' needs, how they operate in the therapeutic session, and how they sometimes define "treatment" and "cure" and even "reality."

Many thoughtful psychotherapists already know this. Some find it hard even to define such terms as "health," "illness," and "normality" without some reference to morals or to discuss the treatment of what they have defined without confronting their own moral commitments.

Moral issues may intrude equally in social problems like prostitution or in apparently individual ones like obsessional neurosis. Neither can be called an illness in terms of invasion by germ or virus or the malfunction of body organs. Nor do people die directly from them. They may be abnormal in a statistical sense, but deviating from conventional behavior by itself does not make us worry about them. Living a century or making a million dollars are also deviant statistically. The thing that makes them objectionable (and that is what "problem" means in this connection) involves the violation of the public moral code, in the case of prostitution, and the experience of seemingly avoidable personal suffering in obsession. In both, the idea of a moral desideratum underlies the definition. For prostitution, it has to do with privacy, promiscuity, and sexual liberty. For obsession, it has to do with the moral values we place on people's preoccupations (obsessions about making money, career achievements, and social success are not judged as harshly, i.e., in need of treatment, as obsessions about health, cleanliness, and sin). In neither case can the moral question be separated neatly from the technical problem of dysfunction which health scientists would like to stick to.

Yet psychotherapeutic training programs in psychiatry, psychology, social work—even in the ministry—often do not deal seriously with the problem of morals. Psychotherapy writing is full of principles of procedure and goals, but seldom speaks to their possible moral implications. Indeed, it often fails to mention that there is a moral as well as scientific side to psychotherapy, though its scientific goals are implicitly rationalized by its moral ones. Are therapists themselves unconscious of these deep difficulties in their work? Or is it the opposite—that they are well aware but find that, as Marie Jahoda puts it, "[it] seems so difficult that one is almost tempted to claim the privilege of ignorance" (1958, p. 77). Either way, ignorance is useless here, or harmful.

At some level of abstraction, every aspect of psychotherapy assumes some implicit moral doctrine. But we need not seek this level to see why it is important for therapists to recognize the moral concomitants of patients' problems and the moral implications of some solutions. Some problems are inevitably moral ones as either client or therapist see them; some can be viewed as more strategic and be treated without reference to morals. In the one case, therapists must fulfill a moral agency in order to function; in the other, they may take the impartial helping role with which they usually identify. But if they do not know the difference, then their own morals will influence their technical activity willy-nilly to mold clients to their own image or lead unwittingly to moral postures they abhor.

MORALS AS TECHNICALITIES

Many problems do not require much moralistic concern by therapist or patient. There are more or less purely technical problems that can be solved on more or less purely empirical grounds. Many phobias will yield to psychotherapy without much thought to the values that underlie its use. Many psychogenic ills may be treated without much invading of patients' value systems or contesting their moral codes or even knowing much of them. Some family conflicts are eased by merely helping people talk and listen to each other, helping them learn that feelings can be voiced without disaster, and so on.

It takes little moral scrupulosity for therapists to want to free people of phobias or psychogenic symptoms and families of conflict. It is precious to belabor these as moral issues, not because they have no moral underpinnings, but because consensus about them almost everywhere is great.

The technical treatment problem that is also a critical moral problem goes more like this: How should a therapist deal with a client who anxiously reports that he has robbed someone or raped someone? Suppose a devoutly religious patient says she has guilty conflicts about sex relations or contraceptives. What is a therapeutic answer to someone who feels that his behavior or his thoughts violate God's will, defile the Church, and are beyond his control?

Or suppose the opposite: a client tells his therapist some awful act that he has done about which he *does not* feel guilt, anxiety, or conflict; suppose he reports some huge violation of the therapist's moral code (Hare-Mustin, Maracek, Kaplan & Liss-Levinson, 1979). What should therapists do for all these? Avoid comment? Refer to the patient's ostensible code but not to their own? Dodge the moral issue and dive into other aspects of the behavior?

All therapy schools try to free people of unrealistic conflicts—but when conflicts revolve around moral issues, can helpers dodge them? Is it possible to decide whether some conflict is realistic without moral involvement? It is specious or irresponsible to say, as some therapists do, that all moral concerns are displays of "resistance" or that therapy deals only with "emotional," not "moral" problems. The common injunction of most treatment schools not to moralize at clients may be good technical advice, but it is a feeble answer to a robust question—will "not moralizing" by itself help with such problems?

Even as a technical question, it is unclear what a therapist should do here. Any of several responses may be good technique. The therapist might reflect, interpret, probe the origins of the problem, or its severity, or its rhythms and recurrences. Some therapists might challenge clients to face their own impulses. Some would disapprove their guilt. Some would soothe their anger or anxiety. Some might inquire of their feelings more, ask them to describe this or think on that or understand some other thing. Common to most techniques, I think, is first, that therapists say something and, second, that what they say almost never gives an opinion of the moral issue itself. Morality, the "*oughts*" and "*shoulds*" of conduct sprung from our ideas of right and wrong, is not the ostensible concern of psychotherapy.

These issues, however, may be deep concerns of clients. Just as most of us look carefully to our material and emotional interests, we also try to serve our moral interests well enough to feel that we are "good," whatever "good" may mean. Most people, sensibly, do not separate emotional and moral in their minds. Both kinds of care, often confounded, bring them to therapists in the first place, and a main thing that keeps them there is hope that treatment will give their lives more meaning and satisfaction in both respects. This very hope moves them to make the psychotherapist more important than many other people in their lives; they see the therapist, more or less correctly, as the agent for resolving their conflicts. The force of this agency, in areas where moral issues figure, puts therapists in the role of moralists whether or not they wish to play it.

Struggling too much to avoid this role can lead to logical ambushes and untenable postures. A supervising therapist I know, for instance, made it a cardinal rule "never to get involved in the politics or religion of the patient." But where a client made them explicit issues, she could not tell students how to avoid involvement other than by not offering their personal politics or religion as models to emulate. This is but half a tactic. Should the therapist list domains of discourse, sets of topics, ideas that are permitted or forbidden in the therapeutic hour? Or allow patients to talk about anything they wish, but say the therapist cannot talk back about A, B, or C? Or what?

A psychoanalyst friend of mine answered a patient's anxious queries about his reactions to her guilt-ridden behavior by saying, "Why should I give a damn how you act?" But another time, addressing the same activity, he said that he would stop therapy if she continued "acting-out." In the first instance, he was expressing his moral indifference to her actions, while in the second he was responding to the same behavior as a technical problem of treatment. Does the distinction make sense? Should we expect clients to honor it?

The logical embarrassment of strained moral "neutralism" is perhaps clearest in the words of a third therapist who says, "Working in the privacy of the consulting room, I don't care if the outside world is coming down around my patient's ears." Would this still be true if the financial world of the patient were collapsing, threatening his fee collections? Or if the client was "acting out" in a way that "interfered" with therapy?

Obviously, the therapist's concern with the patient's life outside the session will be expressed sometimes in ways that pass *de facto* value judgments on it. Some of that concern, and of its expression, will deal with morality.

MORALS AS GENERALITIES

Considering the purely technical problem puts a broader question into bold relief: What does the therapist wish finally to accomplish? What are the ultimate goals of treatment? The technical problem deals mostly with immediate goals, with how to conduct the session, but this asks what therapists wish to happen to their patients, not just in treatment, but in life. How do I, as therapist, want my ministrations to change the client's life?

This is a moral question which therapists answer in practice, whether or not they ever do in words. The answer is made in terms of their own superordinate, if unvoiced, moral codes (Halleck, 1971). Sometimes its moral quality is hidden by the impersonal scientific sounding language of mental health—but it is less subtly masked in the words of the minister who counsels against homosexuality because of its "harmful psychological effects"; of the Catholic caseworker opposing her client's divorce because it is "mentally disrupting"; of the sexual libertarian who helps a client accept the "psychological legitimacy" of extramarital affairs. Such therapeutic goals reflect personal morals, not scientific conclusions.

Perhaps the most general and accurate statement that self-conscious therapists could make about their goals might be: "I want to reshape people's lives so that they will emulate values I cherish for myself, aspire to what I wish humanity to be, and thus fulfill my need for the best of all possible human worlds."

It is a truism that therapists are themselves human beings, that they live in society, and that wisely or blindly, responsibly or casually, they make moral commitments to themselves and that society. My argument only takes this platitude to a logical, if unheeded, conclusion—that the nature of their interactions with patients involves therapists in moral confrontation where moral discourse, even communicating some of their personal morality, may be necessary to their therapeutic work (London, 1981; Robitscher, 1980).

No one seriously objects to this position in the case of the pastoral counselor, for he is commonly committed to a religious moral system which is known to most clients before they ever get to him. No one expects a Catholic priest to "accept" robbery or adultery as something less than sin, regardless of his immediate response to their confession. He may understand the cause, eagerly temper judgment of the act, and deeply empathize with the anguish of its perpetrator— but there is no doubt he sees the act as sin and the actor as sinner, no matter what cause inspired it. For the priest, despite all else, believes that we are responsible individually for our acts, that we choose them freely, and that we must sometime pay the price of that choice—and the person who confesses knows this all along.

That the psychotherapist's situation differs much from the priest's is, I believe, a convenient fiction. To any incident a client reveals, the psychotherapist responds, or so is seen to do. Some may avoid emphatic positive or negative responses—some may show a studied neutral attitude, and may devoutly feel no censure or approval of what they have been told. But to regard this neutrality as an amoral position, to salve one's democratic, egalitarian, or relativistic conscience, to convince ourselves that we "are not imposing our value systems on the client"—because we wish not to—is finally to deceive both clients and ourselves. This belief implicitly denies an essential of the therapeutic relationship: that its main elements are the *interactions* of participants, not their private experiences (Frank, 1973). Psychotherapy is a peculiar kind of social encounter, an interpersonal exchange which differs for the roles of client and of therapist, but which is nonetheless reciprocal.

Several forces compel the therapist to become a moral agent. For one thing, therapists influence the moral postures of patients because they always interpret therapist responses to their moral concerns. If therapists approve clients' behavior, they may reinforce it; if they disapprove, they may change it. If therapists seem neutral, clients may interpret this as either tacit approval or disapproval—and often, it will be one of them, complicated by the therapist's fears of upsetting the patient or reluctance to dictate rules of propriety. Merely permitting these things to be discussed legitimizes clients' efforts to interpret therapists' reactions to them.

Secondly, therapists too have value systems, morals of their own. It is hard to see how they could form relationships with clients in order even to understand them, never mind help them, without privately comparing their values. The ability to *not* respond to such comparisons, to suspend one's own beliefs enough to totally restrain the attitudes that flow from them, must be rare indeed. And carried to its own extreme, does it not remove the therapist from all caring, if not from all interaction? The few studies that have explored the question empirically have found that therapists do communicate their values to patients, with or without intending to and even, perhaps, without consciously comparing their own (Murray, 1956; Parloff, Goldstein, & Iflund, 1960; Parloff, Iflund, & Goldstein, 1957; Truax, 1966; Wolfe, 1977). An extreme of such communication occurs when a therapist threatens to quit therapy if the client does not obey orders. That the value involved for the therapist is technical rather than moral is beside the point. It is the therapist's value, not the client's.

Third, and least important, therapists are affiliated with professional societies which publish codes of ethics setting rules of professional conduct. Breach of these rules may see therapists expelled from their societies. Whether or not they explicate the codes to their clients, professionally ethical therapists act on them in treatment.

IMPLICATIONS

If one accepts the idea that psychotherapists are moral agents and that this agency may be intrinsic to their functions, some important issues take shape.

It becomes clear, for one thing, that many topics of psychotherapy are mental health matters only by terribly broad definition of that term. Some of them are matters of religion, politics, and social and economic behavior far removed from most psychiatric diagnoses. This has always been obvious to American mental health experts watching Soviet psychiatrists hospitalize political dissidents for "psychiatric disability." But the same question applies to social mores within conventional psychiatry. The psychiatric status of homosexuality is one such issue, debated repeatedly by the American Psychiatric Association (Davison, 1982; Paul, Weinrich, Gonsiorek, & Hotvedt, 1982). And it is sometimes painfully clear where political issues overlap visibly with mental problems which are very amenable to psychotherapy. American therapists faced this in the Vietnam War and Israelis in the Lebanon War—soldiers suffering combat neuroses could be treated psychologically and returned to battle. Should therapists who opposed their governments' policies in those wars have treated them or not? Therapists may have no special competence to decide such things, but they must not disengage themselves from concern with them (London, 1979; London, Engelhardt, & Newman, 1982; Shipler, 1983; Watson, 1978).

Such problems are not wholly solvable in free societies. But they would be better handled if, to begin with, therapists became more vividly aware of their own moral investments and thought more about those of their clients. Students of therapy are too often encouraged to view their clients, themselves, and their work exclusively in terms of dynamics, drives, impulses, defenses, relationships, contingencies, and stimulus-response systems. Too little attention has been paid to consonant and conflicting ideologies, philosophies, and moral codes which are important to therapists' and patients' lives and all the more important to know if they are hidden or inarticulate, and therefore subtly mold or sabotage the psychotherapeutic work.

Second, it is apparent that so-called moral neutrality in the psychotherapist is as much a moral position as any blatant one. It is, from the therapist's side, a libertarian position, regardless of how the client sees it (some, indeed, may see it as insidious). Expressed in different ways, this posture is popular with therapists of many schools. Some of the justifying terms of moral neutrality are "democracy," "growth," "fulfillment," "self-realization" or "-actualization," and "responsibility." All these are ideals oriented toward people's freedom to do as they please. Balanced against them, in some therapeutic ideologies, are such terms as "productivity" or "social responsibility." Both terminologies, meant seriously, suggest that psychotherapists see their work as a potent force in people's lives and by implication, therefore, in society. Should they, in that case, feel obliged to represent themselves as social agents to the public or their clients? And if so, then agents for what set of codes? Societies reflect systems of morality within themselves, and open societies, as in the Western democracies, reflect competing codes. Should therapists as moralists, further, feel obliged to take part publicly in the moral arguments of political and economic life—or should they stick to the special area of their competence?

The question may seem less academic in relation to individual patients rather than the whole society: When, and in what ways, may (should) therapists actively be moralists with clients? Should they, or may they, contest the moral intent of clients when they think it inadequate—or immoral? Can they, in good conscience, permit in patients any behavior that serves such therapeutic goals as freeing them of guilt or anxiety? Would this not casually elevate personal adjustment to a supreme value—and is this not an insufficient goal for the human community?

Starting with the technical problem, the string of issues that evolve seems inescapable. Either therapists can intentionally influence behavior or they cannot, and they have little choice of what to claim. To say they cannot or may not in areas of great human concern, and so are not responsible for how their clients live, is to reduce their right to be in business.

But if they claim the ability to influence people, as they rightly can and do, then they must shoulder some responsibility for that influence. They must see themselves as moral agents as they are faced with moral problems. And they are faced with them more and more in modern times as therapeutic discourse broadens to include areas for which traditional moral guides are ignored or incredible to the very people who ask therapists for guidance—with sex, marriage and family, personal responsibility, the worth of ambition, duty to parents, children, friends, lovers, country, principle. Morals are the ultimate values by which we judge our acts. Psychotherapy is one arena in which such judgments now are made. It will not escape that role in our time.

Psychotherapists may be ill-suited to assume this role, but they cannot escape it. In such a strait, they may best serve themselves and those they hope to aid, by studying this agency to see what it entails.

2

The Blurred Boundaries of Psychotherapy

Until recently, almost everyone was content to define health by its absence (in illness) and illness by the presence of symptoms. People went to doctors to be cured of ailments which had symptoms, signs that they were sick. For centuries now, without defining health, doctors have increasingly succeeded at curing illness by finding precise sources of it and specific agents of healing. Good physicians may be indifferent to theoretical definitions of health, but their work takes due regard of the empirical definition of illness. Essentially, it says, illness is defined by the presence of symptoms.

In this view, health is simply the state in which symptoms are absent; treatment is the process of removing them, and cure is the state in which they are continuously absent after treatment ends.

In early use, the idea of *mental* illness referred, somewhat ambiguously, both to oddities of thinking or feeling that resulted from some bodily ill and to oddities of body function that seemed to stem from disorders of thought or feeling. The latter conditions inspired modern psychotherapy when Breuer and Freud began to mine the discovery that some symptoms with no obvious organic basis will yield to psychological assault.

These notions of mental illness are still sound, but they no longer suffice to describe most problems for which people nowadays seek psychotherapy. Most of them, it seems, are "pure" problems of thought and feeling, like anxiety, depression, and discontent. People have "psychological problems" or "emotional difficulties" or "disordered personalities" or are "maladjusted" or, on the face of it, plain "unhappy" (Mellinger et al., 1983).

It is remarkable how this once arcane and obscure branch of medicine, in barely three generations, generated a popular, lucrative, and influential profession which has little obvious connection with the scientific-seeming practice of medicine. Even more remarkably, this once narrowly clinical endeavor has generated a secular moralism which has impressed itself profoundly on the Western world, and without much benefit of scientific "authority." These things have happened, I think, as the result of two phenomena that inevitably resulted from "the talking cure":

First, the psychological approach to symptoms tended to elicit information of much broader scope than just the details of people's aches, anxieties, and obsessions. That begins naturally when a healer thinks to treat someone with conversation instead of prescription, injection, ritual, or incantation. It is extended as the doctor persuades the patient to join in discourse. And it becomes prolific, as in Breuer and Freud's work, when the patient is told to talk about anything that comes to mind. The invitation to talk confers the blessing of relevance, and the presence of a willing, healing audience tempers the stigma of shame or dishonor that may cloud one's private thoughts. What started as a mere report to an alienist on migraine headaches or paralyzed limbs may become a verbal flood of problems in living, of interpersonal conflicts and frightening sexual and aggressive themes, of sin, horror, agony, and fear. If, during this process, symptoms are relieved, it makes sense for doctors to connect the contents of the dialogue with the origin of the symptoms. And it is some tribute to their genius that they invent an orderly explanation of how a mental process creates bodily symptoms when an organic event cannot be found to do so.

The second result of the talking cure was that the definition of symptoms expanded to include problems that previously had no specific relationship to health or illness, such as unhappiness. Once a connection was made between disordered body function and psychological upset, suggesting that mental problems gave rise to some physical ailments, it was reasonable to see those problems as proper objects of treatment before they made someone physically ill. From there, it is just as plausible to treat psychological problems even if they would never create physical illness, because they are themselves major problems of life.

The horizons of psychotherapy thus widened steadily as its advocates found ever better reasons for taking an ever broader range of troubles in its scope. Armed with rationales fit for the spirit of scientific inquiry, without religious messianism or parochial buffoonery or claims to the supernatural, psychotherapy gained appeal among educated people as a useful means of easing their problems of living even when they were not "sick." The goal of "normalizing," as M. B. Parloff said, merged with that of "optimizing" (Parloff, 1982).

SCIENCE AND MORALITY

If the scope of practice was broadened inevitably, so was the scope of inquiry. Expanding the therapeutic dialogue raises the question "What do symptoms signify?" or "What are they symptomatic of?" This suggests an underlying source hidden from the naked eye which, probed deeply enough, makes us eventually confront the question, "What is really wrong?" If the observed symptom is not the "real" trouble, but something overlaid on it, could not what underlies the symptom in turn be but an overlay of something underlying it? The problem is both what to look for and when to stop the search. The idea that there are levels of problems implies that there is some core or basement of concern. Thus working backward step by step, at risk of infinite regress, inquiry gets focused more and more narrowly on the "essential" nature of things. For therapists, the self-imposed limit on the question, the basement of concern, addresses human nature.

The expansion of symptoms raises a less academic but tougher practical question. If any psychological distress is a legitimate target of psychotherapy, then against what cost should the effort to ease it be measured and in terms of what gain should it be valued? Willy-nilly, subjunctives like "ought" and "should" must be called on to decide such things. "How ought people to behave? How ought they to feel? What ought they to want? "How much should they be ready to pay for what they may get—in instability, time, money, effort, pain?"

The first problem poses a question of *fact,* the second a question of value or *moral* judgment. The distinction deserves attention, especially in scientific discourse, for facts define science and moral judgments are excluded from it.

For scientific purposes, a fact is anything potentially measurable. Scientific work concerns facts and their relationships, nothing else. A scientific hypothesis is a guess about facts that have not been measured, and a theory is a body of systematic, logically related guesses, based on known facts, about unknown facts. Scientific work cumulates facts—that is, measurable realities—and tries to predict the factual consequences of their visible or probable relationships. By definition, it avoids evaluations other than factual, that is realistic (as opposed to idealistic) ones. The *desirability* of an event, as opposed to its *predictability,* is outside the scope of science. In terms of "good" or "bad," it is a problem in morals. Science asks such questions as: "What will happen if . . . ?" and "What will then happen if that happens?" But for such questions as: "Is it good or bad that such-and-such happens?" it can do nothing. It only tells what will happen next, not whether you ought to want it to happen.

Morals do not theoretically depend on facts, but the advocates of moral systems always justify them by beliefs about the factual nature of things. Moral theses may start either with the idea that "such-and-such is the way to be" and then propose some factual reality on which the moral rests, or "such-and-such are the facts of nature" and assert some ideal behavior that is consonant with them. Social and religious doctrines develop in both directions. Science starts and ends with thought only of the nature of things. Scientists, however, do not. They care as much as anyone about what is good and bad, desirable or not. Since their work is devoted to the rigors of finding what is true (with respect to facts), moreover, they sometimes think they have a better platform than others for judging also what is good (Skinner, 1971). That is why what they may start as a technical enterprise sometimes ends up as a sweeping world view and moral philosophy that takes in more than they originally dreamed. Far from being intentional, however, this progression may happen almost absentmindedly, with scientists and technicians largely ignorant that their technical adventures verge on moral systems.

THE MEANING OF NORMAL

One such transition in the therapeutic arts is the ambiguous meaning that "normality" has acquired. Technically, "normal" is a term that describes a statistical phenomenon. If a measure is taken of a very large number of individuals, and half of them fall above and half below a certain point on the measuring rod, with most falling close to it and fewer and fewer falling further from the point in equal proportions on both sides of it, then the whole array is called a normal distribution.

Seen this way, normality is not a property of *persons,* but only of *characteristics* shared in some degree by everyone. In statistical use, things like height or intelligence are normally distributed among all people. It would be wrong to say that someone has normal height or intelligence; such a phrase applies to the term "normal" in another sense, where it means *average,* or usual. Thus, to say that people are normally tall or bright is to say they have average intelligence or height. In this meaning, "abnormal" means unusual, i.e., different from average.

Neither of these meanings refers to any moral evaluation—to good or bad, holy or profane, desirable or repulsive. Scientific use of these terms is always purely descriptive. Any scientific evaluation will be evaluative *only* with respect to some fact. Thus, it is good to be abnormally tall (unusual in height) *if* one wishes to be a basketball star, and it is good to be abnormally short *if* one sleeps in the trunk of a small auto. Such statements imply nothing about the virtues of playing basketball or of camping in cars; no such scientific statement is possible except in terms of some function that may be *measurably* served by either fact.

In common talk about behavior, however, "normal" is used to mean "acceptable" or "healthy," if not "optimal," and "abnormal" is used synonymously with "bad," "sick," and so forth. This is not only a popular misuse. It is widespread in professional circles, and one wonders what the mislabeling may lend to misunderstanding. Textbooks in abnormal psychology, for instance, are mostly about pathology, not about the intellectually gifted, the artistically creative, nor the unusually happy, integrated, or productive people who, as statistical "abnormals," deserve some space. Not that they should have; the title is in question here, not the practice.

The idea of statistical normality is most useful to scientists, especially in the life sciences. How has it happened, then, that this valuable notion has been damaged in handling by people who should know better? How has the term "abnormality" passed from a descriptive statistic to a moral pejorative? Maybe it occurred in the same way that science and morality get confounded in psychotherapy—unwittingly, by the thoughtless imposition of value and fact upon each other, by casually assuming that norms can suit values when the one has not been measured and the other not defined, by the failure to weigh means (techniques) against ends (goals) and both against fact. Much of this, I believe, results from the huge variety of topics which must be handled in therapeutic practice. Devoted therapists must address so many pains so variably expressed, that they are likely to use some patchwork of whatever seems to work, mindless of abstractions about science or morals. And if what seems to work works well enough to give their patients some relief, then they remember what they have done long enough to repeat it and well enough to teach it. They rationalize it too, with theory of a kind, but maybe not too well nor very far beyond this case. Dedicated therapists can be fascinated by the case, and even were they not, the public sometimes seems to pound on their doors, pleading for help that they must give as best they can. They are busy folk, intelligent and good willed, but not much given to aloof reflection on their work. If they thought much about astrology or faith healing or the working of priestly castes, or even confidence games, they might see ironic and worrisome parallels between parts of their own and some less scientific crafts. But pure motive narrows vision, especially of busy people. Surfeit of busyness elicits straitness which, lacking perspective, wastes effort which, hindering success, makes more busyness . . . and on and on.

PROFESSIONAL CONFUSIONS

Despite these problems, the results for the public of psychotherapy have not been bad, indeed far better than hostile critics have claimed and possibly far better than many branches of medicine (Parloff, 1983). For the circle of professional colleagues, however, the results have been controversial and prodigiously hard to interpret.

Psychotherapists have responded to ever-increasing needs for service, since the end of World War II, by expanding training and service programs and promoting the use of public funds for this purpose. Training in psychotherapy, as in all healing arts, is mostly by apprenticeship, where one learns to perform in accord with the demands of one's teacher. This is unlike engineering school, where the person of the teacher has no bearing on the performance of what is learned. Bridges stand or fall on their own merit. Nor is it just like learning to play the piano, paint pictures, or carve furniture, skills also learned by apprenticeship, for performance in these arts can be easily submitted to the judgment of large audiences. Nor is it even quite like learning medicine, in which erstwhile patients may, through incompetent performance, become patent victims. In psychotherapy, there is no large body of truth yet that stands apart from its discoverer and no audience to attend its performance; evidently too, nobody dies from it. Finally, if the patients are not always sick before treatment, as many therapy clients are not, how can they be judged well after it? Under the circumstances, training in psychotherapy necessarily involves the perpetuation of error in some unknown degree. For some of its advocates, this ignorance comes to seem less ignorant as it becomes more venerable, expanding error in the same direction. For others, it grows stale with age and pallid, inviting novel truths—or errors. No one knows.

Plainly, in any case, when the main measure of performance is the judgment of the teacher, changes will occur from one professional generation to the next. For bright students will think their own thoughts and have ideas beyond their mentors' conceit. The more personal one's teaching, the more divergent will be some pupils' learning. Then, if the teacher has low tolerance for dissent, and the student has small need to stay close or great need to stand free, they will part (Alexander, 1982; Gitelson, 1962). And when, as often happens, the student grows enamoured of his own experience, gets busy exploiting it and generalizes about it, a school is born. Thus Freud begat Jung, Adler, and Rank; Rank begat Rogers, and so on. It exaggerates to say that there are more therapists than schools only because it takes two to make a school, but there are enough schools now so that one catalogue of over 250 psychotherapies admits to several omissions (Herink, 1980)!

Maybe it is true that the profusion of schools, like Chairman Mao's "thousand flowers," signifies intellectual ferment, but it may also be true that new schools have about the same value as old ones, the more so when they are built on about the same structure. This commonly includes reverence for the founder; fascination with individual cases and generalization from them; some confusion of theory with technique, the former often struck from the latter mint; and the interposition of science and morals. Since most research shows that all kinds of psychotherapy benefit most clients, the abundance of schools shows the weakness of psychotherapy as an applied science; it does not signify different assaults on different problems but, with few exceptions, competing tactics in the same battle. That all treatments tend to work better than no treatment does not prevent many from being what Jerome Frank calls "weak" treatments (Frank, 1973, 1979).

A clue to the weak scientific status of some therapies lies in their close identification with the lives of their creators and with the personal biases of their practitioners. I know few medical students who can identify Sherrington or Fleming or Harvey, much less tell Galen from Vesalius, but still fewer psychotherapy students who freely admit to ignorance about the life of Freud, let alone his theories or techniques. (They are right to blush, in part; psychotherapy has not advanced so far that psychoanalysis can be dismissed, in its "old age," as irrelevant to the therapeutic problems of today. The life of Freud, however, is another matter.) A favorite bait of neo-Freudians, such as Clara Thompson and Erich Fromm, is that Freud's theories cannot be evaluated properly independdently of the intellectual currents of the late 19th century and the social environment of Central Europe, or the emancipation of the Jews from the ghetto or their traditions of religious mysticism. For historical or sociological evaluation, they are right. But for evaluating the scientific truth of Freud's theories—that is, their power to predict unknown facts—the demand for such context is wrong. Newton's physics need not be understood as part of the 17th century or his calculus in the light of his religious mysticism. I have heard therapy students dismiss the scientific worth of C. G. Jung's theories because they think he was a Nazi sympathizer, but no parallel proposal has come from atheistic mathematicians to abolish Cartesian coordinates because their creator was a devout Catholic. There is a striking correlation between how much a science has been validated and how little reference is made to personalities in teaching it.

THE COMPONENTS OF THERAPY SYSTEMS

We do not need to know the history of psychotherapy to study its scientific and moral implications, but we do need to know its components. To do so, we must distinguish *systems* or *schools* of treatment from *methods* or *devices* which claim to be systems or schools, but are not. Most of the treatments involved in today's inflation of therapeutic brand names, I believe, are not systems of psychotherapy, even though they may be therapeutic, that is, helpful in easing the troubles to which they are applied. To qualify as a *system,* a psychotherapy scheme must have three parts: (1) a theory of personality, which addresses the nature of human behavior; (2) a superordinate set of goals, that is, a moral code, usually implying a social philosophy, i.e., an optimal organization of society and of individual relationships to it; and (3) a set of techniques, i.e., of deliberate means for manipulating or influencing behavior.

Personality theories are inherently scientific efforts because they deal entirely with questions of fact. They bear on morals in two respects: First, the theoretical limits of behavior set the theoretical limits of moral expectations. If human nature dictates the way people behave under certain conditions, a sane moral scheme cannot order them to act differently in those circumstances. Second, so little is actually known about the determinants of behavior, that all personality theories are thoroughly speculative. To the extent they are untested, the moral implications one may derive from them have no more scientific value than do the morals of revealed religion. They are based on faith, not fact.

If what scholastics call Natural Law existed, it would be embodied, for our purposes, in the facts that verified personality theory. But few of those facts are actually known, so that no moral code which borrows authority from personality theory can correctly claim much scientific support.

Social philosophies, like other moral codes, are more implied than stated in most psychotherapy systems and are no more scientific. Whether they are derived from theories of personality or from apparent historical or social fact, they pile one speculation on another. No one knows if there has ever been an "original" society or if there exists any "natural" social organization or relationship between society and individuals. Anyway, socially concerned psychotherapists are really concerned with the possibility of an *optimal* social organization, not a natural one. Social philosophies of psychotherapists, therefore, are moral doctrines, suggesting how people ought to live to optimize society or waiving the duties of individuals to social orders unworthy of their efforts.

Therapy techniques are scientific to the degree they predict specific outcomes and processes. Until recently, most therapy systems have been imprecise in specifying either. Most of those that do specify to date have not tested their predictions. Most of those that test have produced mixed results. Most impressive results are protean—hard to assess, controversial, or suspect.

The main moral implications of techniques arise from the assumption that they work. For many treatments, this has been shown enough by hundreds of studies to dismiss the question of whether psychotherapy in general is worth doing. It is. The moral issues surrounding techniques are more immediate than those of behavior theory or social philosophy, for it is technique, not theory, that is actually imposed on people. These issues include the possibility that using a given technique (even if it is unsuccessful) assaults the moral codes of patient, therapist, or society, and that if successful, the resulting change in the client will violate common moral standards or create doubtful new ones.

The bulk of thoughtful psychotherapy writing does not separate moral and scientific issues nor divide treatment into the component parts suggested here. For many years, most of it derived from case studies used to illustrate theory with little mention of technique or social philosophy. Or it would specify theory, mixing technique with it as if they were interdependent, or spell out technique with seeming indifference to the other parts. Social philosophy would get shortest shrift in most psychotherapy books, except in works of social philosophy derived from psychotherapy, such as those of Erich Fromm (1941, 1947, 1955). In them, the actual techniques of psychotherapy had no place.

Early writers on psychotherapy, like Freud and Jung, were aware of the ultimate problems of human life which bear on psychotherapy (Rieff, 1961; 1966). But they were not concerned with its moral implications at the level of everyday conduct. More attention has been paid to them in recent years. It ranges widely in orientation. At one extreme, philosopher-physician Tristram Englehardt, Jr., says that psychotherapy (like medicine in general) involves a "meta-ethic," that is, that it prepares people to choose their own ethical positions rather than offering any ethic of its own (Englehardt, 1973). Allan E. Bergin, at the other, advocates a frank therapeutic moral posture of "theistic realism" to counter the "clinical pragmatism" and "humanistic idealism" which now, in his view, are the dominant (if unarticulated) moral positions of most psychotherapists (Bergin, 1980). Their thoughtful statements, like some intermediate positions, are not characteristic of the therapy literature. In this respect, it is somewhat muddled.

This muddle was a natural result of historical and professional exigencies that were not always avoidable. But it has gone on too long. It obstructs full understanding of psychotherapy by preventing therapists from defining their functions, clients from seeing its limits, and everyone from accepting its ambiguities. The biggest obligation falls on psychotherapists, for they have wares to sell. If they wish to be applied scientists, they must act like scientists, critically examining their work and perhaps discarding some ingrained myths about themselves. If they wish to be arbiters of morality, as maybe they must, they would do well to know it, and maybe to say so. If they hope to discover some scientifically viable moral code, they will have to become sharply aware of the problems involved to launch the search, let alone find anything. In any case, it seems clear that a society as hell-bent as ours on using science to promote a good life will not permit them to muddle through the next four generations plying their trade as they did the last four. In the United States, there have been hints of such concern in legislative rumblings about whether psychotherapy should be covered by health insurance. Such concerns are good for the profession as for the society, for they mean that psychotherapists must examine and improve themselves to earn the decent regard of those they serve.

3

The Modes of Psychotherapy

In its halcyon early days, champions of psychoanalysis sometimes defended it against hostile critics with the argument, innocently borrowed from the Mystery religions of old, that one had to experience psychoanalysis personally to appreciate it. For psychotherapy in general, this argument might read, applied to patients: It is easier to undergo psychotherapy than to describe it. For therapists, read: It is easier to practice psychotherapy than to explain it. Few professions are at once so popular and so hard to articulate.

The reason, I think, is not that psychotherapy is an abstruse or esoteric subject, but because the usual explanations of it contain a theoretical discourse quite removed from what actually goes on. The practice of psychotherapy revolves around some rather concrete techniques, but most efforts to explain it involve some theory of behavior or personality. The connection between technique and theory is often tenuous, and the failure to separate them can create confusion. The upshot is that no one can say precisely what psychotherapy is, or to whom it should be addressed, or how, or why.

It is hard to know how clear understanding can be gained, but a good way to begin may be by studying psychotherapy techniques, which have been the stepchildren of therapeutic discourse. If we do not probe the minutiae of techniques, but their thematic qualities, then we may find, amidst the mass of labels, that only a narrow range of therapeutic schemes exists, with some major differences between them. So let us look at what therapists do or say they do.

PUBLIC CONFUSIONS

One would think that people who need psychotherapy have enough troubles already without having to sort out one kind of therapist from another. But sort they must if they are wise, as endless articles on how to choose a psychotherapist make clear. And if they resort to the ocean of soft-cover case histories, psychic autobiographies, and self-help manuals on the subject, they are sure to have some of these problems:

First and least important, several professions have vested interests in practicing psychotherapy: psychiatrists, psychologists, and social workers all officially use it. Most people do not know the differences between these professions—and indeed, with respect to psychotherapy, most differences that are not financial are fictitious; psychiatrists earn more than psychologists who earn more than social workers. One cannot foretell differences in therapy training or competence from the profession therapists belong to.

It is more confusing, perhaps, that psychotherapy is also practiced in many other professions which differ in functions as well as titles. Some of them find it impolitic, for legal, commercial, or other reasons, to label their work "psychotherapy." Ministers who do psychotherapy call it "pastoral counseling"; educators may call it "guidance"; and a host of persons with credentials in any or all or none of these professions call their psychotherapies "marital counseling" or "psychoanalysis" or "assertiveness training" or "sex therapy" or "*est*" or "encounter" or "TM" or "TA" or "stress management" or "relaxation training" or still other terms. Most of these labels do not refer to a profession and most of them overlap in meaning with several others. All of them are functional equivalents, in whole or in part, admitted or not, to "psychotherapy."

(Psychotherapy, as I am using it, refers to techniques deliberately used for their psychotherapeutic effects in formally defining "help-giving" situations, no matter whether the recipients are called patients, clients, customers, students, or parishioners, and regardless of the formal training, licensing, or social position of the person giving it. A cooking class, by this definition, is not psychotherapy, no matter how great its psychic benefit. An *est* course, on the other hand, is psychotherapy, no matter how much *est* trainers deny it.)

But neither different kinds of tradesmen plying the same craft nor calling it by different names offers the wealth of confusion or needs the delicacy of distinction it takes to sort the many treatment schools and styles whose practitioners, by now, are so used to multiplicity that they see no joke in it.

If this cornucopia of treatments really held hundreds of techniques for different specialists to use on different problems, it would be no embarrassment of therapeutic riches. Medicine or law or engineering have even more distinct "items." But this is not the case. Some psychotherapy "systems," or "orientations," as they are often called, speak more to epithets than entities and more to the eccentricities of their founders than to the facts of human behavior. In today's inflation of names, new labels are given to old methods or, more often, to reconstituted ones, minitheories are paraded as grand insights, and psychotherapists with a weather eye on immortality or referral fees pour old wine in new bottles, hoping that their brand name will give their "innovation" the stature which a mere case study or technical note would never get.

The truth is that for most problems, people do not seem to need very specific treatments, let alone to select them from among the endless and confusing list of names. Almost no one goes to a psychoanalyst in particular to be cured of anxiety or a nondirective therapist to be treated for depression, as one might to a cardiologist for one condition and a radiologist for another. Nor does the same doctor use Freudian therapy for psychogenic ulcers, Rogerian treatment for functional headaches, and Gestalt therapy for phobias, as a physician might use medicine for one ailment and surgery for another. The idea that they could, embodied in the "multi-modal" approach of Arnold Lazarus (1966, 1971, 1973, 1976, 1981) is only slowly gaining acceptance in professional circles, as eclecticism in therapeutic approach does (Goldfried, 1982; Marmor & Woods, 1980). On the whole, being a certain kind of psychotherapist usually has no bearing on treating a certain kind of problem. It more often implies that one will treat all problems from the vantage of a certain ideology, whose champions may see it as so broadly effective that there are few mental ailments it cannot treat.

Most advocates of most therapies, in any case, will treat most people for most problems for which most therapists of most other schools would treat them. Differences among therapists in clientele are largely matters of preference and source of referral and not the studied consequence of system or orientation. And though orientation should tell much of how therapists will treat whatever they lay hand to, it may show less actual difference from others' healing work than therapists, patients, or competitors suspect.

This is not such a bad thing. The indifference of psychotherapists in fact to differences in theory makes it possible for clients to get help without having to know much about psychotherapy or to be shunted around from one specialist to another. The openness of most therapists to most patients is not a cynical attempt to mulct the public nor a fanatical one to missionize any school. It reflects instead what may be the chief article of this profession's faith: that the skillful art of a trained psychotherapist will be helpful to most patients. As we shall see, hundreds of "outcome research" studies on psychotherapy, despite some vagaries and flaws, tend to justify this faith (Chapter 13).

This common creed of therapists belies some claims of differences among the schools, implying that some vaunted differences may make no difference. (Some research has found, indeed, equally successful outcomes among competing treatments.) If we dismiss the nuances of difference among the treatment schemes and seek a topographic outline in the bold relief of major themes, we will lose subtlety but gain perspective. The schools of therapy may then seem fewer, less varied, and more congenial to one another than some of their advocates believe.

The last chapter argued that there are three main parts to a psychotherapy system: a theory of personality, a social (moral) philosophy, and a body of more or less consistent techniques. Of these, personality theory has had most attention in the scholarly literature and in training programs. Argument over theory has been the chief historical cause for the rise of many schools. Differences in social philosophy have not been much discussed by psychotherapists and have not caused much dispute. Differences in technique have always been important to practitioners, but they have also been somewhat disdained. On the one hand, they are the most conspicuous features of a therapy, and so are good foci for argument. On the other hand, many therapists believe that technique is a neat corollary of theory, an almost obvious application of it. This is not so. The same theory may suggest several techniques and a single technique be deduced from many theories—or from hunches that have "worked" and not been theorized much about. But few therapists will join a school just for like of its technique.

Analysis of techniques, however, may serve understanding more than any other approach to psychotherapy. Techniques are relatively concrete, so they are simpler to describe than theories or philosophies. They are also better indices of what actually goes on in therapy. The specificity of techniques gives them three values for understanding therapy: (1) a scientific value, (2) an educative value, and (3) a dialectic value.

Scientific Value of Technique

The scientific value of studying therapy techniques is that they can be exposed and measured in a way that theory cannot. Techniques can be observed in a fairly straightforward way, and they can be described in the operational terms of measurement and experimentation. It is only possible to assess the practical value of psychotherapy in technical terms. As interesting, plausible, and appealing as theory may be, it is techniques, not theories, that are used on people. Studies of the effects of psychotherapy, therefore, are always studies of techniques. Recent researchers, in fact, are using manuals to teach therapists standardized treatments, evidently without damaging their effectiveness (Beck, Rush, Shaw, & Emery, 1978; Klerman, Weissman, Rounseville, & Chevron, 1984; Luborsky, 1984; Strupp & Binder, 1984).

Educative Value of Technique

The educative value of techniques is that they are easy to describe and thus more intelligible than theories to patients and to the general public, the more so as they bear directly on patients' first concern, their symptoms. Symptoms are what make people seek therapy in the first place, and the presumed value of psychotherapists' techniques is what makes them go to them. Patients contribute their symptoms, so to speak, and therapists their techniques to the mutual relationship of psychotherapy. Just as symptoms are easily visible compared to their causes, which may be hidden and must be inferred, so techniques are plain to see compared to theories, which are always inferential and abstract.

Dialectic Value of Technique

The dialectic value of studying techniques is also a function of their explicitness. To grasp the principles of an unfamiliar system, whether of machines or human relations, one must first look at its operations—what it does. Knowing that, one can trace connections backward to their source and forward from the system's operations to its applications. Learning what the machine does, so to speak, precedes learning how it does it, then why it does it in the way it does and, finally, what its doing implies. The efficient means for studying psychotherapy, likewise, is to observe first what therapists do, then how they go about doing it, and finally why they do things just so and what it implies. That means first examining their techniques, then the personality theories that underlie them and, finally, the moral schemes they speak to.

To assess the scientific and moral dimensions of the major psychotherapy systems, we must group them into a manageably small number. Trying to do so from the vantage of personality theories or social philosophies rather than techniques would be harder and less precise. Personality theories are not stated in ways equally applicable to psychotherapy; they must be translated to make them parallel enough to compare in this respect. And with few exceptions, psychotherapists have been silent about the moral ideologies or social philosophies implicit in their work. Typically, these must be read into a treatment scheme because too little has been said for them to be read out of one.

Starting with technical operations gives the best vantage from which to group therapies thematically without much oversimplifying. Doing so suggests that two technical themes dominate psychotherapy. They can be seen as poles on a continuum of activity, with most therapies leaning more toward one or the other pole and some compromises between.

THE TECHNICAL MODALITIES

Most of what psychotherapists do are efforts in the direction of what may be called, respectively, *Insight* or *Action*. These are not the official names of any treatment. The term "Insight Therapy" (not original with me), is commonly used of psychoanalytically oriented methods, but I am using it to include several schools that disclaim concern alike with insight and with psychoanalysis. The name "Action Therapy," as used here, refers chiefly to behavioral methods, though some behavior therapies nowadays use insight-related techniques such as cognition that are anathema in other behaviorist ranks.

Until the 1960s, most psychotherapy in the United States and Europe was

Insight treatment, and Action therapies were little known to the general public. Indeed, psychoanalysis was often popularly equated with all psychotherapy.

Insight therapies have a longer history than Action therapies, but have split more, almost since the beginning of psychoanalysis, into competing schools. They also made fewer claims, early on, to laboratory science as their intellectual anchor, which served them ill in the psychotherapy civil wars of the 1960s and 1970s. Until then, however, they had more impact than Action therapies on the mental health professions. Most universities and training institutes were teaching only Insight therapy. The then tiny literature on behavioral approaches, sometimes dating back half a century and often of high quality, was unknown to most therapists and not studied by most of the rest. All this changed dramatically, however, as the Action therapists raised their voices in a strident polemic, not for equal attention, but for a crusade to do away with Insight treatments. Armed with the canons of scientific evidence, the Action therapists claimed that their adversaries had, at best, failed to prove Insight Therapy and, at worst, had perpetrated an all-but-intended fraud on the public. The public was not convinced, but uncommitted professionals and novice therapy students paid more attention to Action therapy, which by now has equal status in the psychotherapy Establishments of the West.

THE HANDLING OF SYMPTOMS

The technical focus of conflict between these systems helps define the main differences between them. It is about symptoms.

People only seek treatment in the first place because they have symptoms, that is, because something is bothering them. Insight and Action therapists can agree on this casual definition of "symptom," but not on what to do about it. A therapist oriented toward Insight will likely be concerned with whatever caused the symptom, perhaps not even treating the immediate problem. An Action therapist may behave as if the symptom were cause enough and try to remove it. Insight therapists want to undermine symptoms. Where they cannot, they aim to help patients understand the symptoms and control their lives better accordingly. Action therapists try to ease symptoms directly so that clients will feel better, with less concern about their understanding of more fundamental problems.

The technical dispute is thus a function of the importance assigned to symptoms relative to the conditions that sponsor them. The more vital those conditions are, the more cautious must be the attack on their symptoms. There is a lot at stake. But if mental symptoms mean no more than does the rash of measles or even the sputum of pneumonia which, at its worst, is not the essence of its victim's life, then they were best attacked perhaps with gusto and elan and little fear of burning down the house together with the trash.

The goal of Insight therapists is grand and dangerous, demanding (at their moral best) discretion and circumspection. They aim toward the core of meaning in the patient's life, perhaps to reshape and mold it to new designs which, though unknown, may be very great. Symptoms do not occur in vacuo and, however bad they are, they but condense the huge significance of what they symbolize. In such a vital game, therapists risk more by winning than by not. They may thus fear less to fail to cure the symptom than, by curing it, to make a moral golem or a true believer for whom they have no faith. Accordingly, they take a gentle stance, largely of self restraint, exerting no control, but watching, guiding, counseling, and Socratizing, confident that clearing off the cobwebs from the patient's mind will free a better person, better fit to live with human beings.

Not so the Actionists, at first a ruder seeming sort, contemptuous of subtleties. Their fear of symptoms is only fear that other symptoms underly them or that they themselves, once conquered, may recur. If they can solve these problems, they have done enough without studying the meaning of anyone's life. What symptoms mean, in their concern, is pain and nothing else. They are modest folk so far, like mechanics who are proud of their novel repairs but have no wish to patent them. This modesty cuts their risks, they think, permitting a boldness in their work that Insight doctors hardly dare. They shape behavior (in the lower case), not tampering with "souls" or "selves" or even "personalities." If they can, by argument, seduction, threat, or even skillful violence (as a surgeon does), excise the symptom's painful barb, then they have done enough, but not too much. For the moment, they control as much as they can manage, but it is a momentary autocracy only, meaningless enough to the whole of life to be permissible.

Time honors the development of schools, permitting each its institutes, seminars, spokesmen, and prophets, whose identity is crystallized by contrast with their counterparts. So accusations grew between these schools: Insight advocates said that Actionists were sterile, superficial, and mechanical, failing to appreciate the great variety of human ways. Their superficial approach sacrificed the meaning of existence to a quest for comfort and adjustment. By freeing people of the responsibility to discover self and the meaning of their existence, these methods deprive them of their best potential traits. The Actionists' rebuttal said that true compassion sees symptomatic pain as painful and treats it. As scientists, moreover, they decried the house of inferential sand their Insight colleagues burrow out beneath the patient's pain, from which they dismiss the palpable as superficial and spurn felt anguish as irrelevance. "If we are mechanical," said Actionists, "mechanics work some tangible effects that pseudo-scientists do not; and if we seem sterile, we at least refrain from grandiose philosophic quests. And finally," they said, "care for truth dictates that we shed the myths which guide Insight therapy. Whatever meaning or security they lend you Insight therapists, they may give your patients little in the end but great expense and long travail— not meaning, comfort, healing, nor relief."

THE LIMITS OF THE SYSTEMS

Each system, earnestly pursued, leads to points where consistency creates absurdity which reveals delusions of the total scheme. Plainly there are symptomatic wounds which so engross their victims' lives that to neglect them in honor of an unseen underlying cause is idle cruelty. One such ill is anorexia, a sometimes lethal loss of appetite. Another is agoraphobia, a fear of outdoor places which, writ large in urbanites if they merely try to leave their homes, may almost make them invalids. No decent therapist, in deference to insight, will sit quietly through the symptomatic (?) self destruction of a manic state or gently authorize compulsive washers in symbolic flight from guilt to rub away their flesh. For such as these, symptomatic treatments always have priority, if not respect—if nothing else, some vessel must be kept in which to pour awareness.

And as frequently, there must be those who, freed of symptomatic woes, find deeper misery buried underneath their petty ills. No more preoccupied with pedantries, with headaches, phobias, or vile thoughts, they feel an awful emptiness or nameless terror of a faceless life. Must this be a mere symptom, eradicable by some concrete Act, by practicing a habit or association with some pleasantness arousing stimulus pulled from a bag of therapeutic tricks? Do not people jump from cliffs for more reasons than those for which dogs salivate to bells? Are there not meanings, goals, and fears and hopes for which understanding and appraising words dictate pains and balms alike, rooting themselves in consciousness, intertwined with people's myriad thoughts of self? Even the most pious Actionists do not deny their own felt consciousness or will or self. Should they do so, we all know how their actions will belie their words. Whether life means anything or not, people think it does, or can, or should. For some, perhaps the search alone or lack of it brings suffering or repair. Such troubles, by their nature, take orthodox Actionists off guard. Their work is geared to lesser aches and pains.

Happily, the contest between these systems, their mutual allegations, self-delusions and moral implications are not constant in the minds of their adherents, who sensibly devote their practice to their clients, not their colleagues. Since patients do not always fit the mold of theory to which therapists incline, nor always answer graciously to the treatment "of choice," but must be treated anyhow, a certain flexibility comes to mark the doctors' work regardless of their loyalties to any school. The sharp differences argued here then start looking sketchy and simplistic as all but the most extreme therapists are transformed by experience from militant fanatics to quiet eclectics, borrowing from here and there such tools of treatment as seem right for the client and occasion. There is a blending of techniques by artful therapists of any school, and an intuitive reckoning that people are some ways simpler than Insight schools have thought and also more complex than Action therapists have wanted to believe. This is the other pole of absurdity in both systems, where Insight theorists may make too much of nail biting and cigar smoking, while Actionists may not believe that people ever bear real anguish in their hearts for "the suffering of all that lives."

The pragmatism of consulting rooms has been felt in the academies as well. A softening of polemics has occurred, since 1970 or so, as each side, with some embarrassment, began to see some merit in its adversaries' work and their ideas.

All this suggests a caveat on catalogues like mine, but it is a two-sided warning: A straw man is clothed by my model. You must not be seduced into accepting it too exactly or annoyed into rejecting too hastily the comparisons it makes. Whoever has done much psychotherapy knows how the rich variety of people keeps all neat schemes of treatment from working with everyone; no sane therapists are wholly doctrinaire, no matter how worshipful their lip service. But were there, on the other hand, no real distinctions, differences, or cause of argument between the schools, then the learned controversy that goes on in this craft would all be coverup for corrupt purposes, like who shall "own" the market or have power in it. I do not think that is the case. When Action therapists allege, as some still do, that Insight schemes display compassionate incompetence, or Insight advocates portray the Actionists as petty, slinking into scientific rigor to hide their impotence to cope with what's important, each touches on the other's nerve with cause.

However much the compromise and blending of techniques softens the differences, one must not dismiss them, supposing more consensus among schools than there really is. Students of psychotherapy rarely learn both approaches in school, and most places giving practical training are dominated by one or the other approach, with scant attention paid to its competitor. Most practitioners become flexible mostly for practical reasons. It does not make them forego allegiance to the general approach they always took, nor does it nullify the influence of that approach, whatever their adaptations from foreign schemes. The observer who wishes to compare Insight and Action positions may do best to study each one independently, at first, as therapists actually do. But in reality they are hypothetical points on a continuum of technicalities, nothing more.

Approaching therapy via the technical systems serves clarity, but it is not enough. Techniques must finally be seen in the context of their application and connected to the assumptions on which they are based and the goals to which they are addressed. A technique is nothing but a systematic means for doing something. The study of such means in psychotherapy falls midway between studying personality theory and studying the goals of treatment. For means derive partly from some underlying theory and are directed partly at some specific goal. Here we are starting in the middle and working toward both ends. We will finally come full circle to find that the separation of theory, technique, and objectives is largely fictional. It is a useful fiction, however, from which we may best learn to understand and criticize the elusive craft of psychotherapy.

4

Ferment and Inflation

Establishment and Experiential Therapies

Emphasizing the Insight and Action poles of psychotherapy glosses some important historical events of this enterprise. This chapter digresses to tell how these events have made new treatments prominent, blurred the boundaries of psychotherapy more than ever by their variety, and produced a psychotherapy Establishment.

Psychotherapy has expanded faster and faster since the end of World War II, partly for scientific and professional reasons, but also because of changes in modern life. These changes may have affected this craft more deeply than professional interests could have. Like any service industry, psychotherapy is a largely reactive business, in which new methods evolve to meet the needs of new times and situations. The needs and interests of therapy consumers create the market for these services, just as the ideas and abilities of the vendors direct their form and scope. Perhaps this was as true in Freud's day as now.

A SOCIAL HISTORY OF PSYCHOTHERAPY

Professionals sometimes get tunnel vision and think their craft is more their deliberate invention and less a response to contemporary needs than is really so. Probably psychotherapists are like others in this regard. They credit changes in their field too much to the intellectual events that prescribe them and too little to the social events that demand the prescriptions. Social changes have put psychotherapy through three development stages in this century. Each one came in response to a different psychological motif and "modal neurosis" dominating Western society in that period (London, 1973, 1974).

Stage One: Psychoanalysis

Psychoanalysis, the first modern psychotherapy, was a treatment all but designed to serve the needs of Victorian society. The essence of its methods and the timing of its birth are no accidents. It works by exposing unconsciousness, by uncovering repression. It was conceived when Breuer and Freud published *Studies in Hysteria* in 1895; came to term in 1899, when Freud finished *The Interpretation of Dreams*; and was weaned institutionally when the Psychoanalytic Society was founded in 1902.

Now Queen Victoria died in 1901, the namesake of a motif of civilized conduct identified with bourgeois respectability. A main feature of "Victorianism" was sexual "prudery." Psychoanalysis treated the (mostly bourgeois) victims of the Victorian middle class neurosis, as it were—the repression of sexual impulses. The therapy of exposure had arisen to satisfy the needs of an Age of Repression.

By World War II, despite opposition, psychoanalysis was widely accepted as the paragon, if not the prototype, of mental therapy. By then also, Carl Rogers' client-centered therapy was competing with it (Rogers, 1942, 1974). In its early form, Rogers' method is largely an offshoot of analysis, differing chiefly over the need for a transference relationship and the value of therapist interpretations. Like psychoanalysis, the main object of "nondirective" treatment was the achievement of meaningful insight, and its method likewise remained the maieutic of getting people to "open themselves up" to see what they were like inside. Existential Psychoanalysis, another psychoanalytic variant, also grew prominent in this period. Its methods, like the others, made it a late form of Stage One therapies, for which the generic term "insight therapy" or "dynamic therapy" can replace the narrower one of psychoanalysis (Yalom, 1980).

Stage Two: Behavior Therapy & Crisis Intervention

By 1960, treatments based on principles of learning were getting known to the mental health business, first through a trickle, then a swell of books and articles. "Behavior modification" is the best generic name for these methods because it ambiguously emphasizes their behavioristic orientation and deemphasizes the mental and medical implications of "psycho" and of "therapy." By 1970, it had gone from relative obscurity through controversy to general acceptance. Its methods were taught in hospitals, clinics, and graduate schools, and preached to social workers, educators, and nurses. They had joined what was, by now, the Establishment of psychotherapies.

Not far behind, but with less press and academic hoopla, came another set of activist treatments—the *crisis intervention center,* where one could walk in without an appointment, call up while debating suicide, or move in to escape drugs or alcohol while reassessing and revising one's life style. In 1958, Synanon and the Los Angeles Suicide Prevention Center (SPC) independently opened their doors. Since then, the scope of quick intervention, manipulative and straight-to-the-point therapies has reached its apex in dial-a-help telephone counsel of many kinds, from sexual to religious advice, from a great range of counselors, including high school children, and often on a 24-hour basis (Beverly Hills High School, 1983).

In this same period, group psychotherapy came into its own, as T-groups (Training groups) spread from business and industry to college extension programs in "sensitivity" training for lay people. The "marathon" group, a kind of crash course in relationships and self-searching, now became known.

Behavior modification, crisis intervention, and marathon therapy together make up Stage Two. Far apart in their theoretical elegance and sophistication of uses, all share speed, direct attack on presenting symptoms, and a more streamlined treatment than Stage One therapies would even want to offer. Indeed, hostile critics of behavior therapies said they were impersonal, mechanistic, and dehumanizing. But in reality, what could be more suited to an electronic age, to transistors and space travel, let alone nuclear science, than push-button therapy?

These treatments only became popular in the 1960s, but most existed much earlier. The National Training Laboratory at Bethel, Maine, was founded in 1947, and T-groups spread to the universities by 1950. Alcoholics Anonymous was founded in 1935. Many behavior therapies had been used clinically and published between 1918 and 1938. Why were they so obscure for so long?

The reason, I think, is that the social climate was not ready until then for push-button therapies aimed specifically at symptom relief. For the mental symptom par excellence that now had to be treated was anxiety, and the culture had to move from the repression of anxiety to conscious preoccupation with it before a therapy which attacked it could take hold. It had done so by mid-century and was commemorated in 1947 by W. H. Auden's poem, *The Age of Anxiety,* which Leonard Bernstein set to music in 1949 as his second symphony, recorded by Columbia in 1950. Push-button treatments serve the Age of Anxiety.

The polemic between behavior modifiers and psychodynamic therapists over treating symptoms, much the shrillest debate between them, illustrates the professional tensions typical of the shift to Phase Two (London, 1972). In historical perspective, the debate was really about how to treat anxiety. In the dynamic formulation, anxiety is the culprit underlying neurotic symptoms. It is stimulated by conflicting impulses and inhibitions. The symptoms are abortive efforts to defend against anxiety by hiding the fearful knowledge that evokes it. But most of the cases from which early behavior modifiers attacked psychoanalysis were *phobias,* that is, conditions where the symptom *is* anxiety! The Case of Little Hans, for instance, in which a child became terrified by horses, was presented by Freud in 1909 as a case of *displaced* anxiety over the child's repressed oedipal conflict—and reinterpreted fifty years later by Wolpe and Rachman as a case of *directly conditioned anxiety* (1960). The issue for treatment is whether it is more efficient to attack the phobic anxiety which is seen "up front" or whether you must dig for a more complex construction underneath. But in historical terms, it is whether to expect people to feel anxiety "up front" when they come for psychotherapy or to expect to find it hidden by some complex of defense.[1]

Stage Three: Therapeutic Games

It took fifty years for psychotherapy to pass from Phase One to Phase Two, but barely twenty to move to Phase Three. By 1970, the modal attributes of middle class society had spread among the populace. Its members waxed bountifully in affluence, in leisure, in knowledge of life's opportunities and in hope of gaining them, in freedom from the moral restraints which once forbade experiments in living, and in the freedom to champion freedom in personal conduct. Therapeutic preoccupations shifted from the relief of pain and disorder to the achievement of meaning and value in life, from the modest hope of living less afraid to the grand need for existential purpose and positive life goals. For many who were materially favored and morally unanchored, it became an *Age of Ennui.*

By the 1970s, a gloomy view of the era was common to many once merely sober social critics. Economist and diplomat John Kenneth Galbraith had viewed "the affluent society" and "post-industrial society" optimistically in 1958 and 1967, but not in what he later titled *The Age of Uncertainty* (1978). Philosopher Herbert Marcuse showed similar shift from *Eros and Civilization* (1962) to *One-dimensional Man* (1966). So too did sociologists, historians, and psychiatrists—in Philip Rieff's *Fellow Teachers* (1973), Herbert Hendin's *The Age of Sensation* (1975), and Christopher Lasch's *The Culture of Narcissism* (1978). The problems of psychological transition to this era, however, were foreseen most clearly in *The Lonely Crowd* by David Riesman, Nathan Glazer, and Reuel Denney (1950), where they predicted the impact of increased leisure time on society late in this century (Ruitenbeek, 1970).

By 1970, we had entered a period when the traditional values in which many Westerners had been reared no longer justified their life styles, so they had fewer moral referents for judging themselves than had once been true. But these people also had fewer practical referents than before for justifying their life styles, for social survival depended less than it used to on conformity to narrow conventions.

---

[1] In practice, the question of efficiency obscures that of etiology without addressing it. If you can treat the problem directly without risking new symptoms, then the case is made for doing so, whether or not your explanation is correct. All real therapy is impatient with history.

The direction of personal fulfillment, in this social context, shifted dramatically toward "self"ish behavior, in which satisfaction in life chiefly meant serving one's own needs and pleasures and not other people or social or religious or other external ideals. Thus arose what Tom Wolfe called the "me" generation, a special manifestation of what Philip Rieff had named "the age of psychological man" (1961a). Herbert Hendin (1975), Peter Marin (1975), and Christopher Lasch (1978) respectively named the era more acidly "the age of sensation," "the new narcissism," and the "culture of narcissism."

The third or "humanistic" trend in psychotherapy now took hold, spreading mainly by encounter groups at first. More or less officially called the "growth" or "human potential" movement, I have called its many methods "therapeutic games" because they were not aimed at symptom relief and their use was not meant to signify disorder, but to be educational or recreational in a broad sense (Korchin, 1976). They were designed for what had largely become an age of malaise and of existential preoccupation, whose predominant neuroses were boredom, loneliness, and depression (London, 1974, 1983a). In a culture of changed personal needs, the therapeutic games seemed like meaningful efforts to meet them (Back, 1972). Encounter groups and growth centers served social needs by offering instant intimacy to people whose mobility was so great and nuclear families so unstable that neighbors and relatives could not provide support networks. Zen and transcendental meditation offered noncreedal service to the spiritual needs of a society where people no longer believed the religious creeds they had been reared on. Biogenics and sex therapy and food/dance/art therapies and massage/breathing/relaxation therapies served sensory needs in a culture where leisure was so prolific that it had to be much varied and more than "fun" in order to be deeply re-creational. And *est,* Arica, yoga, nude therapy, and such offered combinations of all three, tying friendship, fulfillment, and fun in one handsome package.

THE CURRENT PSYCHOTHERAPY SCENE

Each new treatment ethos developed in competition with the old ones, not in recognition of how times had changed. This happened partly because there was only a finite consumer pie. It also happened for the same reason fish do not recognize water nor people air—because psychotherapists were part of the cultural milieu they were responding to and not fully aware, therefore, that their innovations were reactive to social change. As the whole psychotherapy trade expanded, old therapies did not die or fade away. They joined the conceptual fray. In practice, the three treatment modes borrowed techniques from each other, quietly during the polemic years, openly as the fighting died down. Theoretically, however, they continued to lead what M. B. Parloff called a "dogma-eat-dogma" existence (1979).

The dogmatic dispute concerned not only which therapy "worked better" but also what "working" meant. The main source of confusion, as Barry Wolfe put it, was not professional, but part of a general "social confusion regarding values . . ." which both reflected and generated ". . . definitional confusion of what constitutes psychotherapy" (1977, p. 10).

The psychological ethos that evolved in Western society was a reflection, if not a stimulant, of the social, political, and ideological ferment that characterized the period, just as Black Militancy, Gay Rights, and Women's Liberation in the United States were concrete expressions of that ferment. With ferment went an increasingly visible collapse of conventional life styles and social support networks. As the "me generation" came to adulthood, it had more options and faced more problems of life style choice than its parents had, but with fewer conventional addresses for solving them by *talking*. This trend may have been more evident in the United States than in smaller, poorer, and more homogeneous societies, but it was true of all the developed countries. Increased physical mobility decreased opportunities for dependable social support from family, friends, and neighbors. Increased freedom from traditional moral restraints increased problems of sex relations, marriage, and family, with less opportunity for the counsel of clergymen, village elders, or local sages. The explosion of information from film and television about almost everything made people less willing to accept traditional solutions to personal problems.

Technological innovations also served to multiply options, and thereby ferment, just as social change did. Reliable contraceptives under female control, for instance, increased freedom of sexual action as never before. New psychoactive drugs eased the management of psychoses, depression and hyperactivity, making psychotherapy concentrate more selectively on problems which were more responsive to it, and thus increasing its credibility. Association with science and technology, something psychotherapists always claimed, further increased their credibility, as moral authority in modern society passed from the bearers of "traditional wisdom" to the spokespersons of "technical expertise."

One result of these rapid changes was a net increase in psychological ambiguity and dis-ease and a favorable social climate for seeking expert help with it. Having more choices meant there were more decisions to be made; people had more to talk over than ever before in history. But traditional institutions such as the church had fewer authoritative, credible people to talk to than in the past.

Psychotherapists are entrepreneurial talkers and science-based professionals. Their business could not help but benefit from the turmoil. It grew apace as therapists rushed to fill the psychoeconomic vacuum in society.

Game Therapies for the Well

The psychotherapeutic games that bloomed in the 1960s had to seek markets without running afoul of hostile competing therapists or the law. They did so by saying that they were not "therapies" in the sense of treating mental ills or necessarily even of solving personal problems. The intent, they said, was to spur the psychological growth of mentally healthy people who, as a result, would be more aware of themselves in important ways. They were thus to be seen as educational or even recreational rather than healing activities. Typically done in groups, sessions were called "encounter groups," "sensitivity training," or, in a somewhat later jargon, "consciousness raising." The groups met in varied settings, ranging from group leaders' homes, offices, swimming pools (where "nude encounters" were sometimes held), or hotel rooms to suburban or rural retreats, called "growth centers," where participants might stay for days or weeks. There were 110 or more growth centers in the United States by 1971 (Lieberman & Gardner, 1976).

Much of the curriculum of encounter groups, elaborated and varied in the many workshops people could take in growth centers, was a medley of exercises derived from psychotherapies. Many techniques came from Rogers' "client-centered" therapy (1942; 1951); from Frederick Perls, Ralph Hefferline, and Paul Goodman's "Gestalt therapy" (1951); from variants of Wilhelm Reich's (1961) and Alexander Lowen's (later) "bioenergetics" (1969); and from the "T-group" discussion methods of the National Training Laboratory, originated by Kurt Lewin (Rogers, 1970). The late Abraham Maslow is generally seen as the intellectual father of the human potential movement because of his studies of so-called higher order motivation and self-actualization (1954). Carl Rogers is considered the founder of the encounter group. Maslow, Rogers, and "Fritz" Perls were all active in the movement in its heyday.

It was never wholly clear, either to the public, the helping professions, or the government agencies interested in these matters, how much of the "human potential" movement was really a left-handed, disingenuous incursion on the professional turf of psychotherapists, an earnest effort to use clinical wisdom and skills in "therapy for normals," a utopian social movement, or a commercially motivated confidence game used on people who needed psychotherapy but could not admit it or not afford it (Koch, 1971; Maliver, 1973; Marin, 1975). There is probably some truth in each claim, depending on which of its forms or leaders is studied. The ambiguity, in any case, is structural, that is, inherent in the movement because of its origins, its pretensions, the population it serves, and the way it is funded (entirely by direct promotion and sale of services).

Growth centers have declined or disappeared in the economic recessions of recent years, but the human potential movement abides or expands in some commercial variants. The best known is *est* and its spinoffs, "actualizations" and "life spring," which have standardized, streamlined, repackaged, and sold its games in weekend doses of mixed doubletalk and useful homily. Another is T-groups and nondirective interviewing courses for business managers to improve their dealings with people in group meetings and interviews.

Historically, there is no valid answer to whether the therapeutic games are "really" therapies or not. The legal or professional perspective is also ambiguous. Many customers of human potential workshops regard it as psychotherapy, but most view it as a supplement to other therapies, not a substitute for them (Lieberman & Gardner, 1976). What is clear is that these methods originated as the therapeutic work of distinguished mental health experts and have been incorporated into the repertory of professional psychotherapy, as it is advertised, advocated, researched, and billed for by professionals. Many of them have given formal names to their methods. As a result, not only has the number and variety of therapists increased, but there has been a marvelous inflation of titles and types of treatment, mostly unknown before the Korean War.

Inflation of Titles and Types

Surveying the proliferation of therapies named in the professional literature, a wag commented that we need a psychotherapeutic nonproliferation treaty between publishers and the professions. He may be right. In 1959, when Walter Bromberg revised his 1936 *The Mind of Man: History of Psychoanalysis and Psychotherapy,* its topics consisted mainly of Freud, psychoanalytic revisionists, and single chapters each on group therapy and then so-called "conditioning" therapies. Also in 1959, Robert A. Harper's *Psychoanalysis and Psychotherapy— 36 Systems,* catalogued treatments for both professionals "and the intelligent layman who has heretofore looked in vain for an understandable map" of what seemed a "psychotherapeutic maze." By 1976, Morris B. Parloff had counted 130 titles, which he regrouped into 17 distinct treatments (Parloff, 1976). Picture the convolutions of the maze by 1980, when Richie Herink compiled *The Psychotherapy Handbook: The A to Z Guide to More Than 250 Different Therapies in Use Today.* He found more than 300 treatments named in the literature but, like Parloff, eliminated redundant ones.

Herink's organization of the therapies, sensibly, is alphabetical, Now, alphabetizing is the last refuge of desperate encyclopedists, to be used when no logic of assignment is apparent. That is the case for cataloguing contemporary psychotherapy because the subject matter considered proper to it is now so broad that virtually anything that counts as "problem" has some healing counterpart that can be called "treatment." Early classifications went by setting or method of treatment, so to speak: Psychoanalysis, group therapy, and so forth, shorthand labels which assumed professional control over whatever was called "therapy." Now, typing by domain of problem is commonplace: Sex therapy, family therapy, alcoholism, smoking, obesity, drug abuse therapies, stress therapy. So too is typing by very specific technique: Hypnotherapy, biofeedback, relaxation, and aversion therapy—but also, closer to the fringe of professionalism, occupational therapy, bibliotherapy, art therapy, and such. This is not far conceptually from "Horticultural Therapy" (Relf, 1980), "Cooking as Therapy" (Parrish, 1980) and "Poetry Therapy" (Leedy & Reiter, 1980). Nor is it far from current typing by specific treatment goal: "Natural High Therapy" (O'Connell, 1980), "Integrative Psychotherapy" (Friedman, 1980) and "Burn-out prevention" (Josephs & Khalsa, 1980).

Herink's is not a frivolous book. Its therapies are all practiced and the chapters on the well-known psychotherapies, at least, are written by reputable, even leading exponents of them. There are more psychotherapies than there used to be because the boundaries of what can legitimately be called psychotherapy have shifted radically, and the taxonomy of treatments has had to shift with them. Our notions of problems and goals which could bear the name of therapy have gone in historical sequence from repair to restoration to decoration. Establishing their boundaries now, as always, is a matter of custom and social policy, not scientific truth.

THE THERAPEUTIC ESTABLISHMENT

Most therapeutic games have not been fully accepted by the professions, even when their techniques have been assimilated in the body of professional work, as is true, for instance, of Gestalt Therapy. Being accepted means joining the "Therapeutic Establishment." The Establishment, as I am using the term, is both an entity and an ideology. The entity, our chief concern here, is the body of academic, scientific, medical, and bureaucratic institutions that approve, recommend, teach, study, research, fund, license, and certify the public enterprises of society (London, 1983a; London & Klerman, 1982).[2] The early relationship of "experiential therapies" (the generic term which subsumes many therapeutic games today) to this body was a stew of ambivalence.

Membership in the professional Establishment is not merely honorific. It means status and prestige among the institutional pillars of society and access to the resources they control. In the United States, it means access to billions of dollars across the Federal government, the States, the municipalities, charitable and educational foundations, and insurance companies. Membership, or lack of it, also affects therapists' access to private patients who pay for their own treatment, for the marketplace, even there, is not as freely competitive as it might seem. Most people do not pick a psychotherapist from the yellow pages of the telephone book; they try to find someone "reputable," even if their standard is no more than the recommendation by a trusted friend of a "good" therapist. "Good" is commonly a matter of reputation, and reputation is often defined by one's status among members of the Establishment. They are university professors and administrators, officers of professional organizations, and occasionally influential and wealthy lay persons with special interest in these

---

[2] The ideology is the common belief in a utilitarian, if not normative approach to problems of social regulation. In effect, it is the belief that government should provide the greatest benefit for the greatest number of people.

matters. They write or review the scholarly treatises, serve on government and foundation grant review committees, receive most of the research and training funds, and testify in the courts and before legislative committees.

Even in their heyday, experiential therapies had little access to Establishment institutions. Their language, theories, and methods were little known to most mental health experts or dismissed by them as unscientific and incompetent. Also, many of the new therapists lacked credentials in the health professions; they got involved in psychotherapy via other work, ranging from physical therapy to fine arts to sales. But the main reason was that they mostly excluded themselves by claiming that their work was not bound by the conventional canons of scientific validation or professional practice. They derided both psychodynamic (Insight) and behaviorist (Action) treatments as "reductionist" and "mechanistic," serving a lower order of human needs than the goals of personal growth and self realization to which they were committed. Led by Abraham Maslow (who, like "Fritz" Perls, retired to Esalen, the leading growth center), they called themselves a "third force" in psychology. In fact, they made valuable ideological extrapolations of Insight therapy and invented ingenious technical devices which Insight and Action therapies both have since adopted. But they did not see it that way.

The human potential movement's often intemperate attack on conventional psychotherapy characterized its self exclusion from the Establishment. Frederick Perls, for instance, was eager to "debunk the whole Freudian crap . . . ," and says "The conditioners also start out with a false assumption. Their basic premise that behavior is 'law' is a lot of crap." He is hostile to professionalism in all therapy, including his own. "One of the objections I have against anyone calling himself a Gestalt Therapist is that he uses technique. A technique is a gimmick . . . the sad fact is that this jazzing-up more often becomes a dangerous substitute activity, another therapy that *prevents* growth." "We are here to promote the growth process and the human potential." (All quotes Perls, 1969, pp. 1–2)

Human Potential and Antinomian Religion

What Perls and his colleagues saw as promoting the growth process was, to most psychotherapists, an eccentric theoretical posture which made inevitable their exclusion from the Establishment. They were not promoting a therapy merely of cure, but of personal redemption, whose final product would be the rescue of dissolute modern society:

"Now the problem is not so much with the turner-onners" says Perls, "but with the whole American culture. We have made a 180-degree turn from puritanism and moralism to hedonism. . . . In Gestalt Therapy, we are working for something else . . . interrupting the . . . fall of the United States. . . . To be able to do this, there is only one way through: to become real. . . . I give you the Gestalt prayer, maybe as a direction . . .

> *I do my thing, and you do your thing.*
> *I am not in this world to live up to your expectations*
> *And you are not in this world to live up to mine.*
> *You are you and I am I,*
> *And if by chance we find each other, it's beautiful.*
> *If not, it can't be helped.* " (Quotes Perls, 1969, p. 2)

Pursuing this goal via the "cultivation of idiosyncrasy," as Nathan Adler calls it, put the growth movement and humanistic psychotherapy in the anomalous historical position of antinomian religions and the odd professional position of being anti-scientific and anti-establishment (Adler, 1972; London, 1983a). It was an expression, albeit a wealthy and well educated one, of the same countercultural dissent as that of hippies and flower children. As such, it rejected the Establishment, not vice-versa. Doing so has obscured its position among the modes of psychotherapy. Preaching social redemption always bears this risk, moreso when it is done by amateurs in politics and religion, and most when they promote, let alone tolerate, unconventional behavior. O. H. Mowrer was all but excommunicated professionally for Integrity Therapy, and his socially redemptive treatment pitched normative, if not downright conformist, behavior (see Chapter 12).

This is not to say that these are useless therapies, foolish technologies, or warped ideologies. The goals of humanistic psychotherapy are related to its methods in the same way as are those of Insight Therapy, and its techniques show that it is a variant of Insight Therapy, not a "third force" in the helping professions or the culture. As "experiential therapy," they have largely been adopted (Perls would have said co-opted) into the mainstream of treatment, are part of its ecumenical or eclectic trend, and are joining the Establishment, scientifically and professionally, quietly dissociated from once utopian aims (Wexler & Rice, 1974; Rice & Greenberg, 1983).

In their early years, however, humanistic therapies started ideologically where Establishment therapies end, with consideration of their moral implications. By scorning the very technical issues against which the others aimed to prove themselves, the "game" therapists made the same de facto claims for attention and adherence as do religious creeds. Were contemporary psychotherapy studied for its part in culture, their historical role would be clear in the recurring conflicts between Apollonian and Dionysian forces in society, between nomothetic and antinomian views of reality, and perhaps between the competing doctrines of faith and works as the basis of morality and the price of salvation in Western religion. As it is, even their technical role in psychotherapy, as variants of Insight, was clouded by their indifference or hostility to it.

All therapies, on becoming self-conscious, face the same moral problems and risk being hoist on their own petard by the dilemmas imbedded in the morals of psychotherapy—they address practically how people ought to live, and they lean implicitly on theories of human nature for doing so. The growth movement read itself out of the mainstream not by its bold moral posture, which many other therapists practically endorse, but by its practical rejection of professionalism and of technology on behalf of that posture.

Conventional psychotherapists, on the other hand, have yet to face the moral implications of their technical positions. Clarifying them may help them do so.

II

THE HEALING MODES: INSIGHT THERAPY

THE ARGUMENT

Insight therapy is what most people have in mind when they think of "going into" psychotherapy. Their statements about it may be vague, but their idea of what happens there is correct. They fancy psychotherapy is "talking to someone" in ways which help to understand what "makes" them the way they are, expecting that the understanding thus obtained will relieve their inner stress. In those two simple terms, they grasp the essence of Insight method and theory.

The technical differences that separate Insight schools are not substantial things to lay people. Lying on a couch, sitting upright, saying all that comes to mind, crying, screaming, analyzing dreams, writing fairy tales, admonishing empty chairs, punching pillows, recalling childhood, are all subordinate parts of what they know to be the centerpiece of Insight therapy—expanding consciousness.

This increase takes place chiefly by talking, and to someone who does not reciprocate in kind, does not trade information and experience, and is not sociable or friendly in the usual sense, but selflessly attends the client's self. Insight therapists of different schools answer differently to what patients say and do, aiming at their attitudes, their histories, the contradictions of their self-perceptions or the hidden feelings and ideas which orchestrate the ones they show. All of these are tools for focusing attention on the patient's self, which learns to be responsible for its expressions in the session, as in life, and to treat the therapist impersonally as a mirror of itself, a projection screen for its own ghosts, an instrument to use in hot pursuit of consciousness.

Self consciousness, in Insight theories, is purgative and antidote to poisonous secrets of the heart which "make" us act against our Wills, pervert Will to enjoy transgressions which a better part of self abhors but cannot stop, and fill us with despair and dread because we lose the name of action or forget its cause. Hidden motives, needs, or drives produce the symptoms of disorder. Insight reveals and expurgates them and, in doing so, starves symptoms out. But direct relief of symptoms is less important than the rest because symptoms, though visibly painful, mean less than motives in the lives of those who suffer from them.

Insight treatments have been attacked on scientific and on moral grounds in complementary arguments. The first one says that they do not cure symptoms; the second that, even where they do, their other effects are obtained immorally, by seducing people away from their original purposes. The first claim has, in part, been laid to rest by research which shows fair success of Insight treatments for many problems. The second does not yield so readily.

Many clients spend years in Insight therapy with their symptoms unchanged and their lives altered in other ways. It is rare for therapists to warn of this and to suggest, accordingly, that they think twice before embarking on what may be an endless trip. Maybe they believe the search for meaning or root cause or authenticity is worth more than merely symptomatic cure. But the conveyance still comes in question. Promoting such deep treatment to people who have come for less pervasive help is acting as moralists more than physicians. This can hardly be avoided by the subtle technology of Insight therapy, which at once inspires patients' search for self through heightened consciousness and avoids any sharing of responsibility by therapists for what they find. As long as therapy does more than cure symptoms, says this view, it does too much.

The moral posture Insight therapy promotes, in any case, is the virtue of self-knowledge, personal initiative, and individual responsibility. The politics implied is the right of individuals to live as they choose. The self is valuable because it is, entitled to exist because it does, and not for any role it plays or thing it does. The aim of therapy is to promote the growth of self-knowledge, self-control, and self-esteem, and to do so without manipulation or the exercise of undue influence on patients.

Hostile critics say its blend of deft persuasion and benign neutrality is not so pure, that undue influence of therapist on client is inherent in the dependency created by the treatment setting and the Insight therapist's sympathy, and that the influence must tend to foster self indulgent, socially irresponsible or even psychopathic behavior. The libertarian moral posture is clearly defensible. What stays moot is whether Insight therapists should try to explicate it, since most clients come to them for simple cure, not knowing they may take home moral counsel.

5

Speaking and Knowing

Technique and Theory in Insight Therapy

Magazines, movies, plays, TV shows, novels, stories, essays, treatises, and learned texts have all told much about Insight psychotherapy, and often well. Artists, poets, playwrights, and scenarists have borrowed from it for their work, and even if their opera on it are imperfect expositions, still they show its familiarity in Western culture. Many readers need no introduction to Insight therapy; they have been introduced repeatedly to it in education, entertainment, cultural pursuits, social encounters, and perhaps in their private lives. This is most true in metropolitan areas, for large cities have resources to sustain professional societies of psychotherapists. In such places, the educated public learns some of the trademarks, brand names, and buzzwords of different therapies. The less initiated are more prone to equate all psychotherapy with psychoanalysis, a confusion which gets unwitting support from the many Insight therapists who at once affirm and deny their connection with it by saying they are "psychoanalytically oriented."

Far from belittling their naiveté, however, I believe this gathering of many psychotherapeutic sheep into a single fold is more justified than not (Bellak, 1981; Bieber, 1981). Insight schools of therapy do not differ from each other as much as they claim; they are more united by practical commonalities than separated by differences. The areas of discord, it is true, have caused intense argument among psychotherapists. This has given rise to many schools, some of which feel so strongly about their qualities that they avoid contact with rival schools. (Some even try to protect patients from them, as when a Freudian therapist told a patient to make his wife stop seeing a Jungian because "we can't have two kinds of therapy going on in the same family.") The arguments have also taken much space in professional literature. But as for the techniques involved, which are central to our study, the differences are here seen as less than the similarities.

The prototype of modern Insight therapy, if not of all psychotherapy, is Sigmund Freud's psychoanalysis. It has continued to this day to be bible and whipping boy alike to later developments in therapy. It is with cause; the main features of psychoanalysis are equally vital to its progeny. As prodigal as they may be, they are all "psychoanalytic" in important ways.

Insight therapists vary a lot in the degree of their divorcement from Freudian psychoanalysis and in their reasons for it (Munroe, 1955; Mullahy, 1948). Disciples of the American psychiatrist Harry Stack Sullivan, for instance, a vicarious protégé of Freud, argue some differences with Freudians from a different theory of personality, which asserts a cultural more than biological basis of neurosis. But they also differ in technique: The patients of Freudians must lie down where they cannot see the therapist; Sullivanian therapists let patients sit up and face the doctor during sessions.

The Establishment Insight school which claims the greatest difference from psychoanalysis and has offered the most rigorous statement of techniques and arguments to make its case was founded by psychologist Carl Rogers. It has been known officially as Rogerian, nondirective, client-centered, and person-centered therapy (Meador & Rogers, 1979). Like the Sullivan school, it is an American product. Unlike Sullivan, Rogers was not directly influenced much by "classical" (Freudian) analysis. He admits the influence, however, of Otto Rank, once a disciple of Freud, who emigrated to the United States a decade after he was excommunicated from psychoanalytic circles (he died there almost twenty years later) (Evans, 1975).

Existential analysis, on the other hand, originated in Europe and only became well known in the United States some years after World War II. Sometimes called Humanistic Existential therapy, it blended psychoanalysis with the ideas of existential philosophy. It thereby laid much of the groundwork for the theories (but not the practice) of the Humanistic game therapies which followed it. As presented by its leading figures, such as Rollo May (1953, 1961), Victor Frankl (1963), and Ludwig Binswanger, Existential Psychotherapy has always been a "respectable" variant of psychoanalysis. It does not totally reject psychoanalysis, but claims to be and do more than analysis. Its techniques are more ambiguously connected with the human potential movement than with the mainstream of Insight therapy. Its anti-deterministic rhetoric, on the other hand, sounds unscientific and has damaged its advocates' access to establishment money and prestige (Yalom, 1980). And like most game therapies, accordingly, they have not been subjected to the same scientific scrutiny as psychoanalysis and client-centered therapy, on which we shall focus.

The established position of Rogerian psychotherapy is unambiguous, even though Carl Rogers was a founder of the encounter group and active in the growth potential movement. Rogers was a pioneer in the scientific study of psychotherapy and the first recipient of the American Psychological Association's Distinguished Scientist Award in 1956. He always took pride in the rigor of his theoretical and empirical statements on psychotherapy and was disappointed that they did not receive more attention. He felt that his thinking on psychotherapy broadened over the years, but he never renounced his main ideas, to my knowledge, nor his scientific orientation.

THE TECHNICAL EQUIVALENCE
OF INSIGHT SYSTEMS

There are two common features of Insight therapy operations which dwarf their many differences and their other likenesses:

First, the single instrument of treatment is talk, and the therapeutic sessions are structured so that, from start to finish, the client, analysand, or counselee does most of the talking and most of the deciding on what to talk about.

Second, there is a conservative bias among therapists against revealing important or detailed information about their personal lives. It is deliberately hidden from the patient. (A few therapists even refuse to answer clients' questions about their professional training or degrees.)

There are differences in the details of these practices among different schools, as there are differences in many other details of Insight practice. But these two things are central. They shape the general appearance of Insight therapy sessions, which might proceed like this:

The doctor and patient greet each other and take positions in the consulting room. If the patient lies on a couch (classical psychoanalysis), the therapist sits behind, head toward the side, in order to see the client without being seen. If the patient sits (client-centered, Sullivanian, and others), the therapist usually sits opposite, often with no desk or other barrier between them. Once set, the positions tend to be fixed; neither party ordinarily gets up or moves around the room during the session, nor is physical contact between them common. Talk is the "legal tender" of expression here, not touch and not movement. Some therapists, on principle, never take notes so their attention will be totally fixed on the patient. For some, talk means only speech and no other words. They tell clients not to write agendas or notes to use during the session. Notes are words, but not talk.

As patient and doctor prepare to start, there may be a brief exchange of chit-chat, but many therapists frown on this. In any case, it is always desultory and trivial, about weather or traffic or such, a preparatory busyness, not part of the session. It is likely introduced by the client, not the therapist. The therapist responds minimally, partly because it is social chit-chat, which could be mistaken to mean the therapist has a sociable role in the encounter, but more because it is chit-chat and not the substance of the session. Some talk is worth more than other talk. So, if the client mouths irrelevant pleasantries rather than serious talk, the conversation sooner withers into silence than blossoms into pertinence.

And the silence may last unless the patient starts talking, for it is the rule that, in the ordinary course of Insight therapy, most options belong to the patient. With therapy agreed on, and its business arrangements done, there are no options left except on whether to talk and what to say. Responsibility for them is not assumed by therapists, though their comments or reflections on clients' silence may seem like prods to make them talk.

[Classical Freudian analysis removes some responsibility for talking from the patient as well by the "cardinal rule" of psychoanalysis, which is to say whatever comes to mind. Psychoanalytic hypnotherapists go still further; they may suggest that patients will not have to remember afterwards what they have said while hypnotized.]

Once the patient has begun to talk, the therapist rarely directs the conversation by saying that one topic is more important than another or even perhaps by responding to direct questions. If the client hesitates to choose among topics, the therapist does not prompt—not even if the client asks outright which to speak of. On the contrary, Insight therapists work hard, especially early in treatment, subtly to turn clients' expectations inwards, training them to be wholly responsible for the flow of their consciousness. This is done by practice, not by precept, by waiting silently and patiently, enacting the reciprocal of the role the patient must learn. It leaves the client with the choice of bearing the dialectic ball alone or risking no interaction. The therapist does not say so, but instructs by merely responding suggestively.

This description fits psychoanalysis more than other Insight therapies because analytic training and supervision puts more consistent emphasis on such processes. But the procedural bias of all Insight therapy goes in this direction. Some studies, in fact, show that the methods of experienced Insight therapists of different schools are hard to tell apart (Fiedler, 1950; some but not all—cf. Sundland & Barker, 1962).

To this day, however, many Insight therapists are surprised to learn how similar is the work of different schools, probably because they have heard so much of the differences. Comparing the rhetoric of competing techniques with their actual practice shows how differences tend to merge (Strupp, 1962).

PSYCHOANALYSIS AND
CLIENT–CENTERED THERAPY

Among Insight techniques, some "pet" methods of Freud and Rogers respectively differ mainly over how therapists formulate their remarks and the kind of material they address. Rogerians rely heavily on a method called "reflection"; Freudians give similar weight to "interpretation." Reflection is used to communicate that the client has been empathically understood and to evoke a "re-processing of experience" (Rice, 1974). Interpretation, in addition to understanding, conveys the therapist's elaboration, explanation, or assessment of the patient's meaning. A reflection might repeat the client's very words or paraphrase them; an interpretation, however, might say things that went beyond what the patient said or felt.

The difference between these responses may be less than Rogerians and Freudians think they are. Current feelings are the pivotal contents of client-centered therapy, while analysis is also concerned with their history. Reflection, accordingly, is directed toward feelings alone, as they come up in the session, while interpretation may plumb for more. Reflection naturally has most impact when patients' feelings are implied rather than voiced, for then it is easy to tell empathy from mimicry in the therapist's response. But a reflection is also then interpretive, for to the degree that it speaks to unspoken feelings, it elaborates on what the client has actually said. Even when feelings are explicit, moreover, reflection may work like interpretation by cueing the patient to elaborate on them (Wexler, 1974). If the aim, in fact, is only to convey acceptance and empathy, then a reflection might be less effective than an outright comment. Reflection that says too little may express empathy as poorly as interpretation that says too much. Anyway, the value of what is said will depend on the client's interpretation, not the therapist's intention.

Interpretation, the parallel cornerstone of psychoanalyst remarks, seems to give therapists more latitude than reflection does, but what it communicates may be functionally equivalent to reflection. The main difference between them, I think, is in how they serve therapists' theories of personality. Insofar as the theories yield similar goals in therapy, the techniques achieve much the same thing. The differences in theory make little difference in their practical effects.

The Freudian scheme of personality is more complex than the Rogerian, so it needs a more flexible means of elucidation. It says that emotional problems originate in one's history. Since, for some clients, personal history is not an obvious subject to discuss, the Freudian therapist needs latitude for comments which turn attention to it. Rogerians, in theory, need to direct clients' attention only to feelings close at hand in order to promote the self-acceptance that comes from accepting them. This needs less interpretive flexibility. Rogerians can afford only to reflect because what they say is all contemporary, not preface to history.

The main theoretical difference, for treatment purposes, is that Freudians believe neurosis has a complex evolution. Based on this belief, they construct a plausible treatment scheme to unravel it. Rogerians question the psychoanalytic genetic scheme as unknowable, but do not contradict it. They simply argue that psychoanalytic procedures are unnecessary. Rogerians think that therapy needs to deal with phenomenology but not with history (Rotter, 1963). Their treatment strategy, accordingly, sets the therapist to the minimum activity needed for success. The method is a distillation of the Freudian. It means to economize on it, not do violence to it.

The practical dispute concerns how the therapist should cue the client, and the difference in therapist behavior is far less than differences in interest. Freudians, for instance, see dreams as rich sources of treatment information. But they tend not to solicit or prod patients for dreams, but rather simply to respond with interest if clients bring them up. Similarly, for therapy to work, they think, patients must reenact some emotional encounters of early life, with the therapist seen in the same light as were the loved and hated figures of childhood. But analytic therapists do not lecture or admonish patients to produce this "transference" of feeling nor tell them to watch for some such mental spots to show. They wait for the phenomenon and, when it appears, interpret it, encouraging its scrutiny without demanding it. Rogerians may feel that analysts waste time fiddling with dreams or history, but they use the same method of selectively responding to unsolicited remarks which seem important. Rogerians respond chiefly to expressions of feelings, Freudians to other things as well; but both see feelings as the main events for treatment to untangle.

THE PERSONAL RETICENCE
OF INSIGHT THERAPISTS

Insight therapists, as we have said, do not tell clients much about their own lives. This seems like a tactical corollary to the rule that client-opted and client-centered talk be the focus of therapy. If patients must do the talking, then maybe therapists should not. If patients must learn to scrutinize themselves, then it may be impertinent for therapists to talk about themselves.

But more than relevance dictates this procedure, and it is not just corollary—for by and large, therapists conceal themselves from patients outside the therapy session as well as in it, avoiding all social connections. If that is impossible from the outset, many will not accept the person for treatment. And if social contacts are later unavoidable, they will limit them and probably discuss in treatment the feelings aroused. At all events, Insight schools consider it wrong for therapists purposely to have social relations with clients.[1] As personal as this relationship may be in some ways, it is not sociable—it may look continuous with social states in which people engage each other, but Insight therapy makes clients engage themselves alone. An otherwise natural interest in the therapist as a person must be transmuted into transference projections for Freudians and de-

---

[1] This analysis pays no attention to some mundane reasons which have nothing to do either with technique or theory, such as the fact that therapist and patient may both be embarrassed by a tea party relationship after the intensity of their sessions, or that therapists especially might want fresh company after hours, or that they may reckon clients to be trying company when both change roles.

flected away from themselves and onto others who, by their physical absence, are ghostly extensions of the client's thoughts. For Rogerians, such interest must be reflected back to patients from empathic therapists who feel the patients' feelings proper (not just sympathetic kinship) and who, at their best, are become the patients' self in kindly form, teaching them to see themselves anew in the image of this accepting, even beautifying mirror.

To summarize the methods of Insight therapy: The patient initiates the talking and assumes responsibility for it. The therapist reinforces the more personal and feeling parts of that talk, which is ultimately an elaborate monologue. Therapists guide, as it were, by following the patient's lead, not fully revealing their own identity and not warning the patient where therapy will go, however many times they have guided others on like paths through like forests.

Where does the path go? For Insight therapists, it leads first to the source from which the trouble comes and only then to its solution. They are linked inexorably. Therapists seek the clarification of those ties in clients' minds. Which brings us to the common theory that underlies Insight therapies.

THE MOTIVES OF BEHAVIOR

If "insight" is the key to its techniques, "motive" is the common object at which Insight personality theories aim. The idea uniting Insight schools is that the main problems therapy attacks are products of compelling motives. Solutions to those problems depend on changes in their motivating states. The same proposition gets stated in many ways, but there is no overstating its importance to Insight therapy:

It says there are compelling reasons for everything we do. These reasons cause our acts, and the one sure way of changing the acts is by altering the reasons which compel them.

Again, the theory says that people behave as they do because they are driven to behave so, and they cannot be induced to behave otherwise unless they are otherwise driven.

What motivates people, what drives them, what their needs are, or their tensions, what gratifies them, what their reasons are, or goals—all mean about the same thing, and all are aptly used in the basic formula of motivation theory, that motives determine acts.

Science and common sense both smile on this argument. Its biological side is known to everyone: We eat because we are hungry, sleep because we are tired, evacuate because our bowels are full, and so forth. The acts are driven or compelled or motivated by physical forces we can feel within us. This is as credible of psychology as of biology. In the priorities of mental life too, motives seem to underly behavior. We feel fear because we are threatened, anger because we are injured, thoughtful because we are puzzled, dependent because we are lovelorn. Nor is it hard to see how more delicate and less vital drives evolve from basic ones: An elemental hunger may narrow to a lust for meat or bread or sweets or money to buy them with; or it may broaden to vaulting ambition—to control, to consume, or to possess. By such reasoning, one can explain all behavior by prior motives and believe that all acts seek finally to satisfy unseen drives. Insight therapy theories do just that. At their extreme, acts dangle from their motives like puppets from their strings (Applebaum, 1982).

Put to the problems people bring psychotherapists, the theory understands them as attempts to fill needs or express drives and revelations of longing or fear. Far from being pointless accidents, automated things irrelevant to the essence of one's life (as broken legs and staph infections are essentially irrelevant), these pains are rooted in meaning, derivatives of longing, signifying causes which may seem vague, but which lurk beneath the symptom as surely as it is visible.

This suggests a strategy for therapy. Tracing the symptom to its origin should make it possible to halt the flood of misery at its motivating source. Failing to do so and attacking the symptoms runs the risk of damming up one outlet and leaving the torrent free to flood in other symptoms.

The implication of this doctrine for treatment is more ambiguous than the model of disorder it implies. If there are no meaningless symptoms, then they may all lead to ideas or feelings at the core of one's being. If no behavior is truly incidental, and it is all governed by motives which direct every act, however minute, to their relief, then all mental problems are "behavior which tries to gratify a need and fails." Understanding the disorder means tracing, in "whodunit" fashion, the need whose satisfaction is the symptom's futile aim. For treatment to remove symptoms, it must either undo the need, not often likely, or more realistically, find some means other than the symptom for fulfilling it. At all events, the idea that acts are born of underlying motives forces one to think about what action "means." It must mean the patterns of circumstance that antecede, surround, and "cause" it. The motive of an act is its meaning. This finally demands, when therapeutic discourse speaks to important motives, that therapy becomes an inquiry into the meaning of one's life.

This was not the early aim of psychoanalysis which, even today, is "classically" articulated as a therapy of personal adjustment to help people manage their mental lives with less pain. The search for meaning is fostered more, if passively, by Rogers' system, in its concern with self, because self-value and self-esteem contain the meaning systems people use to judge themselves. The search for meaning is most active and explicit, however, in existential analysis, which all but defines therapy in terms of its concern with meaninglessness, death, freedom, and isolation (Yalom, 1980). The fate of symptoms there is almost moot; they are pawns in a larger war. This is what critics caricature in satisfied patients who say, after therapy, "My tics and headaches have not changed, but now I understand them!" However ironical, the claim has merit in a system which says that visible behavior counts less than what's behind it. The main problem is never what it seems.

The belief of Insight therapists that motivation has such powerful effects lends an aura of indirection to their work. Symptoms must be outflanked and not attacked outright, not because they cannot be, nor even because the changes that result might not endure. The proper task, from the start, is to find the motive complex from which the symptoms spring (McGlashan & Miller, 1982). And this is no simple thing, for not only are motives unknown to others; they are also hidden from the sufferers themselves. Consciousness takes second place only to motivation in the theories of Insight therapists. The main reason symptoms withstand our unaided efforts to change is that our motives stay unknown to us. Therapy's job is to expose them, not to the therapist, but to the patient. Therapy techniques are tools for compelling this exposure, for crafting consciousness. And therapeutic insight means yielding to awareness of things we did not realize about ourselves.

Insight is thus synonymous with self consciousness, and its expansion is the goal of all Insight therapies. The need for detailed understanding of *un*-conscious processes is a moot technical point in Insight therapy, even in psychoanalysis. Freudian theory is concerned with the mechanisms by which information is kept out of awareness, and much scholarly work on personality deals with them. But in the actual practice of all Insight therapies, unconscious processes are inferred, not observed directly, talked about, not induced. Insight therapies work through conscious channels, whether with free association, dreams, or other thoughts or feelings. Even the assumption that unconscious processes exist, in therapy practice, is a means of aiding the expansion of consciousness, for it suggests huge resources in our minds that can be coaxed into awareness.

The basic belief of Insight therapists about personality is that symptoms are motivated, their activity largely sustained and their removal largely impeded by a dearth of consciousness. All Insight therapy therefore involves an insight-bearing sequence of (1) exposure by the patient, (2) therapist operation on the exposed material, and (3) consciousness or insight, intellectual or emotional, growing in the patient.

But what happens then? What is insight supposed to do? How does exposing motives change anything? Where is consciousness supposed to go?

6

The Uses of Consciousness

Science and Morals in Insight Therapy

The techniques of Insight therapy aim to raise consciousness, especially of one's inner self. But what has been gained by it? What is insight supposed to do?

The accounting must be made separately, I think, from a scientific and clinical view, where it is controversial, and from a moralistic one, which raises more questions. The scientific answer is that insight is supposed to relieve symptoms and to give people more control over themselves than they have felt before. The moralistic answer is that insight is not supposed to do anything, that it is a thing sufficient unto itself and valuable in large amounts. Having enough of it marks the point where the doctor can stop treatment and the client be considered cured. Cured of what? Of self ignorance.

SCIENCE AND INSIGHT THERAPY

Insight therapy began with Breuer and Freud's wholly scientific wish to find clinical tools against neurotic symptoms. The techniques of psychoanalysis were meant at first only to deal with them. Freud's personality theory, a brilliant alloy of clinical observation, personal episode, scientific thinking, and literary acumen, aimed largely to deduce how symptoms arose and to navigate the course of psychoanalysis toward their relief. The system started with a technical problem—the presence of symptoms—and worked backward to a theory of their origins and forward to a way of ending them. But theory of any kind was, for a time, subsidiary to practical concern with curing symptoms, and success or failure was judged entirely in those simple-sounding scientific terms.

Insight was seen as the agent of cure because Freudians thought that symptoms were products of a faulty unconsciousness-producing mechanism—repression. Repression prevented its victims from recognizing powerful motives, which operated sub rosa and sometimes erupted in the distorted and wretched form of neurosis. Lifting the repression, permitting consciousness, or eliciting insight, it was felt, relieved the motivational pressure so it need not be forced to surface any more in such corrosive forms. With consciousness, the symptoms might automatically clear up, as it were, without more treatment. If not, having insight still would help patients understand themselves and, thereby, better control their motives in ways that made symptoms superfluous, causing them to atrophy.

[The theory of classical psychoanalysis is more complex than my statement suggests, but its main theme is not. The processes which prevent consciousness, such as "defenses," "denial," and "projection," are variants of repression. Also, those which facilitate consciousness, such as "abreaction," "working through," and "catharsis," all lead to insight.]

This rationale is still basic to all Insight schools that lean toward psychoanalysis because it justifies the therapy of searching for hidden motives. But few practitioners of Insight nowadays would take this doctrine "neat" and unadorned. In late years, they have been battered too much by Behavior therapists' claims that Insight therapy is worthless. Even earlier, however, thoughtful members of their own ranks were noting the flaws and failures of psychoanalytic orthodoxy and were qualifying it (cf. Alexander, 1962). Experienced therapists today would agree that insight, however detailed and precise, into one's motives, however unconscious, does not by itself solve most problems, clear most symptoms, or change people's lives in any but trivial intellectual or economic ways—they have a lot of news about themselves for cocktail party talk and they are out a lot of money in treatment fees.

It is possible, of course, that insight which does not produce relief is false insight, and the true motives remain hidden. Also, insights may be correct but incomplete, with their motive roots deeper and more tangled than was thought. Insight purists make just such claims outright, while analysts who treat patients for ten or twenty years make them implicitly.

[These are literal, not just figures of speech, and not so rare. A colleague told me how the analytic consultant to his mental hospital staff urged therapists not to give up "too easily" on their cases. He was now, he said, in the sixteenth year of treating a homosexual patient, though only the previous ten years had been intensive, At last, he was pleased to report, the man was making such progress that "in another four years he should be able to make a heterosexual adjustment."]

"Interminable analysis," an embarrassing problem even while Freud lived, can be justified by this plausible explanation. But it is flawed argument, logically circular and wasteful. It is more likely that insight alone is simply not enough to solve most therapeutic problems.

Most Insight therapists who say so, however, still think it necessary and helpful to explore motives in psychotherapy. But they also rationalize insight in terms of other benefits than symptom relief: "Gaining insight will not alone resolve all problems or symptoms," they say, "but it will help clients control their behavior better if they are motivated enough to do so." For symptoms, this argument has the same "Catch 22" as the "incomplete" or "false" insight arguments. If relief occurs, it means the treatment worked; if not, it means the patient did not want it "badly enough." We are then back where we started.

The argument for "other benefits" than symptom relief is important, however, if the question of patients' wanting to change badly enough is left out. It is important because it shifts and broadens the grounds for assessing what psychotherapy does, implying that it gives a more general and less specific kind of help than one might think. The idea that self-control is one of its general benefits particularly reduces the responsibility of the therapist, who is no longer required so much to cure clients as to help them cure themselves!

In a way, this position is more consistent with the actual techniques of Insight therapy than is the argument that success is defined by relief (Menninger, 1958). Throughout the actual course of treatment, initiative is the patient's and so is responsibility for what is done in the session. So why not responsibility for the cure as well?

The scientific "rub" of this position comes, not by making patients responsible for the cure of their own symptoms, but by exempting symptom-removal from the requirements of success, for this removes the most visible index of what psychotherapy has achieved. When the connection between insight and symptoms is so loosened, as it is here, it is equally fair to "successfully" end treatment with the symptoms still there or to say that therapy failed even with the symptoms gone unless insight was achieved. The one says that treatment cured everything except what bothered the patient in the first place, and the other says, never mind if patients get well unless they get self-aware. Finally, since insight is applied to motives whose force and volume is unknown because they are hidden, how does one know how much insight is enough? The scientific status of this therapy depends on measurable relationships between the insight it produces and the objects of that insight. No object is more obvious than symptoms.

MORALS AND INSIGHT THERAPY

Despite all, it is still sensible to divorce insight from such practical effects as symptom relief. Even if symptomatic trouble is what inspires the search for motives in the first place, who can say that the discoveries which result must ipso facto satisfy the impetus for the search or, for that matter, that the search should be for no more than its initial ends? Columbus's failure to find a new route to India did not make the discovery of America less real, less important, or less rewarding. Should he have regretted the trip? The Insight therapist, by the same token, may propose to start on the motivational path suggested by the client's symptoms without knowing where it will lead, with only the faith that it will lead somewhere worth going. But doing so practically abandons the commonly accepted notions of treatment and cure applied to most ailments; it makes of insight an end unto itself which, as it does not relate to symptoms, forces a redefinition of psychotherapy. That definition makes the therapist a moralist.

As long as the prescription of insight is rationalized by its effect on symptoms, the therapist can claim that treatment is a technical activity, scientifically conceived and aimed at some measurable end. But the more such concrete ends are attenuated, the less is this possible. The most distant of such connections, perhaps, is the claim that treatment is a preventive against some future symptom-generating condition. It is a weak claim to practice. When the justification of insight does not bear on some known distress, but on different ends, the fitness of dispensing it is more a moral than scientific matter.

The simplest moral problem in its dispensation is seen if we think of insight as having a benign effect in every way except in its effect on symptoms. The doctor may then be trying to sell something other than what the patient meant to buy, which is morally questionable. The same question might still be apt, however, if insight also cured symptoms, for so long as it did more than that, it would do other than that. But in such cases, we usually overlook the side effects (sometimes to our peril, as studies of long-term drug effects increasingly reveal). The point here is not about professional ethics, some of which are merely guild rules of trade, but about the nature of the profession. I am not saying that Insight therapists, by doing something other than treating symptoms, are immoral rather than moral, but that they are moralists as well as technicians. It is the generality of their effort, not its efficacy, which forces this conclusion.

What is the morality they promote? In precept, it is the virtue of insight or consciousness or self-knowledge. In practice, it is the necessity for each of us to take our own initiatives in the quest for insight and to be alone responsible for finding it. By implication, it is the right of individuals to live as they choose.

For Freudians, the unknown self that needs knowing has a core of violent and lustful impulses, denied as one's own, often angrily attributed to others, the antitheses of the familiar heroic virtues decreed by the culture and charged to be emulated by the individual. For Rogerians, it is a self of discrepancy, where deprecation of self worth produces neurotic misery and treatment restores healthy self love. For existentialists, it is a self alone in a hostile universe who, to become capable of knowledge, must realize its isolation as the first step toward imposing meaning upon chaos. Regardless of the content to be exhumed, all Insight theorists make the same moral supposition: that the self is valuable, that it is worthy of being known, and that its title to explication and intelligibility is its sheer existence, not the role it fills or acts it does or moves.

A technical reason clients must take the initiative for self-discovery in therapy is the belief that they will refuse to hear or understand or absorb the meanings of self if those are delivered from outside. But this rule also reinforces the moral doctrine of selfhood by making patients be alone with self even in treatment sessions, thus forcing independence. The moral goal this tactic serves is autonomy, freedom to experience the self, to enhance it, to gratify it, to unbind it, to test it, to give it rein to palpate itself and, so doing, to be fulfilled. What concrete actions serve this end and constitute therapeutic deeds? No special ones—any, or all, or none—what serves the self, or fairly represents it to itself, can qualify.

The virtues of this morality are so popular among liberal people in democratic countries that it would be redundant to recount them at length. For secularists and civil libertarians, it exonerates the individualism of the Protestant ethic in a more plausible context than could any religious creed. It grounds the justification of political autonomy in science. It affirms individual human rights to independence in more fundamental and more final terms than could the best of 18th-century rationalists, offering a more probable "natural" order than Encyclopedists or natural theologians ever could. It frees the artist from suspicion of perversity, assigning the same perversity to all humanity, and casts on conformism the shadow of hypocrisy to boot. It offers the ultimate justification of individualism, and so it has since its earliest, most conservative exposition at Freud's hand, and despite his own social conservatism.

At the extreme of existential analysis, Insight therapy strives to establish or restore meaning, not function, to life. The object of treatment is not so much surcease of pain as finding a meaningful context in life of which the pain is an intelligible and tolerable part. This, of course, is what religions have long tried to do. And it is what, when their doctrines become incredible to people of any era, secular philosophies criticize and replace. They, in turn, often are corrupted or co-opted by old and new religions, cults, and ideologies in the endless struggle of humanity to make life meaningful. So, in the ancient Hellenistic world, as classical religions lost their strength, Stoicism and Epicureanism grew. They were then co-opted by the mystery religions, and they by Christianity, which spun off cults and creeds and took in classical philosophers, and on and on. Now Scientology, *est*, and many cults in the almost faithless Democratic West proliferate to the same end. Mostly nonprofessional, sometimes commercial counterparts of existential analysis, they all strive to replace the personal meanings that are lost when the extrinsic morality of religion, common custom, and community loses its authority in people's minds.

THE PROBLEMS OF INSIGHT MORALITY

To the extent Insight therapy fails technically to restore functions, its scientific pretensions as an applied healing art must be discounted. But its technical success, long a polemical bete noire against which Action therapists made a case, is now better supported by research reports than it used to be (see Chapter 13). It is precisely of the meanings implicit in Insight therapy that the most important moral questions must be asked, especially about the implications of hidden motives and of individualism. These questions speak to more than social philosophy and political science. Insight therapies, particularly psychoanalysis, are the psychological orthodoxies of our age, and like all familiar orthodoxies, leave us too thoughtlessly comfortable with the moral orders they imply.

The system says it works, for instance, by lending all initiatives to the client. But does it really do so, or is the proposal itself part of a seduction of patients to voluntarily exercise their doctors' preferences? If the latter, then the seduction is made perfect by therapists' sharing the myth of their own midwifery, just as placebos work best when doctors think they are giving active drugs (London & Engstrom, 1982). By this delegation of responsibility, Insight therapists insulate themselves from all assaults; if they fail to heal symptoms, they are not much to blame because cure resides in the patient to begin with. But if they succeed in changing people otherwise in opprobrious ways, they are not so culpable there either—for all they did is put clients in contact with themselves (their selves), catalyzing their behavior. The choices patients made were their own, not their therapists'.

But are the choices really the patients' either, according to this system? The endless seeming chain of motives, especially those *unseen* (and thus needing *insight*), suggests that they are finally free of choice, or will, or all executive capacities. As Anna Balakian suggests, does not "the preoccupation with the subconscious . . . anesthetize the sensitivities of that faculty which used to be called 'conscience' [1962]?" Perhaps any moral sense is stretched beyond recovery by introspection of a causal chain that puts events so far from their origins in time and space that the idea of responsibility becomes absurd, literally *ab-surd,* rootless, unanchored in a recognizable self.

If so, then the doctrine that espouses the search for a self hidden beneath the surface of behavior nurtures this rootlessness by saying there is a "real self" different from what is seen. The assumption of massive complexity, the mental iceberg Freud describes, is limitless and, accordingly, always witnesses in defense of nonresponsibility, leaving individuals free to feel stainless and justified in anything they do.

Maybe this is the heart of the problem. It is not whether Insight therapists really can confer free choice or whether they should want to. It is rather whether their successful efforts might shape people who, schooled in all the erstwhile hidden references to self, could be best described as well-adjusted psychopaths. Such persons might not be amoral, by their own lights, but theirs would be a moral order whose referents all lay within themselves. Would the broad acceptance of this doctrine sponsor an individualism which could support no social order and, perhaps, which no humane society could afford? If the methods of Insight therapy make people "self conscious" enough, may they not see their selves fulfilled in isolation? Does the "ultimate aloneness" of human beings now graduate from an existential observation to a therapeutic recommendation for facing the world with self-interest as the standard of choice for every social act we do?

Where sociality means crude conformity or mindless service to the brutal dicta of tyrants, nurturing the lonely self preserves humanity. But mostly it does not mean that, at least in societies where psychotherapy most flourishes. There, individuals are most secure from just such harm. For them, the moral burden of freedom is the temptation to endless selfishness, to indifference, not servility. As C. P. Snow so clearly put it: "Most of our fellow human beings . . . are under-fed and die before their time. In the crudest terms, *that* is the social condition. There is a moral trap which comes through the insight into man's loneliness: it tempts one to sit back, complacent in one's unique tragedy, and let the others go without a meal [1959, p. 7]."

The asocial implications of Insight therapy have troubled its advocates as much as its critics, and some have tried to weave a prosocial imperative into the rationale of Insight treatments. One such argument says that the real self is fully realized only in interpersonal relationships such as love offers, and therapy prepares us for this experience. Another says that since the therapy relationship provides the medium for self-discovery, it creates a general need for fulfillment through relationships with others. The sophisticated genetic theory of H. S. Sullivan says that, since the child's self comes into being via its social context, adult selfhood, at peril of insanity, must be maintained in one. Victor Frankl says that love for other persons is the most vital meaning life holds. But none of these answers fully satisfies the question. They say that sociality is good for self, not how good self, fulfilled, will then be for society.

The question is somewhat tangential to the purposes of Insight therapy because its main themes, to begin with, aim less at social functions than personal meanings and less still at conflicts between them. Even so, people's social roles and functions, in this view, are finally meaningful only as they serve their selves. I think that this idea commits all Insight therapies to a moral posture in which individuals, pitted against societies, have prior right. It is a right without mandatory commitment or responsibility. This differs sharply from classical social theory which, as Philip Rieff says, sees society as the true therapeutic agent and good citizenship as the final mental prophylactic (1961b). But it also dissents from classical definitions of virtue, both religious and secular, which hinge human dignity, or worthiness, or right to self esteem, to moral codes that stand outside the self, whether revealed in thunder and inscribed in stone or elected into law by common counsel among peers.

If older moral codes have no more claim to truth than Insight does, and age alone surely can give them none, at least their demands are familiar. There is emotional refuge in duties we can in common recognize, discuss, measure, discharge, or reject. Thus comes a final moral question of Insight therapy.

Where are the boundaries between understanding and tolerance or responsibility? Granting that our behavior is explained by the motives which underlie it, should it become acceptable to us, let alone to others, by virtue of the explanation? Suppose we view it as weak or stupid or vile? should the wish to change it waver with understanding? And if it does, then does not the distinction between explanation and excuse become confused and arbitrary? There is the danger, since this system must in any case proceed this way, that the wholesale quest for insight into self which occupies so much of intellect in these times, may be less a quest for cure, or even for control of self, than grand apology for impotence or willful deviance. Where this is so, the search for meaning becomes a desperate substitute for functions which were lost or never had.

CONCLUSION

The early efforts of Insight therapists were to cure neurotic symptoms. Later, they broadened to help people better understand and control their lives, regardless of the fate of symptoms. At first, psychotherapy dealt mostly with phobias, anxieties, obsessions, and hysterias. Then its topics expanded to all uncontrollable impulses, sexual deviations, depression, and so-called character disorders, and finally, to a general concern with existential problems of a traditionally moralistic rather than scientific kind. It is impulse, deviance and guilt, with their obvious problems of social perspective on behavior, which demand the nicest distinctions between the roles of moralist and clinical scientist. If Insight therapists have failed to concern themselves with the distinction, it is as much because they live in a society which is sympathetic to individual liberty and rich and powerful enough to tolerate a lot of deviance as because they reject the role of moralist. That is also true. Were they to specify their moral role, however, their theoretical positions suggest that they would promote libertarian, individualistic morality. They sometimes soften the harshness of this plain doctrine with the qualifier that people, in doing what they please, should not hurt others. Many lawyers, theologians, social utopians, and other moralists might say this is an incomplete morality by itself, however therapeutic it might be for individuals. Some critics of Insight therapy would say it is not therapeutic either.

Some professional opponents of Insight therapy have been, if anything, even less concerned with morals than have Insight therapists and, by their own lights, have been more concerned with science. Their indictment of Insight therapy has little to do with problems of meaning, which some of them see as a meaningless idea and, until recently, had little more to do with the moral implications of social deviance. They have chiefly addressed themselves to the technical problem of symptom removal, proposing stridently that Insight therapy is rarely able to relieve symptoms, that it is grossly wasteful when it does work, and that its successes have nothing to do with insight anyway, but are either accidents or the results of mislabeled *action* methods. Let us now look closely at these Action therapists to see their origins, indictments, techniques, prospects, and their flaws.

III

THE HEALING MODES:
ACTION THERAPY

THE ARGUMENT

"Science" and "symptom relief" are the battle cries of Action or Behavior therapies. As champions of these ideas, they warred on Insight treatments in the 1960s and won space in the professional Establishment. Some Behavioral methods were published decades earlier, but they made little impact then. After World War II, clinical psychologists especially, steeped in scientific method, armed with public funds for training and research, hungry for academic accomplishment, and eager for professional independence from psychiatrists and psychoanalyst physicians, were attentive audience to these scientific sounding treatments. They are still its main exponents.

In pure and early form, Action treatment is reactionary to Insight therapy's main premises and practices. It attacks symptoms, not motives; saddles therapists, not clients, with responsibility for the treatment agenda; speaks to damaged functions, not existential pain; and promotes repair, not insight. Planning and economy are clinical corollaries of this attitude and professional cudgels against the slower work and vaguer goals of Insight therapies.

From theories and experiments on how animals and people learn, Behavior therapists drew inspiration, argument, and strength for new treatments of the same ills Insight worked on. But Action methods were more pragmatic than their inventors thought, and sophisticated pragmatism more than theory made their novel interventions valuable. The principle which guides them, not quite theory, says: "Neurotic problems are resolved by healing experience." The therapist's task is to decide what healing means, to plan the action leading to it, and to guide the client's movements down this path—by whatever methods work, in whatever setting serves as operating theater, not limited to talking as the only treatment tool nor requiring consciousness as curative response.

The upshot, from the start, was a variety of remedies for varied ills, both in the work of pioneers and in the tropical growth of treatments from the seeds they sowed. Action therapy is not rudely empirical, but its pragmatic emphasis makes theory sometimes an afterthought. Its scientific sobriquet, "functional analysis," is a prescription for therapists to plan their work precisely and judge it by standards everyone can understand. Doing so has made these treatments paragons of scientific virtue for studying psychotherapy results. By firmly linking what they do to what they undertake to treat, it has also made finer technologies of them than Insight therapies have, with techniques for sex, for tantrums, for timidity, for terror or stuttering or aggression, and more. This has happened, not because Behavioral methods come from novel theories, or are themselves so new, or so successful, none of which is wholly true—but because they have transcended, in their practical variety, the common constraints of most psychotherapy, including dependency on speech as the sole medium of communication and control.

Action therapies get the obverse of criticisms laid on Insight therapy. They are faulted as clinically simplistic and morally presumptuous. The clinical complaint says treatment is hobbled by its specificity, which lets symptoms be sustained by nourishment from motives that go untreated or which, suppressing symptoms, risks their resurrection from those hidden roots. Neither claim is well supported by the evidence, but neither can be totally dismissed. Action therapists now are less insistent that "the symptom is the problem" and more inclined to guard their motivational flanks with more "multi-modal" views of problems than was true before.

The moral allegation is that Action therapists take too much responsibility and are too ready to manipulate clients for their supposed therapeutic good. Whatever may be gained by easing symptoms is lost by stealing people's freedom of choice and responsibility for themselves and promoting dependency on therapists by giving them the final word on what the goals of psychotherapy should be.

Action therapists would answer that their moral duty is to diagnose and treat, much as physicians do; that their treatment obligation is to give relief, not self direction; that they must do so by the thriftiest and safest means at hand; that decent attention to symptomatic woes does not violate patients' freedom but protects their privacy; and that it is self-deluding to think that therapists can avoid decisions about the goals of psychotherapy, like it or not. Within that moral framework, skill at manipulation, anathema to Insight treatment, is prize beyond purchase to Actionists, whose right to influence is as clear to them as their duty to cure is certain. Once therapy's goals are mutually agreed upon, manipulation is not a merely useful tactic to them, but a moral imperative which they must satisfy to have the right to offer help at all.

The "rub" for Action therapists comes when the goals of psychotherapy are not mutually agreed, which is the common case when people ask for help with more than tidy symptoms; or when their symptoms are socially deviant, not mentally disordered; or when their goals in treatment change; or when alternative remedies all are horns of moral dilemmas for client, therapist, or both. For Behaviorists, who approach therapy with narrow purpose and precise intent, moral counsel is no more part of the therapeutic bargain than are hidden motives or heightened awareness. But moral issues insinuate into helping relationships as functions and meanings intertwine and overlap in people's lives; what's symptom for one problem turns out to be the heart of another; "adjustment" and "fulfillment" are less separable than they seemed; and therapeutic contracts change, expanding to include more things than either side had bargained for. Action and Insight therapies, in the end, face much the same burden of moral issues for most of the same reasons, intrinsic to this relationship and to these times.

7

An Epitaph for Insight

Polemics and Policy in Action Therapy

When Breuer and Freud made the odd discovery that hysteria could be cured by talking and listening, they had no idea what impact it would have on their own craft, let alone on the intellectual life of the next century. Their early goal was as modest as their view was short: to find a treatment for hysteria that would cut its symptoms near enough the root to stop their flowering again. Hypnosis had long been used with some success, but it was undependable. Some symptoms did not yield to hypnotic suggestion, and some of those that did later gave way to new ones. Even at its unpredictable best, moreover, hypnotic cure was as strange as hysterical illness, compounding the medical puzzle even when it worked.

Their cathartic method, which Freud later expanded into psychoanalysis, differed from hypnotic treatment in two main ways: It needed no instructions by the doctor for the symptoms to retreat, and the doctor's role was reversed; instead of doing most of the talking, he mostly listened. This kind of listening, morever, was not preface to the treatment, like taking a case history, but was the essence of it. This shifted the doctor's role from a very active to a more passive one. With the shift of function, responsibility shifted. Since the doctor had to be listener in order to treat and could not force on the patient the consciousness vital to cure, there was less chance of bungling by errors of commission than of simply being ineffective; there were fewer ways for therapists to err.

If the doctor was not so responsible for the treatment, neither was the patient so responsible for the ailment. Freud was loyal to the scientific determinism in which his medicine was schooled; it argued that neurotic people were ill. Neurotic behavior is the product of its motives, which are unconscious and therefore not in one's control. In this, neurosis is like an infectious illness; once contracted, the victim cannot be blamed for the germs. If anything, neurotics are even less liable, for we may increase the risk of infection by abusing our physical health; but since Freudian theory put the origins of neurosis in childhood, and in circumstances beyond children's control, its symptoms could not come from collusion between a liably self-destructive psyche and a cooperatively banal environment.

Even near its beginnings, when Insight therapy aimed only at specific ailments, not at larger questions, it was ripe for some enigmas and embarrassments. Deterministic theory made patients not responsible for their illness, so how could they be responsible for their cure? Yet this therapy seemed to hold them responsible for the treatment process. The studied indirection of analytic method, moreover, proscribed the use of blunt, direct, or surgical-like procedures. So how did cures occur? When the accidental products of the client fit the delicate interventions of the doctor? Or by some activity of therapist or patient for which neither was quite responsible? How does treatment work?

And what does "cure" mean? It cannot be the mere erasure of the "presenting symptoms" which send people into treatment, for theory says they are not the main problems: Symptoms are signs of covert maladies of motive. If cure means the exposure of those motives, must the symptoms also disappear or not? In either case, how much discovery of motives suits what criterion of cure? Do not motives themselves have motives, and must these not also be exposed and analyzed?

These questions may seem like casuistry, but they are important. They apply to early psychoanalysis, to neo-Freudians, ego psychologists, Rogerians, and existentialists alike. They are intrinsic to any system that makes insight the main event of treatment and that views symptoms as results of disorder rather than its core. Much as they have deviated from Freud, other Insight therapies have stuck to these principles.

It is here that Action therapies open their polemic. At the extreme, they deny that symptoms have disorders underlying them and that insight has more than an incidental role in cure. Their dissent merely starts here; they depart from Insight therapists on many counts of technique and of theories which support it. Also, Action therapies speak fluently in the language of today's hardest intellectual currency, that of experimental science, and make their case only in these terms, as Insight therapies often have not. They have made many friends in doing so, and the relative status and popularity of the two systems, accordingly, has changed. Action therapies have not "done in" Insight schools, as they once angrily hoped to, but are now firmly seated with them in the Mental Health Establishment. The polemics have not ended, but are more subdued. They have been replaced in part by a politely disingenuous mutual lip service muttered across the high walls of their still separate and fortified academies—few professors or programs teach both modes to graduate students, interns, or residents.

But equal status has also produced a growing ecumenical trend—more practitioners call themselves "eclectics" than used to (Garfield & Kurtz, 1976; Norcross & Prochaska, 1982); some research is showing that different modes work better for different problems (Barlow & Wolfe, 1981); and calls for ecumenism are more frequent than before (Goldfried, 1982; London, 1983b; Marmor & Woods, 1980).

THE GENESIS OF ACTION THERAPY

Who are the Action therapists? What are their origins? Their intellectual pretensions? The 1959 revision of Walter Bromberg's history spent only one chapter on "conditioning treatments," a good name for them at the time. They were then calling themselves "learning theory-based psychotherapists" or "behavior therapists," often with the "psycho-" removed, and some were calling their methods "behavior modification" rather than "therapy." Their obscurity was not limited to the laity; psychology courses did not talk of Action therapies under any title, though most textbooks discussed Insight therapy and Freud and Rogers in particular. Social workers and psychiatrists then knew still less of these things than did psychologists.

This began to change around 1960, largely through the efforts of Hans Eysenck in the United Kingdom and Joseph Wolpe, then in transit from South Africa to America. Eysenck, an experimental psychologist, was already the *enfant terrible* of psychotherapists because of articles he wrote saying that conventional psychotherapy was useless (1952, 1960). Wolpe, a psychiatrist, went from relative obscurity to infamy for a single closely argued book which rejected psychoanalysis, described some new treatments based on his (1954) theories, and gave some statistical data on their effectiveness (1958).

These were not the first iconoclastic attacks on psychotherapy nor the first innovations based on the psychology of learning, but they appeared at a time when the therapy "industry" was ripe for change. The vanguard of this change was clinical psychology which, after World War II, became an increasingly independent profession. Previously, few clinical psychologists were trained in psychotherapy. Then, huge funding was given to university psychology departments by the United States' National Institute of Mental Health and its Veterans Administration to expand the profession. Most of its aspirants wanted psychotherapy training, which then meant Insight therapy. But the psychology departments which trained them were dominated by experimentalists, who saw to it that budding clinicians also spent a lot of graduate school time studying learning, an area of prolific experimentation over the previous half-century. Other mental health professionals had no training to speak of in learning except, perhaps, a whiff of Pavlov's dog in a college psychology course.

Equally important, perhaps, was the attraction of academia for psychologists. Despite the lure of clinical work, it remained for them the symbol of professional status. So, relative to other mental health professions, they did more research, more reading, and more professional writing. The American Psychological Association claimed, in 1954, to have become the largest publishing house in the world by virtue of its many scholarly journals. The aim of American clinical psychology professors, in a 1948 conference, was to train psychologists who were skilled both as scientists and clinicians (Raimy, 1950).

They succeeded in some degree. From then on, research in psychotherapy became chiefly the province of psychologists, as were most of the scientific disputes about it. Most of the storm over Eysenck's articles was in psychology journals, and most of the audience which welcomed behavior therapy was psychologists. They did most of the studies comparing treatments, published the books, journals, and articles about it, and staffed the professional societies and lobbies which propagated it. Though they have dealt abundantly with all of psychotherapy, most of their work has gone to behavior methods which, since about 1970, have dominated scholarship in this field (London, 1983a).

PROGENITORS OF ACTION THERAPY

The forebears of Action therapy were laboratory scientists, not clinicians. Ivan Pavlov, who won the Nobel Prize in 1903 for his research in physiology, is sometimes considered the grandfather of these methods because of his monumental studies of learning. His younger contemporary, however, the American psychologist Edwin L. Thorndike, made equally important scientific contributions to learning. In fact, Pavlov got the idea for his 1904 study of "conditional" responses from Thorndike's doctoral dissertation, *Animal Intelligence* (1898–1901). Their work formed the bases for the Action therapies, but neither man counted a therapy school among his many contributions to applied psychology. Late in life, Pavlov grew interested in treatment based on his research. It got little notice in the West until Action therapies became popular, but it is the basis of all Soviet psychotherapy for political as well as scientific reasons.

Thorndike's ideas were widely publicized in the United States as "Behaviourist Psychology" in the 1913 and 1914 writings of John B. Watson. Watsonian Behaviourism, so called, became the dominant psychology of the United States in the 1920s and 1930s. Some clinical applications were made in those years by Watson himself; by Mary Cover Jones; by Edwin R. Guthrie; by Molly and O. Hobart Mowrer, and by others. But almost no one pushed them much, and they did not "take" professionally until the 1960s. Learning studies were theoretical or were applied to educational, not clinical, problems.

The therapists who first transferred the psychology of learning from laboratory to clinic were mostly vicarious students of their scientific mentors, having neither studied with them nor, in many cases, ever met them. Most were reared professionally as clinicians and trained in a variant of psychoanalysis. Then they grew disaffected with the therapy they used and sought alternative methods and rationales for their work.

Curiously, the intellectual roots of Action therapy are largely independent of Insight therapy, but its historical roots in the careers of its founders are not. Some of them tell us the reactionary process of their development, and we may guess it about others. It may explain why, despite differences among themselves, the early Action therapists tend to attack Insight therapy so vehemently. Most of the second generation of these therapists, on the other hand, was trained only in Action techniques and theories. Having come to them without sin, as it were, with nothing to recant, their writing on the topic is less polemical. Conflicts between the systems may thereby be obscured. It is useful, I think, to mark the differences in warlike tones, as the founders did.

THE ASSAULT ON INSIGHT

Their assault on Insight is mounted on several levels: They accuse it technically of producing useless knowledge at the cost of needed action, theoretically of inferring motives when it should be observing behavior, and philosophically of wallowing in sentimental humanism when it should be courting tough-minded mechanism.

As for goals of therapy, the Actionists allege that Insight therapists delude themselves and, at their worst, defraud society by claiming to sell self-knowledge, which almost no one comes to buy. Knowing that their clients seek relief, not information, they still post their walls with certificates that license dispensation of a balm they do not have. Face to face with customers, they then produce a diagram of illness and a blueprint for repair, which always says the same: "You suffer from illusions that must dissipate when once you know yourself. First among them, and most illusory, is the belief that what you think is wrong really is what's wrong." By sleight-of-mind, it seems, the sufferers' felt troubles are demoted, and they are launched on an introspective voyage which can last forever—for when do people really know themselves? This might be justified, says the Actionist, if in course of this winding trip, the trouble went away. But mostly it does not except for random errors in which the therapist slips and, accidentally using Action methods, cures. The Action therapies claim to rightly prevent the spiraling inner search by anchoring treatment to the proximate source of pain: the symptom. In this respect, they are truly reactionary, for they thus return to what was also once the goal of Insight.

Far from bringing hidden motives into consciousness, the early Action therapies' attack on symptoms dismissed their source and disavowed the crucial need for consciousness. This probes the very core of Insight treatment, for it implies that symptoms may not represent motive states, but may be nonsense learned by chance connection with unhappy circumstance, and consciousness may be no

help in gaining freedom from it. Were this the case, and the labyrinth of motives a fiction, then not only might symptoms stay when motives became conscious, but even if they left, it would not prove that they were products of the
motive! If not, the personality theory which informs Insight therapy would
shake, for its main foundation is the hypothesized connection of symptoms to
their sources.

There was another reason, though, for questioning Insight theories, especially
humanistic ones. They imply that therapy problems involve uniquely human
attributes of clients which are helped by human acts of therapists. Action therapists said the opposite: Most neurotic problems involve learned behavior of kinds
which are as visible in other species as in human beings. The proper treatment is
less the right display of humanity than the artful exercise of mechanics in which
the technical problem is finding which organismic buttons to push or switches to
throw. This is why early Actionists, angrily opposing a "disease model" of neurosis and treatment, ran to animal laboratories to find learning models of human
mental ailments in creatures simpler than ourselves. Humanistic Insight therapists reject such studies as poor analogies. They know that neuroses and stress
disorders can be produced experimentally in animals, but they doubt such states
are just like human troubles.

Finally, Action therapists had an economic complaint. Insight therapy is so
time-consuming and expensive, they said, and so few people are helped by it,
that it is doubtful even as a luxury of the rich. When they first said so, psychotherapy clients did have to be better off financially than most, and there was evidence that Insight Therapy worked worse than Action methods. Both situations
have changed since. But the demand for all psychotherapy also has increased so
much that echoes of these old wars are now come back to haunt the whole
industry. Since so many people want psychotherapy, and there have been such
storms over its value, some champions of national health insurance in the United
States want to consider psychotherapy insurance "cost ineffective," meaning
that it will be too expensive for what people get out of it. Action therapists may
be hoist on their own petard, along with their enemies, if this idea prevails, at
great disservice to the public.

GENERAL TECHNIQUE OF ACTION THERAPY

In addition to common hostility to Insight therapy, Action therapists share
some positive ideas about treatment.

Perhaps their most important common technical ideas are relative indifference to the motivational origins of symptoms and deep concern with the detailed goals of treatment. Contrary to Insight therapists, who are concerned with
tracing symptoms to their sources and more casual about where doing so will
lead, Action therapists are eager to eliminate symptoms and more complacent
about their origins. They want to get specific behavior changes as quickly and

precisely as they can—and in doing so, care not a whit what clients know about themselves except as these are useful to the changes to be engineered. Like Henry Ford, the Action therapist despises history.

Two tactical results of the planful, goal-directed character of Action therapy are all but inevitable: First, the therapist takes more control of the treatment sessions, and at times of the outside life of the patient, than Insight therapists would. Second, the therapist is more responsible for the outcome of treatment, that is, for how the client changes, than are Insight therapists.

If the goal of Insight therapy is to free people, that of Action Therapy, it is fair to say, is to cure them. It may seem ironical that these therapists, though rejecting the disease model of neurosis, would no more ask patients to conduct their own treatment than doctors would ask them to prescribe their own medicines. But neither would the teachers of a complex skill ask students to compose their own lesson plans, and it is with educators that the closest analogue is found. By and large, Action therapists plan specific treatments according to their understanding of the specific needs of each patient. The formal planning process is called "functional analysis."

They do not force these plans on clients, for the most part. Most therapists find it useful, if not vital, to have the client's active cooperation in planning. Sometimes they even make a formal contract. Patients who help plan treatment understand it better and are more motivated to work for its success. But this does not make insight critical to cure. At best, the Action therapist may say it has some minor benefits—but it is change in act or feeling which defines cure here, not understanding. The value of patients' helping to plan treatment is that it fosters a positive attitude to the general enterprise and to specific tasks like "homework" assignments. Anyway, insight into a treatment plan is not the same as insight into one's motives or unconscious processes.

Most Action therapists, in any case, do not design treatment around patients' understanding of it, and all are very active in the treatment session. A few argue and exhort; some use hypnosis often, which means they do much of the talking; some do most of the talking anyway; some plan and control the program in a way that makes discussion irrelevant.

Just as they are responsible for conducting sessions, Action therapists take much responsibility for therapy's outcome by deciding in advance what changes they wish to promote. This is more true of some Action therapies than of others. Even so, in common contrast to Insight therapists, who do not wish to control patients, the extent to which Action therapists are unable not just to predict, but to control outcomes, is an index of their failure. They are not scheming Machiavellians or power-hungry mad scientists who use human pieces in infernal chess games, as some adversaries have said. Selecting specific goals is part of the planful character of treatment. Success means that therapists have met them. And they no more make patients responsible for their plans by discussing them in advance than a physician does so by cataloging the available medicines. Even when they propose many possible goals, Action therapists say what goals they think are realistic and take some responsibility for meeting them. Insight therapists put the onus of setting treatment goals more on the patient.

So much for the common methods of Action therapies: The therapist actively designs treatment plans rather than passively awaiting the introspections of the patient; plans specific details and goals with only secondary attention to the problem's history; and assumes serious responsibility for the changes resulting from the treatment (Goldfried & Davison, 1976).

Naturally, no such plans, controls, or responsibility are possible without therapists' making some assumptions about symptoms and the conditions which control them. Ideas of personality underly Action therapy as they do Insight therapy, and its procedures are linked to theories that inform the plans.

POLICIES FOR ACTION

Action methods are not based on theories of personality, in the narrow sense, for that term is commonly used for theories of human behavior alone. They rely more on theories of learning, which try less than personality theories to explain uniquely human behavior but are more general in that they apply to other species as well as us. This makes them easier to study in the laboratory and, therefore, easier to prove. Despite disputes among themselves, Action therapies all agree that a few laws of learning explain the conditions which psychotherapy can treat. These rules, by and large, apply as well to other creatures as to human beings.

The principles have all been connected with the term "conditioning," either as "classical" conditioning, so-called of Pavlov's work; as "instrumental" conditioning, which Thorndike discovered; or as the "operant" conditioning of B. F. Skinner, a special case of instrumental conditioning. After almost a century of fruitful study, these processes are still not understood in some respects, including how and how much they dominate human behavior, especially of adults. This problem is not urgent to Action therapies. They use "conditioning" simply as a formal term for "teaching and learning"—which human beings certainly can do. More important, they assume that all teaching and learning can be seen correctly as stimulus-response patterns. Learned behavior is lawful behavior, this says, and the laws apply equally to human beings of any age, sex, or degree of sophistication as to rats, cats, and dogs. Humans are not the same as other animals, of course, but the same principles of learning apply to them, regardless what they learn. This says nothing more dramatic than that the circulation of the blood works the same way in humans as in chimpanzees despite other differences in their physiologies. But it is important in connection with another learning principle: that of the interchangeability of stimuli and responses. This says that animals will learn to make the same automatic response to a once-trivial new stimulus if it happens to occur when the response is already being made to some other very affecting stimulus. It also says, conversely, that a new response will become habitual to a stimulus if it is made just as the arousing properties of that stimulus are reduced. Now the exact conditions in which these things happen are complex, as the principle may seem to be. But the upshot is clear: it says that under the right conditions, any stimulus can be attached habitually to any response.

Talking, for instance, may be valuable in Action therapy, but maybe not for its meaning so much as for its stimulus value, that is, its capacity to get linked with a response the therapist wants from the patient. This will be apparent in the "conditioned avoidance" treatment of Joseph Wolpe. It is a bit more subtle in the "flooding" therapy of Thomas Stampfl, who uses speech as a convenient substitute for physical objects. And it is more subtle still in the Cognitive Behavior Therapies, a second generation of Action treatments, whose rhetoric and concepts depart somewhat from the strict conditioning analogues of the pioneers.

Viewing all learned behavior as stimulus-response patterns, the picture of psychological disorders that emerges is one of learned disabilities; the untoward things that have been learned are symptoms. In some cases, people have learned bad responses to innocent stimuli, as in compulsive rituals or sexual fetishes. In others, they have accidentally connected a once-trivial stimulus to an arousing one and now make the same automatic response to either, as in phobias. The task of therapy, in either case, is the same: to identify unwanted stimulus-response connections and to intervene in ways that loosen them, on the one hand, and that help in learning new and better patterns, on the other. The goals of Action therapy sometimes seem naive because they are so specific. But this specificity is central to their argument that symptoms are at the core of therapeutic problems, not at the periphery.

Another statement of difference between the systems is now possible: Insight therapy, with its emphasis on motivation, is sometimes called "dynamic" because the motivation theory which informs it works on a "pay-off" principle, also called a reductionist or homeostatic principle. It says that action gets its meaning from the drives it reduces or the motives it satisfies; it becomes meaningful as it is reinforced and made habitual by repetition. That meaning may be hidden from the self, however, and thereby puts action beyond the individual's control. In psychotherapy, meanings become evident through experience which awakens consciousness and makes choice possible. The process of evoking and understanding it defines therapy.

Action therapies, where they attend to drive reduction, attack the problem at the stem, not at the root, by changing the conditions which elicit action rather than fussing over the motives which sponsor it. They also attend to the principle of "contiguity" or "association," which says that new actions may be learned by chance associations between important events and previously irrelevant ones. In such cases, the new behavior may have no meaning in the sense that there is no underlying motive that it affects. The job of treatment is to find the stimulus-response connections which constitute the symptom and to create conditions for their unlearning and the learning of better patterns. Implementation of this plan defines therapy.

The epithets I have used to label the systems should now make sense: "Insight" is the technical goal of treatments that use cognitive and emotional processes for raising consciousness of one's motives, consciousness of self, and sometimes of the meaning of one's existence. "Action" is the technical goal of therapies that deliberately manipulate stimulus-response connections in order to change specific behavior from one activity pattern to another. The most self conscious (sic) intellectually and best studied of these are called, as a group, "behavior therapy" or "behavior modification," names I interchange with "action therapy."

We have yet to portray the actual methods of action therapists and the intramural differences between them. These grow in number all the time. We shall look closely here at the first generation of these therapies, all still widely used and studied, for treating anxiety and for shaping new behavior for other problems.

8

Antidotes for Anxiety

Counterconditioning and Flooding

If learning is the most studied topic of psychology over the past century, anxiety is a close second. Freud's theory of anxiety was the basis for his view of neurosis and, in turn, for much of the rationale of psychoanalysis. It is no surprise, therefore, that early opponents of Insight Therapy took anxiety as the core problem from which to differ in theory and practice. Their ideas of how anxiety is learned, is expressed in disordered behavior, and can be combated have inspired several treatment models and methods. We shall look here at the work of Joseph Wolpe and Thomas G. Stampfl in particular, and its implications for psychotherapy.

DISCARDING BAD HABITS: THE WORK
OF JOSEPH WOLPE

Joseph Wolpe was a psychoanalytically oriented psychiatrist in 1944, he says, when he grew interested in the work of Ivan Pavlov and American learning theorist Clark Hull. He credits them chiefly with the theory from which his treatment system comes. He named it, and his first book, *Psychotherapy by Reciprocal Inhibition* (1958). Wolpe later renamed the system, and the book which supplanted the first, with the more general title, *The Practice of Behavior Therapy* (Third Edition, 1982). In the generation between them, his innovative work has become such standard practice that it is now copied, expanded, and elaborated often without mention of him. Much evidence has testified on behalf of his early claims. His writing, in turn, has been remarkably consistent, and his view of Behavior Therapy is much the same now as then.

The term "reciprocal inhibition" is borrowed from physiology, where it refers to the way in which one set of nerves or muscles acts antagonistically to another, so that they cannot both work at once. Wolpe applied this idea to psychotherapy with methods for antagonizing healing responses to neurotic acts in ways that dissolve symptoms. Symptoms, he says, are learned or conditioned habits. The responses that suppress them become new habits, so this mode of treatment is also called "counterconditioning."

Wolpe believes that neurotic behavior is the expression of anxiety, whether in phobias or compulsions or sexual impotence or shyness. He also believes that there are many psychological states, in both humans and other animals, that are antagonistic to anxiety or, as he put it, reciprocally inhibitory of anxiety. When people act in ways conducive to these states, they cannot be anxious at the same time. If the therapist can find anxiety-inhibiting actions to counterbalance a symptom, and can teach the patient to produce them at will, the symptom will dissipate in face of its pleasant antagonist. The object of the procedure is only to break the old behavior pattern, not to teach a new one. Where a stimulus once provoked an anxious or symptomatic reaction, the treatment inhibits the reaction, which loosens its connection with the stimulus. In a while, the stimulus loses power to evoke anxiety, and the symptom disappears.

Over years of clinical work before he wrote his first book, Wolpe found a repertory of methods to use as anxiety inhibitors. Some have become the basis for therapeutic "industries" of their own.

The prototype of his treatment, he says, is the feeding response which Mary Cover Jones first used clinically in 1924 to cure a small child's fear of a rabbit. She would show the rabbit at a "safe" distance while the child was eating. Over many feeding periods, she moved the rabbit a little closer each time. The soothing effect of eating, it seems, prevented fear of the rabbit, seen at a distance, and the distance could be shortened as the child's tolerance increased. Eventually, the rabbit provoked no fear up close, even if the child was not eating when it appeared. Eating had inhibited anxiety until the rabbit lost its stimulating value. Wolpe did not use feeding with his patients, but seeing its suitability for treating children's fears, he modeled his techniques along those lines.

ANXIETY–INHIBITING TECHNIQUES

In his clinical practice with adults, Wolpe used four main means of inhibiting anxiety: (1) conditioned avoidance responses, especially "anxiety-relief responses"; (2) sexual responses; (3) assertive responses; and (4) deep muscle relaxation, mostly as a preliminary to "systematic desensitization." All of these methods existed in some form previously, but they were little known to the professional world until Wolpe discussed them in his 1958 book. Since then, the latter three have become the basis for a large fraction of all the behavior therapy done in the world.

Conditioned avoidance responses, especially what Wolpe calls anxiety-relief responses, are not used much but are good illustrations of how any stimulus (including words) and any response may get linked to each other. Anxiety-relief therapy uses a harmless but painful electric shock continuously. Before turning it on, the therapist tells the patient to say the word "calm" when the shock becomes excessive. At the word "calm," the shock instantly shuts off. Repeated many times, the word "calm" gets attached to the feeling of relief, so when clients say it to themselves in everyday situations, anxiety abates. Technically, any word could be conditioned to elicit relief, but "calm" is obviously a good one.

Sexual responses, in Wolpe's treatment, were used largely for impotence in males. The technique trains a man to attempt sex relations only when ". . . he has an unmistakable positive desire to do so, for otherwise he may very well consolidate, or even extend his sexual inhibitions" (1958, p. 130). The training requires that he learn to identify and avoid situations in which sex is anxiety-arousing and that he learn also to seek out women who are clearly capable of arousing him "in a desirable way . . . and when in the company of one of them, to 'let himself go' as freely as the circumstances allow." If he already has a sex partner who will cooperate to help him learn successful sex without getting anxious, so much the better. At all events, "If he is able to act according to plan, he experiences a gradual increase in sexual responsiveness to the kind of situation of which he has made use . . . [and] the range of situations in which love-making may occur is thus progressively extended as the anxiety potentials of stimuli diminish . . ." (1958, p. 131).

Surely no treatment could be more "symptom specific" in method—the problem is the inhibition of sexuality, so the treatment is the disinhibition of sexuality. The trick of therapy is how to exchange one action pattern for another. There is no concern here with insight, motive, or meaning except as they may be used to affect the patient's acts. Even Wolpe's theory of anxiety as the root of the problem is only important because it is useful, not because it may be true. It gives the therapist a rationale for making demands on the patient, and it gives the patient "reasons" from which to take courage to comply.

Assertive and *relaxation* responses are as specific as sexual ones. For clients who are deferential, shy, and easily intimidated, the treatment gets them to assert themselves more often and more forcefully; if they are tense and anxious in unwarranted situations, the treatment gets them to relax.

Assertive responses. Wolpe views Andrew Salter as the father of assertive treatment and says his own method is about the same as Salter's. In 1958, he rarely used assertive responses as the sole technique of therapy. They were intended to help anxious people in verbal dealings with others. Wolpe teaches them to express hostility and resentment. He assumes that anxiety inhibits self-expression, and that angry self-assertion inhibits anxiety.

Relaxation responses. Wolpe's most original method extended the use of relaxation from its obvious use in tension reduction to problem situations ". . . that make irrelevant the use of direct action, such as assertion, on the part of the patient." He named the technique "systematic desensitization" because it works methodically to make people insensitive to things they fear. The general method is that the therapist gets the patient to vividly imagine more and more frightening things while remaining deeply relaxed, sometimes hypnotized. The relaxation inhibits the anxiety usually caused by these images until the client is eventually unmoved by them. The benign indifference then generalizes from the imagined fears of the consulting room to the real ones of everyday life.

Initiating Treatment

It is easy to see how the therapist conducts systematic desensitization treatments where all the patient has to do is to relax and fantasize what the therapist says. This is ". . . a method in which the therapist has complete control of the degree of approach that the patient makes to the feared object at any particular time." But in the case of sexual and assertive responses, where the consulting room is only a classroom for instructing the patient, and the therapeutic action must be self-administered outside, how does the treatment get put in motion?

Getting the action going is "a matter of common sense" to Wolpe, whose "Approach to the Patient" (Chapter 7 of *Reciprocal Inhibition*) seems simple and straightforward. "To begin with, there is the gathering and organizing of information. . . . Then there is the routine of preparing the patient for the specific procedures . . ." (1982, p. 86), which is like that of most physicians at initial examinations. Wolpe listens to the problems and takes a careful case history in which he tries to find related problems and symptoms that have appeared at other times. After the history, he administeres a psychological test to measure neuroticism. He then explains at length how neuroses develop (by conditioned anxiety responses) and how they can be treated (by reciprocal inhibition). He uses the case history to illustrate the origins of the patient's problems and suggests ". . . the formal use of particular responses that, through inhibiting anxiety . . . weaken neurotic habit" (1958, p. 112). The stage is set. The rest is argument, persuasion, or any means at hand to get the healing action going outside the office and to help its guidance and control. "If little was said of these . . . in the early writings of behavior therapists," he later explains, "it was because to do so seemed as superfluous as to state that a syringe was used when recording that a patient received an injection" (1982, p. 86).

WHAT INHIBITS ANXIETY?

That the inducements to action are no problem for Wolpe may reflect his great skill with his own methods. But it may also reflect his belief that the treatment merely eliminates anxiety rather than creating new behavior. "Common sense" might then suffice to decide what action to provoke; anything which reduced anxiety would do.

This is easy to say of desensitization, where the only action required is in the patient's head, and the work of the therapist is only to "talk up" imagery. But getting people to go out and do what is needed in sexual and assertive treatments is something else. Can those things really be seen simply as anxiety inhibitors rather than important actions in their own right? Notice that, for these treatments, Wolpe does not link the frightening stimulus to any old anxiety-inhibiting response; he does not feed a man who is sexually fearful or tell him to have an erection if he is anxious in company. And it is well technically that he does not, for however much the assertion of anger inhibits anxiety, it inhibits sexual arousal too. And a man who is afraid of his boss may fear him just as much across a lunch table as across the desk. Plainly, Wolpe's anxiety inhibitors are as specific as could be to the source of anxiety. His treatment consists largely, then, of getting people to do the things they fear. As this grows habitual, an old response pattern is willy-nilly traded for a contrary one. The old anxiety is gone, as intended, but in its place is new conduct, with the therapist as sire and midwife to its birth.

SIGNIFICANCE OF WOLPE'S WORK

Over the years, Wolpe has remained an energetic scholar and practitioner, well aware of novelties in therapy theory and research. His ongoing books and articles sometimes fit them to his perspective and sometimes do not. The perspective itself has not changed greatly since *Psychotherapy by Reciprocal Inhibition* (1958). The importance of Wolpe's work, however, does not depend on the finality of the learning theory from which he derived it or the precision of his deductions. Desensitization, for instance, does not have to be explained as reciprocal inhibition. That theory seems to describe how some therapeutic actions work, but it is as speculative a foundation as the motivational systems of Insight therapists. We now know for certain, after many centuries of common experience and one generation of research on the techniques, that if you can get people to do things they needlessly fear, under the right circumstances, the more so to do them repeatedly, their fears will diminish—but the reasons are still elusive.

The importance of Wolpe's therapy comes in the method of its construction and presentation, in the fact that, having formed the theoretical conceit he did, he invented specific tools for using it in treatment. Elaborating different procedures for different problems did wonders for a field as full of vagaries as psychotherapy. This was no less true even though he proposed a loose theory for them and even if that theory was wrong. Therapeutic cookbooks are not elegant intellectually, but in medicine they are far more useful, and may yet be in psychotherapy. When Wolpe began publishing, they were all but unheard of there. His status as a pioneer is safe.

SYMPTOM RETURN AND OUTCOME STATISTICS

Two aspects of Wolpe's work were important to the polemics of Action therapy: His theoretical challenge to Insight therapies, particularly psychoanalysis; and his statistical reports of success and failure.

Symptom Return

Like Freud, Wolpe sees neurosis as the result of anxiety commonly attached to sexual and aggressive drives, which warps their expression. Now, Wolpe's learning theory is taken mostly from Clark Hull, whose "drive" theory of behavior is so like Freud's instinct theory that Dollard and Miller used it to translate Freudian theory into learning terms (1950). Wolpe does not say so, but his sexual and assertive therapies depend on assumptions which the late O. H. Mowrer quite rightly dubbed "thoroughly Freudian."

The big dispute between therapies, with terminology equated, is procedural— Freud tried to expose the hidden drive so that the anxiety which attends it will dissipate, and sex and aggression will be disinhibited (and expressed or not, as the patient chooses). Wolpe tries to produce the sexual or aggressive behavior itself, so that the anxiety attending those drives will not arise. Both systems aim to free the behavior and reduce the anxiety that blocks it.

The argument of Insight therapists against direct action has been that eliciting the behavior without exposing its motives would relieve anxiety only for the moment. As new forests grow from old roots after fires and lumberjacks, so new symptoms will erupt from motives still rooted in unconsciousness when old symptoms are excised. But Wolpe works from much the same framework and finds that symptoms removed by his direct methods are not replaced by new ones. If the motivational theory is correct, then his work challenges the practical need for "uncovering" motives more than it would were he arguing from a different premise.

Outcome Statistics

Wolpe's writings typically include statistical summaries of how many cases he saw, their presenting problems, the number of treatments, the degree of improvement, and the rate of relapse on followup study. He is not a sophisticated statistician, and his data can be considered inconclusive on many grounds. All such criticisms pale before what was, in the psychotherapy business of 1958, the astonishing fact that he gave outcome statistics at all. Psychoanalysis was the bête noire of Wolpe's writing, of course, but some of his prejudices were justified by the plain fact that almost seventy years of psychoanalytic work by thousands of therapists had yielded little data and less incentive among analysts to submit their work to the scrutiny of the scientific community. One of the rare corporate studies of psychoanalytic outcomes, in fact, was all but suppressed in 1958 in a way that clouded the good name of psychoanalysts (Weinstock, 1958). This one man, working mostly alone, invited the examination, not of an isolated sample of his work, but of his whole career as a therapeutic innovator. Wolpe's willingness to expose himself to actuarial evaluation set a model of intellectual good faith that all pretenders to innovation in psychotherapy must finally emulate if they want public license and legitimation.

TEACHING FEARLESSNESS: THE IMPLOSIVE THERAPY OF THOMAS G. STAMPFL

Thomas G. Stampfl never rushed into print. He developed "Implosive Therapy" as a young professor at John Carroll University in Cleveland, Ohio, in the late 1950s, but published nothing about it until 1967 (London, 1964). Since then, it has been elaborated, altered, and sometimes supplanted by other "flooding" and "exposure" methods which, as a class, are the most effective treatments for extreme fears. Stampfl's work is a good practical example and an interesting theoretical one because it integrates learning and psychodynamic theory.

A caveat on terminology is necessary. There is no firm convention among scholars for the class names of these treatments. Some sharply distinguish implosion from flooding (Bandura, 1969; Wilson, 1982); others use them interchangeably (Levis & Malloy, 1982). Neither side argues unambiguously. The trend of current usage, as I read it, is to use "flooding" to mean *in vivo* stimulation of anxiety, and "implosion" to mean imaginal stimulation. I am using the terms more precisely: "Exposure" is the generic name of all the treatments of this chapter, after Marks (1978); "flooding" is the subclass of exposure methods meant to provoke high anxiety; and "implosion" is the subclass of flooding which uses so-called "hypothetical cues" to repressed material, as we shall see.

A DYNAMIC LEARNING THEORY OF NEUROSIS

Stampfl's theory of neurosis is, like Wolpe's, a learned anxiety theory, but his use of learning theory is more complex than Wolpe's and his treatment simpler.

Stampfl owes less theoretical debt to Pavlov, Thorndike, and Hull, than to the "two-factor" theory of O. H. Mowrer, which tries to explain how fear-inspired "avoidance behavior" is maintained. The first factor in learning neurotic fear, says Mowrer, is the accidental conditioning of innocent things to some frightening episode. The classic illustration everyone cites is the case of "Little Albert," based on a 1920 article by John Watson and Rosalie Rayner. It may not have worked, was never fully verified, is confusingly reported by them, and has been misrepresented in many texts and theories since. But the mythical power of the (maybe valid) principle it meant to illustrate has had huge influence (Harris, 1979). As commonly told, they taught a 9-month-old boy to fear a white rat by startling him in its presence. Once learned, the mere sight of the rat, or of other hairy/furry/white objects, frightened him.

Indeed, such fears, once learned, seem to last forever. They are unlike other classical conditionings, whose longevity depends on reinforcement. Were fear like any other Pavlovian learning, it would require the occasional recurrence of something like the original trauma in order to last. It is not so with conditioned fears. They abide and endure.

Mowrer explains this phenomenon by means of Thorndike's "Law of Effect." So, says Mowrer, anxiety is learned in the first place by contiguity (conditioning), a la Pavlov, but a second factor maintains it, namely, fleeing from the things we fear. Successful flight reduces anxiety and so is self-reinforcing. The two factors in sequence make the pattern last.

Applied to clinical problems, this theory says: Neurotic anxiety is the fear of an innocent stimulus as if it were truly harmful. A symptom is an avoidant act that tends to reduce that fear. By doing so, it becomes fixed in the person's behavioral repertoire (memory). Though the avoidant act may itself be painful, it will endure so long as it reduces more anxiety than it arouses pain. It is "neurotic" because the anxiety it reduces is not realistic in the first place.

This theory, so far, is compatible with both Freud and Wolpe. The Freudian version says that anxiety is the motive for neurotic symptoms; insight into the unrealism of the anxiety reduces its motivating quality, and the victim, freed of fear, no longer needs the symptom to relieve it. Wolpe, replacing insight with counterconditioning, also uses this model.

In Stampfl's view, Wolpe fails to appreciate the persistence of neurotic behavior and wrongly concludes that reciprocal inhibition is the best treatment for anxiety. Stampfl does not aim to countercondition neurosis, but to extinguish the fearsomeness of the cues that cause it in the first place. The difference connects him, almost perversely, with Insight therapy.

Like dynamic theorists, Stampfl says not only that anxiety is at the core of neurosis, which Wolpe accepts, but that repression is its sustaining mechanism, which Wolpe rejects. Like psychoanalysts, Stampfl thinks that cure requires the lifting of repression. But he does not expose motives to this end or analyze symptoms; to him, symptoms are meaningless gestures to escape from the complex memory of absurdly frightening accidents. His treatment plan resembles Insight therapy in having one cure for all ills. But it gives the patient no options and no responsibility for treatment, and far from encouraging insight, seeks only to evoke emotion, and only one at that—anxiety.

A NEW VIEW OF REPRESSION

In learning theory terms, psychodynamic therapists also aim to extinguish rather than inhibit symptoms. Symptoms, they believe, are maintained by repression, which forces things out of consciousness, a process reversed by insight. All these processes, in their view, are more or less uniquely human. Stampfl rejects this notion. His idea of repression fits rats as well as people. From it, and from experimental work following Mowrer (Solomon, Kamin, & Wynne, 1953), he proceeded to produce "neurotic" avoidance behavior in rats and to cure it without insight. He applied the same paradigm to human beings in Implosive Therapy.

Stampfl's theory says: Neurotic behavior is the fearful avoidance of harmless things which are symptoms of other fears. They were once trivial cues which became frightening merely because they appeared in the context where we were already fleeing from some trauma. So we ran from them too, not realizing that they were innocent and remote from the cause of fear. From then on, as long as we do not face the original trauma, it never frightens us. And we are not likely to confront it, nor even remember it, because we get frightened first by secondary cues and flee from them. We have repressed the main fear and are unafraid of it because we are unconscious of it. If we became aware, it would frighten us more than the symptomatic stimuli from which we now flee. But buried, the underlying fears cannot be extinguished. And the symptomatic fears remain because we get no chance to see that they are harmless. Their power to scare us away remains forever fresh.

IMPLOSIVE PSYCHOTHERAPY

Neurotic fear is made permanent by this pattern, says Stampfl. Victims of trauma feel unsafe until they have escaped, and then wrongly conclude that flight saved them, not that it was needless. Correct treatment would make them see the truth.

Its strategy follows the homely wisdom that experience is the best teacher. The most convincing lesson, it says, would come from facing fears until their groundlessness is evident. If people were exposed enough to the fearsome stimuli while their anxiety went unreinforced, the fear would extinguish, burn itself out, so to speak, for lack of fuel to nourish it. The "trick" of treatment is how to keep people from running while keeping them exposed to fear until it has lost its power.

Stampfl does this in a simple way: He frightens clients as much as he can for as long as he can at a sitting without hurting them physically. He persuades them to imagine themselves in situations he describes—and he describes, in copious detail, and with compelling urgency, a thorough catalogue of horrors, as gruesome a set of ugly death, sex, havoc, filth, violence, and mutilation scenes, with the client the main participant, as could be conceived to terrify the hardiest souls.

The treatment works best, he says, when he can frighten people most. Per theory, the effects of extinction then generalize from more- to less-frightening stimuli. As the main sources of anxiety succumb, healing spreads to the minor ones, domino fashion. With this in mind, he provokes maximum anxiety as fast as he can. He does not want to soothe patients or gradually raise their tolerance of fear by starting with small doses, but to terrify them, to cause an explosion of panic. Thus the name "Implosive" therapy, treatment by inward explosion. Its practical principle: If you can deal with big fears, you will not need to get at little ones. People who learn to handle torches need no instruction for matches.

Sessions last usually from 60 to 100 minutes; long is better because implosion, like other exposure therapies, works best if it continues longer (Levis & Malloy, 1982). Each session lasts until all signs of anxiety are gone. People usually start to improve after the first session (Stampfl & Levis, 1967). Therapy ends when the therapist can no longer elicit anxiety in session and the patient is free of it outside.

If anxiety and immobility are the only necessary conditions of treatment, and if extinction effects generalize, then Implosive therapy has another treatment economy—the therapist should not need accurate information about the patient's problem. Knowing it may give leads about what ideas are most frightening, so Stampfl spends some time interviewing and testing before treatment starts. But convenience is not necessity; if the material is frightening enough, and the fears it evokes are truly groundless, implosive tales should work, even if they are false and unrelated to the patient's life.

Inaccuracy is not intentional here, but an unforeseeable result of trying to cope with repressed material. Other flooding therapists usually confine themselves to so-called "symptom-contingent" cues, i.e., fears reported by the patient, but implosive therapists use "hypothesized" cues as well. They make guesses about fears underlying those the client reports and use those guesses to compose their scary stories. This is why at least part of the treatment must be done in the consulting room, not live. *In vivo* flooding treatment of a flying phobia, for instance, would put patients on airplanes until they grew unafraid. Implosive therapy, however, ". . . would hypothesize that it is not airplanes or even flying per se that the client fears, but rather the possible *consequences* of flying—crashing, bodily injury, and death . . . Since these . . . cannot be presented *in vivo,* they are included in . . . an imaginal implosive scene" (Levis & Malloy, 1982, p. 97).

Now this is the theoretical oddity of Stampfl's system: He counts repression as vital to neurosis, and ingenious animal studies of his and even more of Donald Levis are nice heuristic supports of the hypothesis. But the idea that extinction generalizes, which he also believes, makes repression into excess theoretical baggage, whether for rats or people! The serial context of conditioned anxiety becomes a mere curiosity, and the experiments proving it rigorous academic irrelevancies. Neither really bears on the extinction process; there, the strength of unreinforced anxiety is all that counts.

The irrelevance of repression to Implosive technique has important implications: First, it suggests that Stampfl is less psychodynamic than he thinks, with his theory and therapy both purer cases of Action than he knows. Second, it raises the bigger question of the link between his theory and technique. If the treatment works, but is not uniquely explained by his theory, its practical value is unpredictable and understanding is "up for grabs." The problem is a plague on every therapy. Stampfl does not escape it.

THE STATUS OF EXPOSURE TREATMENTS

Wolpe's and Stampfl's therapies are variants of the same general theory and its supporting empirical studies of how neuroses are learned. Their respective approaches to anxiety reduction seem to be opposites, one of which should not work, but the experimental evidence has long shown that intense fear would yield to either gradual exposure or sudden bombardment.

In both methods, at all events, the activity of the therapist is meant to procure specific, not general behavior changes, and the use of instructions and verbal imagery has a wholly noncognitive aim. If Wolpe reasons with people, it is to persuade their effector systems, to prod their muscles into needed movements, not to convince their intellects. If Stampfl tells nasty stories, it is to arouse anxiety, not to convey ideas. (Indeed, Stampfl's patients try to get scared, in session and as homework.)

Their very use of language, in contrast to Insight therapists, is a needed encumbrance, as it were, that should not belie their intent. The sexual and assertive acts Wolpe counterconditions must be done outside the consulting room, so he must use words to instruct and guide them. But most of his desensitizations, like Stampfl's implosions, are done in the office, where verbal efforts to program imagery must substitute for live exposure. When it can be provided, indeed, both *in vivo* desensitization and flooding typically work faster, and often in more cases, than do imaginal methods (Emmelkamp, 1979).

Since Wolpe and Stampfl first published their work, exposure treatments have been more studied empirically than any others. Some findings have been equivocal—some studies (but not all) of desensitization, for instance, can explain its success as "nonspecific," meaning that it worked like a placebo, only because of people's positive expectation that it would (Rachman & Wilson, 1980). And many have shown that such details of Wolpe's procedure as relaxation and the ascending hierarchy of fears, are not important. Comparative studies of implosive therapy likewise cast doubt on the value of hypothesized cues and some, indeed, of all imaginal treatment. No challenge has proved conclusive. Wolpe's and Stampfl's early work is no more at the cutting edge of new methods, but it still stands.

Two things are clear in this connection: First, exposure methods, including desensitization and flooding, among others, are best among all forms of psychotherapy for treating the extreme fears called phobias, especially "simple" phobias, where fears have very specific objects (Barlow & Wolfe, 1981; Wilson, 1982). Second, it is now clear that phobias are a medley of different conditions, not by any means the prototypes of all neurosis, and that there is no single treatment most effective for them all (Emmelkamp, 1979; Marks, 1978). These facts have important implications for Insight and Action therapies both. They offer empirical testimony, for the first time in this traditionally contentious business, that there may be separate domains of use and value for each modality.

Their complexity also helps explain why early exposure treatments, despite their practical value, are not necessary and sufficient outcomes of theory. This is true of all psychotherapy, but it threatens behavior therapies' need to be theoretically rigorous as well as specific and precise (Wilson & Franks, 1982). Even if their manipulations work, as long as their explanations are in question, they feel pushed into rude empiricism, which lacks scientific authority.

This is only a problem for therapists whose methods pretend to be deductions from substantive theories of personality or behavior. For "operant" therapists, to whom we now turn, reliance on the "experimental analysis of behavior" makes their stark empiricism anything but rude and spares them this embarrassment.

9

Shaping New Behavior

The Operant Methods

B. F. Skinner was never a psychotherapist, nor were some of his protégés who invented many of the therapeutic uses of "operant conditioning" or "behavior shaping" methods, as they are called. Yet their ideas apply so broadly to so many areas of human concern, that the term "behavior modification" is sometimes used exclusively to mean Skinnerian techniques, as if no others counted. With respect, it is not a stupid error.

Skinner's elaborations of learning theory and their implications reach far beyond their status as treatment tools. They have been used in education and in social rehabilitation and control as well as psychotherapy; applied in hospitals, prisons, schoolrooms, clinics, nurseries, and outdoors; to litter control, toilet training toddlers, computer learning programs and social utopias, real and imagined. Skinner has personally been a subject of great public interest, and of some scorn, despite his dry, professorial style and gentlemanly bearing, because his ideas are so provocative. The *New York Times* has called him the most important psychologist of the century. He concurred. They are probably correct.

The principles of operant technique are intuitively known to everyone. Parents, animal trainers, and wise rulers have always relied heavily on them to raise children, pets, and support. Before 1850, they were the basis of successful education and rehabilitation programs whose likes were not again seen until the late 1960s (Kazdin, 1978a). In psychotherapy, Skinnerians have been models of the engineering approach to human behavior since 1953, when they demonstrated their ability to systematically change the behavior of chronic psychotics (Lindsley, Skinner, & Solomon, 1953). Since then, their methods have had more therapeutic applications, perhaps, than any other system—to psychosomatic medicine, pain control, biofeedback, speech disorders, learning disabilities, hysterical blindness, habit disorders, child autism, and adult schizophrenia (the list goes on). Sometimes treatment has been only an afterthought of experimental work, and sometimes it has delivered in practice less than it promised in principle. Even so, the operant method, with its step-by-step experimental analyses of behavior, utterly free of theoretical cant, sets a standard for all behavioral approaches to psychotherapy.

Practically, operant methods try to shape new patterns of behavior rather than to erase old ones, the aim of exposure therapies. Theoretically, they are important to us because Skinnerian ideas are an extreme version of the kind of argument to which Action therapy is disposed. They differ more from Insight therapies than does any other Action system.

THE BASIS OF BEHAVIOR SHAPING

Skinnerian treatment is based on two main principles: First is Thorndike's Law of Effect. It says simply that an animal will learn to repeat acts for which it is rewarded and to avoid ones for which it is ignored or punished. The second principle, one of Skinner's original contributions to learning, says that complex behavior patterns, including all skills, are gradually learned in small steps that progressively approach an optimal level of performance.

A scheme of treatment flows directly from these principles to the solution of many behavior problems: The therapist needs to know chiefly what things patients find rewarding and what not. These can be found by watching their overt behavior and analyzing their activity patterns to see how they unfold. When the product of an act is such that it causes the act to be repeated, we say it is "positively reinforcing," that is, it strengthens or rewards the act. When, conversely, what follows an action causes the act to be discarded or avoided, the result is negative or nonreinforcing; it fails to strengthen or punishes the act. (Positive reinforcement is the same as reward, but negative reinforcement and punishment are different processes). Since learning depends on patterns of rewards and punishments, in this conceit, it should be possible to control what is learned by controlling the rewarding, indifferent, and punishing features of the environment that determine those patterns.

The operations of operant psychotherapists follow:

1. First, they analyze the problem behavior to see what rewards and punishments in the environment mold and support it.

2. Next, they decide what new behavior pattern they wish to promote.

3. Then they evaluate what they can use as rewards or punishments, whose dispensation is totally in their control.

4. Finally, they manipulate the environment so that patients are likely to

perform the desired behavior. When they do, even approximately, they are rewarded, while irrelevant or interfering acts are disregarded or punished.

Punishment, however, is a tricky technique; unless used with great precision, it can have unforeseen side effects (Bandura, 1962). This is one reason why Skinnerian therapists tend to avoid "aversive" or punitive methods. Another is that one can usually minimize undesirable behavior by withholding positive reinforcement, without resorting to punishment. So operant therapy works mainly by watching for desirable behavior or creating situations where it is likely to happen, then rewarding it (or its approximation) when it occurs and ignoring unwanted acts when they occur.

This system can also be called "contingency learning" because it teaches people that getting rewards depends (is contingent) on how they act.

CONTROLLED ENVIRONMENTS AND CONTROLLING REWARDS

The theoretical course of operant behavior shaping is simple, though it is a far cry from a workable practical formula for any problem. Environments differ and so do the things that are reinforcing to different people. The therapist must control both, so it takes ingenuity to plan a treatment program.

Controlled Environments: Token Economy

The "Skinner Box" is a totally controlled physical environment. Originally designed for operant experiments on small animals, Skinner later expanded it into a chamber for human infants. The ideal environment for human development, he reasoned, is the one which loving parents create for infants. It keeps them warm, clean, fed, burped, rocked, smiled to, talked at, and crooned over. Control of this cornucopia is what gives parents their great power to shape infant behavior. The best teaching atmosphere, likewise, is one which offers most control over the environment.

The societal equivalent of such environments is what sociologist Erving Goffman called "total" institutions—hospitals, prisons, dormitories, and such (1961). It is no surprise that Skinnerians observed the parallels and, accordingly, that some of the boldest therapeutic applications of operant technology, called "manipulation of pay schedules" or "token economies," have been made in such settings.

A token economy is a therapeutic organization, such as a hospital ward, operated like a business. Tokens are used for money. When patients are admitted to a token-economy ward, they are given free tokens. From then on, they must earn them as payment for good behavior. Tokens are made valuable by rules which require that they be used to pay for necessities as well as luxuries. The value of a purchase is manipulated by how much is charged for it. In some token-economy wards, patients have had to pay to eat, to go to bed, to shower, to sleep, even to use the toilet. The purpose of the system is to train psychotic or retarded people in the habits and skills of normal social intercourse which they need to get along outside a hospital. Also, it makes their lives, and those of the staff, more comfortable within the institution. The same principle has been used in prison rehabilitation programs, rewarding good social behavior with creature comforts.

Since they were started by Teodoro Ayllon and Nathan Azrin in 1961, token-economy programs have had some success and much criticism on legal, ethical, and practical grounds (Kazdin, 1978a). One inevitable problem is that, while the technology is basically an incentive system, implementing it requires the control of resources whose withdrawal is punishing. A token economy in a mental hospital, for instance, rewards patients for making their beds, for using utensils to eat, and so forth; that is good because it teaches them to act as they must to get on in the world. But the training process is often harsh—failure to make the bed may cause its removal, so the delinquent patient cannot sleep on it; not using utensils may cause the food to be withdrawn, so the patient goes hungry for that meal. The program bosses may plead that this only increases bed-making and utensil-using incentives, but many patients, like anyone else, feel punished rather than challenged. And the courts agree with them. This is even more true in prisons, where one is only there in the first place to be punished (Kazdin, 1978b). Operant methods have been used abusively in such settings, and efforts to "shape people up" (an unhappy phrase from the often clumsy argot of this field) have violated their rights. So much control of the environment is needed for these methods that they can easily add to the punitive ambience of places where one's dignity or rights are violated just by having to be there (Stolz et al., 1978).

The relative success of operant methods with chronic psychotics and mental retards in institutions, on the other hand, has so much exceeded that of other treatments, that they are worth the care and caution that must be exercised in using them (Paul & Lentz, 1978). This is true despite the fact that, in absolute terms, they have done better at reshaping specific acts than at fixing the general debilitating patterns of psychosis and better at getting people out of institutions than at keeping them out (Rachman & Wilson, 1980). The alternatives to date are costlier, crueler, or both.

Skinner's writing implies that, while operant techniques are not most effective in a free environment, they can be used politically to create one where people function freely. The climate of his utopian novel, *Walden Two,* does not differ much, in principle, from clinical controlled environments. It uses operant methods for the "social engineering" of a society where children are instructed and motivated by positive incentives, not by fear of punishment, and where self control is taught as the cardinal ethical virtue. Doing so requires general control over society in order to manipulate behavior for everyone's good. This is as true, in this conceit, for behaviorally disordered people, who must be manipulated into rapprochement with so-called normality, as for normal people who must learn to take constructive roles in society.

Controlling Rewards

More environmental control is possible in hospitals than in other settings, but operant methods with chronic psychotics have not proved wholly effective even there, in part because each unit of behavior that can be taught by this means tends to be very small. Still, Ivar Lovaas and his collaborators at the University of California at Los Angeles have had more success teaching schizophrenic children cognitive and social skills than have most workers with other methods. And they teach nonprofessionals the same therapeutic functions as Lovaas's senior staff—another instance of the economic promise of operant technology (Lovaas, 1977, 1978; Lovaas, Ackerman, & Taubman, 1983).

Environmental control is only important in behavior shaping to begin with, of course, in order to turn people's attention toward therapeutic rewards. A great variety of things can be made into rewards, and their orchestration can be done in many settings and conditions. Most of them do not need anything like total environmental control. David Premack, for instance, treated child problem eaters by first observing that they like to play with objects and then telling them they could not do so until after they ate. He reversed the process on children who like to eat but not to manipulate. In the same vein, but more urgently, Bachrach, Erwin, and Mohr induced an anorexic woman (anorexia is neurotic self-starvation) to eat by controlling access to some of her pleasures, such as classical music and social chitchat (1965). Many variants have been used for obesity, thumbsucking, and other problems. Grandma knew the method in principle; Skinnerians use it most systematically.

Some operant treatments work best when professionals act as consultants to people in a better position to regulate the target behavior. Therapists have little control of the environment outside the office, but there are people who do. Teachers and parents control enough contingencies in the lives of children, and husbands and wives over each other, so they can be the therapists if they understand the situations to control, the reinforcements to use, and the schedule by which to present them. As consultants, Skinnerians have taught them therapeutic skills for problems ranging from administering medical treatment to stuttering, juvenile delinquency, school failure, and social adjustment. The consultation need not always be face to face either. Nathan Azrin, for instance, who invented many institutional operant treatments, also wrote a valuable popular manual for teaching mothers how to toilet train their children without trauma in only one day (Azrin & Foxx, 1974).

Biofeedback and Behavioral Medicine

Operant methods are among the "behavioral medicine" techniques increas-- ingly used to treat medical conditions. They are used for psychosomatic problems such as sleep disorders, headaches, allergies, and gastrointestinal ailments, and for what were once viewed as purely physical ailments, such as hypertension and chronic pain.

"Biofeedback," perhaps the best-known behavioral medicine technology, is not much recognized as an operant technology, but it is. All biofeedback works in the same way: People receive an external record or signal of an ongoing internal body process—they see a graph of their heartbeat or hear a buzzer synchronized to their brain wave or watch a counter rise and fall with their blood pressure. Then they learn to correlate the behavior of the gauge they are watching to their own mental or physical state. They gradually find that by manipulating their thoughts, imagery, and mood, they manipulate the gauge as well, and with it the internal process changes.

In principle, this technique makes possible a direct psychotherapy for somatic conditions. It is now widely used for relaxation training, lowering blood pressure, relieving headaches and asthma attacks, and for many other problems. Results have often been mixed, but the developmental promise of biofeedback remains intact (Cohen & Ross, 1983).

THE IMPLICATIONS OF SKINNER'S "ANTI-THEORY"

The relative lack of explicit formulas for operant treatment, as opposed, for instance, to those of Wolpe or Stampfl, is some evidence of its more experimental character. Skinner's empiricism is not merely free of the restrictions imposed by theory, however, but leans strongly biased in what some consider an anti-theoretical direction. For most of his influential career, he advocated that scientific psychology avoid making theoretical assumptions about internal, invisible, and especially unmeasurable events to explain observable behavior. This operationism writ large, with its implications for personality theory as well as practice, makes Skinner the purest of Action therapy theorists. In effect, he takes as the total measure of human beings, the acts we can know they do.

In their early polemical concern with symptom relief, Action therapists were often accused of superficiality, of failing to address the internal source of behavior problems. To some extent, Wolpe's and Stampfl's theories refute such claims by offering anxiety as the inner motive of neurosis. Not so Skinner. He not only denies the need for insight and the significance of motives, but he questions their very existence—and doubts equally the motivating significance for behavior, of thoughts, ideas, and intentions. He casually admits that there are physiological drives, but he thinks it is generally a waste of time for behavior scientists to study them. Late in his career, he allowed it might be useful to study such "private behavior" as cognition, but only if its students beware of postulating "mental way stations" to explain what they cannot well describe (1963). It is wasteful, he says, to build psychological theories that require inferences about events that cannot be observed. Finally, in the ultimate ideology of action (and paradigm for Action therapy), according to Skinner: It serves no purpose to explain behavior except to learn how to control and change it (1974).

This extreme view, aptly titled "radical behaviorism," can be seen historically as Skinner's extension of philosophic pragmatism to behavior science. It is a reaction to idle scientific speculation and a plea for better research method and analysis of ideas in psychology, and its effects on behavior science have been powerfully salutary. But leaving it at that, I think, misses the larger meaning of this work for psychotherapy. Radical behaviorism offers technique par excellence to approach treatment. By "turning problems into behaviors," it demands the functional analyses from which behavior changes can be deduced to solve them (Baer, 1982, p. 284). But the purely functional view also implies that the business of psychotherapy is finally that which affects people's relation to the external environment and not to their (hypothetical or expressed) internal states. Therapy is an adjustment process to produce optimal interaction between people and their environment. Optimal interaction is partly defined by the therapist, partly determined by experiment, and partly, but never solely, by the stated wishes of the people being adjusted. Their "verbal behavior," as Skinnerians call it, has no priority claim for attention. It, and (the behavior system which is) they, are parts of a system bigger than themselves. In it, they may or may not be allowed, for any practical purpose, to have a self-turned-inwards or to indulge it. This system is pure method. As such, it cannot say what behavior to promote or how executive decisions should be made about it. The political implications of the question should make psychotherapists (among others) fidget. Skinner has been reviled, perhaps for facing too squarely, if not for solving too glibly, a problem which most helping professions would rather never face at all. For thoughtful psychotherapists, it is inescapable, however painful, and we shall return to it.

For their immediate purposes, meanwhile, the problem is largely academic, for the empirical issue at hand is how well operant training methods can shape the behavior of psychotics in ways they will themselves approve, free neurotics of habits they dislike, civilize small children, and so forth. If Skinnerians have little use for our internal states, they have careful regard for how we act, and most of us have enough behavior that needs reshaping to lay aside the other issue for a while. For now, it is enough if Skinnerians can satisfy their own criteria for cure. This is no easy thing, for operant psychotherapy has the vices of its virtues: The very specificity that functional analysis permits and behavior shaping demands often limits too much the variables that a program can deal with and takes too long and costs too much to work. It is marvelous to get psychotics to ask for gum after years of total silence, as Ayllon and Michael did, even if months of effort are required, as they were. But it is a long distance from this kind of gain to leaving hospital and functioning at large. Operant therapy has produced far more important changes in psychotic behavior, in fact, and seen modest success at increasing hospital discharges and halfway house membership, though not at cure. But it is a method, after all, limited absolutely to the power of the reinforcements it can muster for the acts it can evoke. The demands of biochemistry on behavior, and of states of mind concealed from therapeutic probes and thus from benign stimulation and reinforcement, continue to elude it.

Even so, we may be sure that, for too many other purposes to catalog here, operant technology is here to stay, and to be used therapeutically in hospitals, in prisons, in clinics, in schools, in offices, in life—not because it is a wondrous new invention, but because it is the scientific distillate of the ancient elemental laws by which skills and habits are learned throughout the upper echelons of the animal kingdom, including humankind. Nothing changes in this domain but how cleverly people learn to use these principles to teach. This means that this technology will always be important to behavior control, and hence to treatment. It is not so sure that Skinner is right that whole societies can be organized this way or that only by doing so can people be happy or learn the self-control demanded by the complex interdependencies of modern civilization. Even so, behavior shaping is the essence of all skill training, which is much of what psychotherapy is, like it or not—so the technology that does it systematically can only grow more widely used and more accepted, and the scandal and drama from abuses and confusion over it must wither and decline (London, 1977).

10

The Uses of Specificity

Science and Morals in Action Therapy

Though they do not share the Skinnerian's disdain for theory, neither Wolpe nor Stampfl nor other Action therapy theorists would rest their scientific claims too heavily on the intellectual elegance of their theories. The scientific pretensions of all psychotherapies tend to be afterthoughts, based on their practical results. For Action therapists, "results" means their potency for symptom reduction. The scientific status of Action therapies has been easy to judge on this basis; either they remove symptoms or they do not. The evidence, with qualification, is that, by and large, they do.

Insight therapists used to insist that symptom removal without treatment of motives would eventuate in new symptoms or the return of the old ones. This has happened sometimes, and dramatically, but the bulk of evidence says that such events are atypical. The statistical odds against it are great enough so that, given the choice, most patients are wise to take the risk of future symptoms against the certainty of present ones. Whatever their other failings, the Action therapies are not very vulnerable to attack on the grounds that their criteria are unclear or typically unmet. How worthwhile their satisfaction is another question. But by itself, the claim to empirically testable results was enough to quickly lend to Action therapies the scientific status to which Insight therapies' claims had grown clouded.

But their scientific status is not so neat as Behavior therapists might wish. There are too many gaps between their therapy techniques and the theories that guide them (London, 1984). Deducing a treatment from a learning theory and applying it successfully does not assure the validity of the theory or the virtue of the therapy. In the history of the healing arts, plenty of silly-seeming treatments deduced from intellectual muck have produced real cures. Why this is so is poorly understood, but it has long been known that "faith healing" and "placebo effects" work as well for mental as for medical disorders (Frank, 1973; Rosenzweig, 1936).

There is a legend in the psychotherapy trade, at all events, that whatever is new and enthusiastically pursued seems, for a time, to work better than what went before, whether or not it is more true. Eventually, novelties join the Establishment of techniques and turn out much like what went before. It is clear today that this is not so. But maybe it is not pure fantasy—maybe the common denominators, and the most vital factors in all successful psychotherapy, as Jerome Frank argues, depend more on qualities of their advocates than on the mechanics of what they think they do (1974, 1982). Freud and the first psychoanalysts thought for a while that they were getting cures in what now look like almost instant analyses, sometimes in one or two sessions. An eminent analyst I know has observed that young, fresh psychoanalysts seem to get more cures than their more experienced colleagues; and Carl Rogers once noted that client-centered therapy, after many years, seemed on balance not to have done much better than any other. This may have happened to the Action therapies as well, even in areas where they are statistically superior to Insight methods. Later statistics of success never equaled the early ones announced by Wolpe and Stampfl, and the failures of behavior therapy have lately gotten some attention (Foa & Emmelkamp, 1983). New treatments fare better competitively against hostile criticism and emotional denunciation than against the pallor and flaccidity of sympathetic acceptance, familiarity, and the slow growth of careful assays.

MORALS AND ACTION THERAPY

The main moral problems of Action therapy presume its success rather than its failure. Just as the fascination of the search for meaning in Insight therapy may make the participants forget to ask if symptoms are being cured, relief from symptomatic pain in Action therapy may cause its parties to disregard the cost or consequences of that relief.

The methods of Insight therapy, for better or worse, vest control of treatment in the patient, which has its problems. But Action therapies do not; they assign to therapists, as far as possible, control of the treatment scheme. Responsibility for outcome thus rests more with them than with Insight therapists, maybe more with them than with their patients. But what are they responsible to do? The naive answer, consistent with one moral tradition of Western civilization, is to remove pain. But for psychological troubles, the pain in question commonly involves some dissonance between one's mental processes and one's overt behavior. The term "symptom" may refer to any part of the complex. Removing it may mean inducing changes in the way people feel about themselves, but not in how they act, or changing how they act to harmonize with how they feel. In either case, the Action therapies imply that the decision about which to try rests largely with the therapist.

Now suppose a man comes to a psychotherapist to be treated, say, for homosexuality. He may define the symptom as doing or wanting homosexual acts, on the one hand, or as the anxiety and guilt he feels over it, on the other. Either way, the pain results from the discrepancy between these aspects of his experience, and it would presumably disappear if they were harmonized. But in which direction? Harmony could come equally from renouncing homosexuality, and thus maybe escaping guilt and social remonstrance, or from giving up the moral posture that condemns homosexuality. Which is the better choice? Maybe it is that which follows the line of least resistance. So, if the man wants to stop being homosexual, the treatment should encourage that outcome. If he wishes to be homosexual but not be bothered by it, the therapy should help to do that. Where relieving pain is the only issue, line-of-least-resistance arguments look best.

The true line of least resistance is not always found easily in such cases. When it can be, however, chances are good that it will be the line that rejects the prohibiting moral code rather than the prohibited behavior. For the prohibition is poorly clothed by a tissue of religious legal scruples whose moral authority in this culture is almost vestigial, and it is opposed by the appealing political rationale of personal liberty. The forbidden impulse itself, moreover, is driven biologically, so the tensions it creates are most easily reduced by being gratified. This is exactly Wolpe's position in curing a man's anxiety over homosexuality; he persuaded him to reject the religious code that condemned it (1961).

In this case, the client was overtly homosexual, and the therapist treated the discomfort that went with it. But the opposite situation is also common, where the guilt and anxiety concern an impulse which has not yet been enacted, and where the therapist suggests indulging it to resolve the symptomatic feeling. The attack on *feeling* only characterizes all Stampfl's work, on *behavior* only all Skinnerian treatment, and on either or both, Wolpe's varied methods. For all three, the choice is the therapist's. Wolpe does not shrink from responsibility for his decisions, and the Skinnerians do not allow responsibility to rest anywhere but with the therapist. Stampfl, more like Insight therapists in this respect, holds his breath as to the behavioral outcome, hoping that ridding people of anxiety is not also fostering unsociable, if painless, feelings to fuel vile behavior in them. Stampfl also comforts himself with the belief that "conscience cues" are aroused by implosion, i.e., self-civilizing stimuli that had little previous chance to work (London, 1964).

That the locus of control in therapy should reside in the therapist, not the patient, may seem a bad idea to partisans of Insight treatment models. But Actionists may fairly claim, from the framework of their assumptions, that they are doing much the same thing physicians do in treating the symptoms of physical illness. Seen that way, the worst they can be accused of is using their own judgment to plan therapy. Most would cheerfully plead guilty. The outcome of treatment may greatly change the patient's life, but that is no grounds for either trying or rejecting it. Surgery may greatly change one's life, and so can the prescription to change climate, take exercise, or stop smoking. It may be less presumptuous of the doctor, after all, to treat the symptom with some disdain for its role in the patient's total life than to think too far ahead of treatment's aftermath.

It is typical of most medical problems, on the other hand, that there is an implicit consensus among physicians and patients about treatment's goals. For psychological problems, even such evidently narrow ones as phobias, goal consensus may not be so clear. Where it is not, the readiness of Action therapists to be "responsible" may be too blithe.

THE LIMITATIONS OF ACTION

In any case, as long as they tend only to symptoms in their narrow sense, Action therapists can be less concerned with the rest of their patients' lives, even as physicians can. Repairing functions seems, after all, a fairly straightforward job. To that extent, they may not be faulted for the social philosophy implied or lacking in their treatment, no more than a mechanic can be blamed for fixing a car which later has an accident or a physician for splinting the broken finger of what turns out to be a hired gun. Everyone cannot be responsible for everything, and while society obviously has the power to curb its specialists in whatever ways it wants, it can hardly ask them to foresee and legislate all their own powers and restraints. In this respect, Actionists may seem less subject to moral scrutiny than Insight therapists, who have, to start with, broader interests in the patient's life.

But not all troubles people bring to psychotherapy can be seen as wholly functional, and even when they can, repair may still demand great changes in what things mean to them. Some phobias are clear-cut ills which can be fixed outright, and so may many other psychic troubles be, as Behavior therapists say. But who can speak so glibly of the "dysfunctions" of friends and lovers torn by friction with their consorts; or husbands unhappy with their wives; or parents with their children, all seeking counsel? Or of young people who, facing an unsafe and shadowed future, fear to cast themselves into it in love and work and seek to borrow courage? Or of the aged, whose fear of what's ahead mingles with regret for what's behind, and who seek both solace and repair? Nor is it so easy to specify the ills of homosexuals and whores and hoods and gamblers and drunks and all the hosts of people whose malfunctioning defines their public lives and not just stains them, and for whom the very definition of disorder may be more imposed from outside than it is felt within. And least of all can we be sure that dysfunction is a meet word for the discontent of those whose lives bear all the outward badges of success—prestige, accomplishment, power, fame, and wealth—and for whom dissatisfaction is itself a dark shame, emptiness a guilty secret, and boredom, loneliness, and depression, not anxiety, the hallmarks of despair.

Behavior therapies, in their purer forms, are not well equipped to handle these or to translate unhappiness or insecurity into problems of function rather than meaning. It is not obvious how they would help people who were socially deviant without addressing meaning systems which would inspire changes in life-style. And the existential crises of the rich and well endowed are not easily soothed by even the best of functional analyses. The same modesty which makes Actionists limit their aim to symptom relief, gives powerful scientific impetus to their work and frees them of some moral concern—maybe also forces them to curtail the range of problems they address. Courting specificity, the Actionist risks wedding triviality.

The only inevitable alternative to self-restriction, in this trade whose customers are ignorant of vendors' capabilities and whose needs are many and diverse, is to expand the concept of "symptom" or "malfunction" to include a wider range of troubles. This is just what many Action therapists have done. But the further this expansion goes, the more tenuous and presumptuous grows the definition, hinted or outspoken, of what good and bad functions are. The effort produces precisely the same expansion through which Insight therapists passed, as we have seen in Chapter 2 (and to which the American Psychiatric Association seems to have committed itself in its all-inclusive *Diagnostic and statistical manual #3* [DSM III], 1980). The only difference is that problems of happiness, crisis, life change, and life style are now called problems of functioning rather than of meaning, and the definition of good functioning now becomes the property of the therapist.

Skinner looks forward to such a situation in his utopian novel, *Walden Two* (1948). In that ideal society, people are engineered to function in a perfect blend of society's needs with their own. Concern with freedom does not arise, for well-functioning organisms do not feel enslaved. Unhappiness does not arise, for good functioning in Skinner's human society, as among the ants in T. H. White's *The Once and Future King* (1958), obviates unhappiness and insecurity. And the society itself is organized by planners whose power, in their own view and that of the citizens, is just a job, a social function, unprivileged and unburdened, serving the community.

The convergence or overlap of "functioning" and "meaning" is not an embarrassment to Action therapists because they define meaning, in effect, as the subjective aspect of what objectively is functioning, much as "feeling" gets defined as the subjective aspect of what is objectively "emotion." The implications of what they do to patients' lives are the same whether they choose to call them meanings or functions. The real problem is that of the breadth of the problems they tackle and the degree of control they try to exercise over the selection of goals and their achievement; it is not a problem of the semantics of labeling. The broader the problem, and the greater their control, the more their patients are at risk, when they succeed and when they fail alike.

CONCLUSION

On balance, the Action therapies made some advances over Insight therapies, though not just the ones they thought to in their early polemical writings. Their relatively mechanistic techniques were more subject to direct scrutiny than the often esoteric-sounding Insight schemes, and their early efforts used more rigorous standards for assessing psychotherapy than had generally been true of their competitors. Their theoretical formulations suggested direct lines of inquiry, exploration, and innovation in the field. For these, the gain in intellectual precision alone had great value, let alone any comparative rates of greater therapeutic success. And restricting their application to things which can be considered personal malfunctions may itself serve a social function too valuable to be dismissed by an excess of concern with social philosophy or with the relation of meaning and function.

But even the scientific gains were not all clear-cut. In the early works of behavior therapy, the range of techniques was too narrow at one extreme (Stampfl) and not very practical at the other (Skinner). In the one case, the underlying theory argued too narrow a basis for disorders (anxiety), and the broad concept of behavior shaping in the other seemed to need a whole social order for its best fulfillment. Both theories, moreover, treated too much of human behavior as a tidy extrapolation of two basic principles of learning, which is as much too neat a concept as that of meaning is too vague. This rigidity was breached when Cognitive Behavior therapies began to confront the obvious capacity of human beings to use their heads, as we shall see in the next chapter. But this timely notion was not so clear at first or so agreeable, and it was done at the cost of more, not less theoretical diffusion. The gains of Action therapies came finally from the rigorous standards they essayed in the analysis and assessment of psychotherapy and the improved taxonomies of disorder and treatment that resulted.

With respect to their moral implications, the lack of overt concern with social philosophy or a hypothetical moral order does not free Behavior therapists from involvement with these issues. When all is said and done, they can no more escape the moral dilemmas and conundrums of psychotherapy than can Insight therapists. At best, if they are careful, they may get into them with their eyes wide open. Specifying goals or limiting attacks only to so-called symptoms will not prevent immersion in these problems. Indeed, their view of responsibility for treatment sould make Action therapists more alert to therapy's implications for the social (moral) order and for their own and their patients' role in it. Most of them have not yet recognized this problem or, like Wolpe, have elected willy-nilly much the same moral goals as have most Insight therapists. Preferrring comfort to meaning as a goal, they are committed to the welfare of the individual and, in conflict, are more agents of the individual than of society, often unwittingly. Like Insight therapies too, the more they try to comprehend people's welfare in terms of their total lives rather than their symptomatic pain, the more they pose a moralistic end which is finally no less problematic or perplexing for all its scientific gains.

IV

HUMAN COMPLEXITY AND INTEGRATIVE THERAPY

THE ARGUMENT

Today's orthodoxy was yesterday's radical idea. Novelty crystallizes if it gets the chance. The chance comes best when contemptuous but imperfect isolation greets a serious new idea. In psychotherapy, this used to happen more than it does now. Psychoanalysis once produced an orthodoxy which now embarrasses its brightest advocates. Later Insight methods, like client-centered therapy, never did, nor did Behavior therapies (though they came close) because they matured in an era of great publicity and in intellectual circles committed to scientific open-mindedness. The publicity prevented any group from making its ideas private property and forced its members to talk with critics from all sides or risk deserved contempt. Doing so was good for all of them; it exposed their flaws.

The less than fatal flaw of early Action therapies was that their models were weaker than their methods. They failed to reckon consciousness or cognition in their formulae while they used them in practice. This is clear from the apparent contradiction of Wolpe's desensitizing and Stampfl's implosive treatments of anxiety. Opposite methods, both depend on imagery for their effects, but neither one admits it. The cognitive aspect of Action therapy, long observed, did not give rise to new treatments at first because the early models in vogue were not yet understood as metaphors. The animal analogs of neurosis which Behavior therapy borrowed from the learning laboratory were correct enough to be taken too seriously. Hostile critics, on the other hand, did not take them seriously enough and scorned the models as simplistic or irrelevant and the methods as trivial or immoral.

The less than fatal flaw of Insight therapies was the opposite; their methods were weaker than their models. They ascribed too much to awareness and cognition, thinking these had more power than they often do to relieve symptoms or reshape goals by changing motivation or adjusting behavior to it. They may also have presumed too much on people's ability to steer their own course in treatment. Hostile critics, however, denounced their motivational models but used the same models cloaked in different terminology, creating confusion about what symptoms mean. They also wrongly condemned Insight methods as useless, failing to see that listening sympathetically to clients, evoking feelings, and expanding consciousness is a true technology and not seduction of the innocent nor mere icing on the therapeutic cake.

Action therapists, in time, were pushed by their pragmatic bent and its functional ideology, which champions therapeutic novelty, to see and use the fact that people are cognitive, not just reactive animals. This gave impetus to what is now called Cognitive Behavior Therapy. And Insight therapists are seeing that we are reactive, not just cognitive animals and, like Behaviorists, are writing standard treatment manuals and essays on rapprochement.

This hopeful trend suggests that, except at the most orthodox, know-nothing fringes, both kinds of therapy should improve at symptom treatment as they blend ideas and methods. But neither one is thereby well equipped to treat problems of meaning in clients free of functional defects or of symptoms whose solution rests on what life means to people. Such problems are common because much of today's psychological misery is caused or worsened by the impotence of creeds, the weakness of families, the decline of communities, and the lack of customs and ceremonies to which people can refer their life goals. But therapies for them are rare because the view of mental health required is bolder and broader than theorists or therapists like. It demands that therapy speak to people's need for purpose and commitment outside themselves. Religious creeds and social utopias are the conventional agents of such goals, not secular psychotherapies.

Freud, Skinner, and others have theorized about this problem, taking "society" as the object of commitment. The late O. H. Mowrer, however, invented a practical psychotherapy to address it. He argued that symptoms reflect social transgressions in socialized people, whose cure requires their social rehabilitation. Therapy helps them to expose their sins and guides their acts of restitution. Mowrer's is an uneasy blend of Insight and Action treatment, in which mental health rests on self-esteem, and it in turn depends on action to affirm one's social integrity. Alienation from real people and from a normative order, he says, is the root of psychological "dis-ease," and it is psychotherapy's job to "re-connect" them. "Integrity" means wholeness, one-ness, being all of a piece, as people's lives are, however fragmentary their neuroses seem. Psychotherapy is morally bound to serve it.

11

Orthodoxy, Novelty, and Cognitive Behavior Therapy

If psychiatry still seems a somewhat backward branch of medicine and psychotherapy a scientific folly to some psychologists, it is not for lack of splendid students of these fields, but because knowledge comes harder here than in some other disciplines. The disease model of psychosocial disorders gained ascendance over demons and dybbuks only lately, as progress in human thought is measured. And two centuries after its demise was augured by Pinel's idea of "moral disorder," the term "mental illness" still has not been abandoned or replaced by a better one that includes disorders of learning, of behavior or of meaning, which might be another forward step in thinking on this theme.

At each stage in psychotherapy's development, yesterday's innovator is today's reactionary. The champions of the structural disease or defect model of mental ills which sired "organic" psychiatry in the 19th century opposed the functional, nonorganic model of disorder that produced psychoanalysis. And, in turn, the dynamic psychiatry born of psychoanalysis despised at first the new technology that learning theory spawned.

Clinical psychiatrists and psychologists, who invent most of the novelty in psychotherapy, are disadvantaged relative to some close colleagues for gaining firm new knowledge—much of medicine and psychology deal with smaller units of behavior and clearer problems than does most of psychotherapy. Unlucky in their scientific subject matter and hungry for clinical confidence, psychotherapists may clutch too hard, generalize too much, and stick too fast to weak theories and eccentric observations. Since their topic is dreadfully complex, and since the techniques they invent take struggle, work well enough to use again, and lack better known or proved alternatives—once learned, they tend to stick.

It is hard for psychotherapists, like the rest of us, to transcend hard-won convictions, whether to see faults in the familiar or to explore new horizons.

This ossifying process overtakes the sponsors of therapeutic novelty as well. Reinforced by sympathetic colleagues and disciples and by the happy testimonials of patients and publishers, in due course their innovations become new orthodoxies. Then, immured against new ideas or inquiry themselves, they spurn past work too much for its faults and disregard the future's sure discovery of weakness in their schemes.

This came to pass with some Action therapists, whose reactive zeal against the Insight schools made them forget some virtues of insight systems and overlook flaws in their own.

THE LIMITS OF THE EARLY SYSTEMS

Although their conflicts go beyond one issue, the battle between Insight and Action therapists was joined historically over what symptoms meant and how they could be cured. For some symptoms, it turned out, Action therapies had a better case. They made the most of it.

The excess of Insight therapies, in this respect, was the notion that consciousness inevitably drives behavior. It does not, at least not inevitably. Empirical studies of therapy outcomes could have told us this long since. But they were not much done or done halfheartedly or ineffectually, and it was largely the statistical pricks of polemical antagonists like Wolpe and Eysenck that made outcome studies be taken seriously. Action therapies score heavily for that.

But the early Action therapies had a parallel excess. While Insight systems made too much of consciousness, insight, and meaning, Action systems made too little of them, both in theory and technique. In their righteous rebuttal of the sanctity of insight, they dismissed *thinking* as a means of behavior control. Hurrying to the animal laboratory for models of learning transferrable from cats and rats to human beings, their zeal to find species' similarities made them forget the differences. The most obvious one is that humans have language and other animals do not. With it, they can take instruction, observe and report their own private behavior, and can separate the processes, recount them, and remember them. Early action therapists disregarded these facts in their theories even while they used them in practice. Their models credited the words of psychotherapists only with the simple stimulus values that analogy with cats and rats attributes to them, while the thoughtful responses they asked of patients, like imagining, remembering, and mentally rehearsing, were not part of the models at all. The scientific posture of the Actionists rejected not just "fuzzy" humanism, but the very parts of evolutionary biology in which we are most unlike our fellow creatures. But the seeds of a "cognitive therapy" were already embedded in their methods, as evidenced in Wolpe's and Stampfl's apparently contradictory procedures for treating the same kind of anxiety.

A COGNITIVE THEORY OF EXPOSURE TREATMENT

Wolpe and Stampfl clash head on at the point where, treating the same condition, Wolpe claims to "desensitize" people to anxiety by a method that avoids arousing it, while Stampfl claims to "extinguish" anxiety by producing it. In practice, each creates as vivid a mental image as he can of things that make the patient anxious. Wolpe does so while keeping the client relaxed, so the feared object will not feel frightening. Stampfl does so while frightening patients so the feared object will come to seem harmless as the fear goes unsustained by danger.

Neither model deals with vivid imagining itself as the likely key to healing: Anxiety, after all, is both a mental and physical experience. By practice at imagining, the client learns to discriminate between cognitive and affective aspects of experience, on the one hand, and sensory-muscular and hormonal aspects on the other. Imagining, in this case, teaches one to separate mentally what is "imaginary" from what is "real" or, to be exact, what is harmful from what is not. Anxiety declines as people learn to tolerate awful imagery, and this tolerance comes from discriminating between anxiety-provoking and other aspects of experience. The better the imagery portrays experience in one's thoughts without support of the sensorimotor response it simulates, the more one's expectation of disaster declines. By this means, people learn that even extreme thoughts, feelings, and motives need not force them helplessly to disastrous action and consequent punishment and pain. Thus they learn control; the differentiation or "mediation" process gets efficiency with repetition and becomes an alternative to anxiety in the face of provoking stimulation. It allows "thinking over" the frightening stimulus instead of automatically shrinking from it. Since by definition (of neurosis) the stimulus is harmless, its discrimination becomes easier and less important both, and its stimulating value sinks beneath the threshold of observation.

The principle of discrimination is not news to students of learning, and it is, of course, learned alike by cats, rats, and people. So far, its use does no violence to either Wolpe's or Stampfl's formulation. But the *cognitive* aspect of discrimination here has two uniquely human features: First, it makes the therapist's talking central to the treatment process, where it is only incidental to the animal-anxiety model, a mere mechanism for inspiring imagery. Second, it suggests that the main therapeutic action, spoken or otherwise, is eliciting imagery, not a direct assault on anxiety. If so, neither Wolpe's verbal brinkmanship nor Stampfl's verbal brutality count as much toward success as the skill they both have in vivid description and perhaps the luck they have in patients whose imaginations can be so aroused.

So far, this says only that cognitive behavior can be part of Action models for treating anxiety. But maybe any animal-anxiety model, without cognition, will not explain the varied human anguish which does not parallel that of a caged animal to an electrified floor. It cannot take full account of people's long memories for the past or large plans for the future, delaying rewards and stabilizing action or changing it more than other creatures can. With all that the animal laboratory has done to find the fundamentals of behavior and of neurosis—and it has been much—we will not fully know them in people without models for the special traits of human beings (Bandura, 1983).

Many scholars have addressed these qualities. Although Watson and Skinner saw speech and language as special cases of classical and operant conditioning respectively, Pavlov considered human language a "second signal system" (the first was conditioning) by which learning occurs without conditioning (Kazdin, 1978a). Edward Tolman's later theory of "purposive" or "molar behaviorism" argued that behavior is goal directed, not merely associational, and guided by cognitive as well as reflexive (conditional) processes (1932). Still later, students of classical conditioning in humans proved that awareness of the process makes great differences in people's reactions to it (Grings, 1965). And most empirical results since, in a raging debate on the role of awareness in human learning, suggest that, while operant conditioning of people can occur unconsciously, precious little does (Bandura, 1969; Kazdin, 1978b). Most of what people learn, therapeutically or otherwise, takes consciousness.

Oddly, direct evidence of the role of consciousness, as in the studies above, had far less pro-cognitive impact on behavior therapy than did studies of "observational" or "vicarious" learning, in which one learns an act by watching others do it rather than by doing it. This capacity, vital for much of human learning, hardly exists in nonprimate species. But neither does speech, of course, which made little impression on early behavior therapists. The impact of observational learning research came from its timing and from the high quality of the studies which promoted it. Led since the 1960s by Albert Bandura and his students, studies of imitation and modeling, which are the mechanisms of observational learning, gave rise to contemporary "social learning theory" (Bandura, 1977a; Bandura & Walters, 1963). It gave behavior therapists an innovative latitude they had not felt before.

"Social learning theory" is not a theory in the sense that Wolpe or Stampfl or Eysenck mean. It is not a deductive system of lawful principles for predicting behavior. As Ted Rosenthal, one of its leading exponents, says, it is ". . . a rather general theoretical approach toward human thought and action . . . an integrating framework for a broad swath of empirical data . . . [which] play [s] a heuristic role in pointing out new and needed directions for study" (1982, p. 340).

Functional Analysis and Behavior Therapy

The idea promoted by this work, which gradually gained currency, added to the behaviorist creed the legitimacy of studying other principles than conditioning. As it did, new treatments abounded.

Some were fairly direct analogs from animal studies, as in Wolpe's and Skinner's work. Others were more metaphorical, as in Implosive therapy, where Stampfl speaks of storytelling as if it had the same frightening properties as an electric shock. Yet a third group made little pretense to "fancy" scientific theory, but used the idea of behavioral "models" or "orientations" or "paradigms" as heuristics for strategic planning, making commonsensical arguments for plausible treatments. They claimed kinship with Behavior Therapy because of shared disapproval of Insight therapies or specific similarities in language, theory, or technique. What they had most in common, though, was clinical interest and admiration for scientific method. They were loosely allied ideologically under the banner of Science, but the alliance was as much organizational as intellectual.

The true intellectual bond among what finally called themselves "Behavior Therapies" was an implicit common commitment to functional analysis as the main intellectual tool for clinical diagnosis and psychotherapeutic treatment. Honed by operant psychologists in particular (see Chapter 9), it consists, in essence, of a precise statement of the problematic situation, precise plan of the operations meant to attack it, and precise standards for results by which to judge success.

Obviously, functional analysis has nothing to do with psychotherapy per se or with animal laboratories or models. It is a tool for dealing with scientific experiments and technical problems. And since the scientific structure of the psychology of learning rather than its content is probably what attracted clinicians to Action therapy in the first place, they welcomed others with like scientific ideology into their confederacy.

As treatments proliferated for a host of problems analyzed this way, a systemic weakness of behavior therapy was laid bare: Its theoretical structures could not gracefully carry all the practical techniques which functional analysis was enabling. The methods were often better than the explanations of them. Classical Conditioning, the Law of Effect, Successive Approximation, Observational Learning, and the whole bundle of extant behavior theories could not meet the need of many therapists to understand how they managed to work mostly by talking and listening, which is what they did. Some stopped worrying and, instead, simply used the license that functional analysis had given them to evolve and rationalize what are now called generically "Cognitive Behavior Therapies." Their loose theoretical lines range from "common sense" to information processing and computer models (Mahoney, 1980). Among the best known are "Cognitive Therapy," developed by Aaron T. Beck (1976); "Rational Emotive Therapy," chiefly the creation of Albert Ellis (1980); and an integrative collage of well-reasoned techniques, some derived from the notion of "internal speech," by Donald Meichenbaum (1977).

COGNITIVE BEHAVIOR THERAPIES

The methods of "cognitive behavior modification," as it is often called, are all connected to things people say to themselves, especially things about themselves. The techniques derive as much from personal experience with everyday behavior as from observations of patients or learned musings on behavior theory or research. Donald Meichenbaum says frankly that his methods come from his family history. (Not new—Freud said that he learned the interpretation of dreams and psychopathology of everyday life largely from self observation.) Understandably, therefore, there is a "homeliness," a familiarity about them, which gives a simplistic seeming cast to all these treatments and, indeed, to the descriptions of the problems they treat. A. T. Beck's *Cognitive Therapy,* for instance, as summarized by A. John Rush, is based on the theory that ". . . how a person thinks determines how he feels and reacts . . . The symptoms of a disorder are related to the content of the patient's thinking . . . people who develop depression have schemas concerned with self-deprecation; those developing anxiety states have schemas concerned with the anticipation of personal harm . . . Cognitive Therapy techniques are designed to identify, reality-test, and correct maladaptive, distorted cognitions and the dysfunctional beliefs (schemas) underlying these cognitions. The patient learns to master problems and situations that he previously considered insuperable by reevaluating and correcting his thinking. The cognitive therapist teaches the patient to think more realistically and adaptively, thus reducing symptoms" (all quotes Rush, 1980, p. 91–94).

The *Rational-Emotive-Therapy (RET)* of Albert Ellis makes much the same argument, but more brashly: People "condition" themselves to feel disturbed, tend ". . . to think 'crookedly' and to needlessly upset themselves . . . to invent and create disturbing beliefs, as well as . . . to upset themselves about their disturbances." Withal, they have ". . . unusual capacities to change their cognitive, emotive, and behavioral processes so that they can: (a) choose to react differently from the way they usually do; (b) refuse to upset themselves about almost anything that may occur, and (c) train themselves so that they can semi-automatically remain minimally disturbed for the rest of their lives" (all quotes Ellis, 1980, p. 543–547).

The specific techniques, often ingenious, are also commonsensical: The therapist challenges the assumptions and premises on which the patient's irrational or misguided thinking is based, if necessary, as Ellis says, using ". . . verbal force and vigor . . . in order to powerfully help uproot these clients' self-sabotaging ideas and behavior." With or without vigor, the process, to cite Rush, first gives the patient "a didactic explanation of the rationale for Cognitive Therapy. Next, he learns to recognize, monitor, and record the negative thoughts associated with incidents in which he felt particularly upset. . . . The cognitions and underlying assumptions are discussed and examined for logic, validity, adaptiveness, and enhancement of positive behavior versus maintenance of pathology."

More than argument is needed, of course. Extensions of it include lectures and confrontations, role playing and behavioral rehearsal, workshops, seminars or group therapy for mutual discussion of problems and feedback and reinforcement of therapeutic effort. Familiar techniques of behavior therapy, such as assertion training and desensitization, are also used in cognitive behavior therapy. Varied self instruction and homework assignments teach patients literally to talk to themselves in rational and constructive ways that ease anxiety, lift depression and improve performance; to keep a Daily Activity Log; a Mastery and Pleasure Schedule for rating activities in the Log; or to do Graded Task Assigments of things hitherto thought impossible to accomplish. Above all, practice! The methods are whatever teaching devices the therapist can construct. For the name of the game of Cognitive Therapies, when all is said and done, is to teach people to understand what is wrong with their lives and give practical lessons on how to set it right. "Teach," understand," "wrong," and "lessons" are used here in superficial as well as subtle meanings. They mean the same things in cognitive therapies that they mean in ordinary conversation.

It is easy to dismiss these treatments as naive because they sound so much like the traditionally insensitive and useless "shape up!" counsel known to everyone: "You shouldn't feel that way!" "You're not being rational!" "You've got to pull yourself out of this!" "You can do it if you really try!" "Start off by making a list of all the things . . . !" and so on. Such a view is wrong. Cognitive behavior therapy fills in for the failure of Insight and Action therapies to notice people's capacity to evaluate and change their lives by deliberate effort—to listen, to understand, and to act (Meichenbaum & Cameron, 1982). Our common familiarity with teaching should not breed contempt for it. These methods simply teach directly by skilled and sensitive means what prior therapists assumed (but did not test) could not be taught directly at all.

Internecine Warfare in Behavior Therapy

Despite differences among cognitive behavior therapies, they share an emphasis on thinking, that is, on consciousness as an important part of therapeutic work. This did not at first arouse much thought of rapprochement between Insight and Action therapies. It did provoke quarrels among behavior therapists over the role of cognition in treatment and over the gerrymandering of learning theory to fit it into the rubric of behaviorism. Wolpe accused cognitive behaviorists of making too much ado over cognition; it was already fully incorporated into behavior theory and therapy practice, he said (1978). They accused him, in turn, of confusing learning, which is central to all therapeutic change, and conditioning, whose relevance to psychotherapy is less than Wolpe thinks (Beck & Mahoney, 1979; Ellis, 1979; Lazarus, 1979).

Despite acrimony, both sides of the argument stick religiously to the scientific credo of behavior therapy, to the idea that it is the artful application of what must be empirically verifiable techniques, regardless of its theories. Cognition broadens the scope of Action therapy but does not take it beyond the pale of functional analysis. It legitimizes essential procedures—for what real therapist works without instructing, let alone talking? It permits inventiveness. It takes verbal tools like Ellis's persuasive arguing and Meichenbaum's internal dialogues into the behavioral framework. And it allows richer discourse about what goes on in people's heads than does the "black box" idea which was once so useful to academic psychology (London, 1983a).

Ecumenism in Psychotherapy

Its combined emphasis on consciousness and scientific method might make cognitive behavior therapy seem to be a natural bridge for reconciling or integrating Insight and Action therapies. There is some truth in this. Interest in integration, synthesis, or reconciliation has, indeed, grown in recent years. A few treatises on the "interface" of psychodynamic and behavioral therapies have tried to join them, the moreso as research suggested that they are about equally effective (Goldfried, 1982; London, 1983b; Marmor & Woods, 1980; Wachtel, 1977). And a "Society for the Exploration of Psychotherapy Integration" now exists for that explicit purpose (Goldfried & Wachtel, 1983). But cognitive behavior therapists have not yet rushed to partake of this trend and, indeed, the idiom of their discourse still is mostly a variant of the terminology (and jargon) of behavior therapies, not of insight methods. It could hardly be otherwise, since "consciousness" here and in Insight therapies is so disparate (Franks, 1984; Messer & Winokur, 1980).

Even so, cognitive behavior therapists' scrupulous attention to the role of consciousness in behavior change creates a domain of potential compromise and harmonious discourse, so to speak, between the earlier and more puristic insight and action orientations (London, 1984). Both of them are on the same side of the intellectual fence when considered in what Barry Wolfe has called "the cultural context of psychotherapy." As much as their origins, theories, and methods differ, they both advance the same kinds of therapeutic goals.

THE NEED FOR MEANINGFUL ACTION

In the evolution of behavior therapies, it seems, the more complex the problem in question, the less early Action treatments are suited to its solution. They lack action mechanisms for achieving broad goals and, for complex issues, they are unable to specify fruitful goals. They can do so only by confronting (exploring or supporting or attacking) the large meaning or value systems to which patients adhere. The cognitive "insert" into behavior therapy helps to broaden its dealings with more problems than pure stimulus-response models could. But it addresses the problem of meaning systems, including that of existential systems, only in terms of the individual reference values of the therapist. It says nothing of meaning systems for which people need validation outside themselves and more general than their therapist's.

Within limits, not all psychotherapy needs a system of meaning in order to work. But considering what everyone knows personally of how life shuttles us subjectively between misery and joy, it is hard to see how any but the smuggest psychotherapy can long avoid concern with meaning. People may come to therapy seeking relief, not knowledge, and maybe should get surcease of pain without the necessary imposition of self-consciousness. Still, many will seek awareness, once healed, if only because, at their most thoughtful, undistracted by personal suffering, people see themselves as creatures of purpose—and worry about how to see themselves when they do not.

If this is true, then one may ask of all the Action therapies, including the cognitive ones, whether an excess of modesty limits them to too demonstrable empiricisms. Ultimately, the functional analysis and treatment only of "symptomatic" questions begs all ultimate questions, which are questions of meaning.

Insight therapies may seem to escape the question, at first, because they talk so much to start with about meaning, with easing symptomatic suffering a perhaps prior, but less important, task. But they too cannot quite take title to the profundities they claim to have. They mostly run into the same problem as do Action therapies in trying to effect some broad improvement in people's lives: Their referent for a meaningful existence, by and large, is the individual standing alone. But maybe people cannot find their lives meaningful except in a context where their sense of hope, of control, of support and of commitment revolves around things outside themselves and greater than themselves. For theistic people, their religion would provide that context. For most others, the most likely context would be a social one. Many of the folk who attend psychotherapy sessions are drawn from the secular group; their quest for meaning most needs attention.

The need for social validation has worried students of psychotherapy, from early Freud and Adler through Sullivan, on the psychoanalytic and neo-analytic side. More recently, and more broadly, Erich Fromm, whose posture derives from analytic insight, and Skinner, the purest of Actionists, posit the necessity for sane societies of rather similar kinds. Fromm finds it truly meaningful, Skinner truly functional; to both, involvement with society is vital to the best development of human beings. But in all their works, the "social interest" is academic therapeutically because it gives no concrete counsel for therapists or patients in this society. Knowing that societies may be abstractly "sick" or "well" or that relationships may be "authentic" or phony does not tell people how they can relate their lives to a social order or the people in it.

A psychotherapy that tried to do all this would use insight and action to attack both symptomatic and existential problems. Insight, in such a system, would connect the motives and behaviors, present and historical, that prevented an orderly relationship with the (commonly social) context that makes life seem meaningful. Its aim would be to steer a new action system which channels the individual's functions within that context. The context itself, the reference that makes the whole thing meaningful, would not be the painful symptom nor the wounded selfhood beneath it, but something outside the individual. For most such therapies, serving secular clientele, a social system, real or ideal, must provide that context.

Most psychotherapies which try to integrate insight and action do not speak at once to the ideas of meaning and action and to a social order for their fulfillment. Perhaps the first psychotherapy to do so was that of the late O. H. Mowrer. His research of many years concerned both psychoanalytic and learning theory. His therapy transcended them.

12

The Price of Personal Integrity

The Therapy of O. H. Mowrer

Radical scientific theories must sometimes pass political tests to become respectable objects of inquiry. When they assault established positions, such theories tend to irritate in the extreme. An index of the seminal quality of a new theory, indeed, may be the extent to which it is scoffed at. If so, then the theory of neurosis and treatment which the late O. H. Mowrer proposed around 1960 may deserve more serious attention than any such theory since Freud's, for in the few generations between them, no more respected psychology theorist has suffered such noisy and contemptuous attack.

The fault therein does not lie wholly with the critics. Mowrer's theory of disorder and treatment did not get very systematic treatment in most of his own writing. *The Crisis in Psychiatry and Religion,* his first long work on it (published in 1961), is a potpourri of essays that collectively contained his then current thinking about therapy. It had two great flaws, one intellectual, the other political. First, none of the essays tried to present his theory step-by-step. One had to wade through them all to capture it, which was not easy. And if it was hard to do for the theory, it was impossible for the details of therapy, for the book says nothing of the techniques Mowrer had devised. His next large work, *The New Group Therapy* (1964), began to correct this flaw, but without removing the language barriers it presents to many mental health professionals.

These barriers are the political faults of his work, more germane to its polemics. Mowrer had some genius for sensing the rawest intellectual nerve of his audience and then addressing himself to it in a way that incited to riot. In these early works, he would first use conventional religious language to advocate secular ideas; thus endeared to the clergy, he would then assault choice bits of their theologies with gusto, wit, and venom.

Some scholars were not amused, including many who esteemed Mowrer's great scientific contributions to learning, personality, and psychotherapy. Unable to judge the theory on its scholarly merits because of the foreign sounds religious language makes in scientific ears, many of them failed to recognize the important and sophisticated argument expressed in these writings. In later papers, Mowrer and his colleagues obligingly used more conventional psychological language to explain "Integrity therapy" and the "Integrity groups" which are now its sole method of operation (see Vattano, 1981).

But some momentum of interest was lost, and "Integrity therapy" is less talked of in "the trade" than it used to be. That is unfortunate, for its effort to integrate Insight and Action therapies in a social context within the existing political and economic framework of Western society is almost unique in concept and in scope.

His concept was almost lost at the beginning anyway, for Mowrer's statement of what was wrong with neurotic people and how treatment should fix it seemed scandalous. It looked simple-minded, cruel, and opposed to all the scientific and humane ideas of mental health which had won the minds of experts everywhere. A few colleagues thought he had lost his mind.

Briefly, Mowrer said that neurotics had acted badly, that guilt was the mental hell that signified their misconduct, and that cure demanded discovery and compensation for their misdeeds. He was even blunter: Neurotics, he said, were sinners; their guilt showed the reality of their sins; and confession and expiation alone would cure them.

This got people's attention. We must now look at his work in more detail to see that it merits some support as well (Mowrer, 1972).

THE GUILT THEORY OF NEUROSIS

Mowrer proposed that neurosis expresses distress that comes from breaches in people's relationships with "significant others." Its symptoms include anxiety, depression, delusions, and hallucinations. Mowrer used the term "significant others," borrowed from George Herbert Mead (1934), mostly to mean specific people, like mother, spouse, friend, or employer, but he also used it to mean abstractions that may embody the principle of relationships, such as Community, Society, or God.

People who suffer neurotic breakdowns, says Mowrer, were partly socialized during childhood. They learned to attach enough importance to relationships with others that they are hugely distressed at their violation. The mechanism that maintains this attitude is "conscience." Mowrer discussed it at length in *Learning Theory and Personality Dynamics* (1950), long before he invented Integrity Therapy. He sees the role of conscience in neurosis opposite to Freud.

Freud, he says, views neurotic suffering as a product of the merciless activity of an overdeveloped conscience. Mowrer, however, sees it as the paralyzing anguish resulting from the conflict between self-reproach and restitution in one whose conscience is normal but whose activity has betrayed it. Freud's neurotic has been "emotionally oversocialized"; Mowrer's has been "behaviorally under-socialized."

The theory thus does not apply to every kind of psychological disorder. Psychopaths or sociopaths, for instance, are not neurotic because they have not been socialized enough in the first place to suffer from disrupted sociality.

Symptoms and breakdowns follow a destructive course of development that goes like this:

First, the person indulges some selfish impulse in a situation where he or she had learned, as part of early social training, to inhibit such acts.

Next, the person is made anxious either by the absence of punishment for it or from recognizing the breach of sociality created by the act, and conflict results from the simultaneous fear of the negative effects that might come from its discovery. The most obvious and most significant negative effect is the loss of social and self-esteem, but all punishment may be feared.

Not revealing the behavior to significant others—maintaining secrecy—sustains the conflict, which is made worse by the same impulses whose indulgence got the person in trouble to begin with.

Thus trapped between revulsions over one's own behavior, on the one hand, and reluctance to either pay for it or be done with it, on the other, one may be overwhelmed with conflict and get symptoms of guilt, anxiety, and depression. Of these, the most favorable prognostically is guilt.

Like others, Mowrer's is an adjustment theory. But it differs in important points from other such theories, whether they are oriented toward Insight or Action:

First, it argues that, once such primary drives as sex and aggression have achieved a modicum of gratification, they grow less important to mental health than do secondary drives of importance to interpersonal relationships, such as the need for trust which motivates openness and honesty with others.

Second, Mowrer believes that people's reaction to their acts causes conflict leading to breakdown not, as in other theories, that purely mental events are sources of such conflict. People who *feel* guilty, says Mowrer, have *done* more to arouse this feeling than merely thinking or feeling some "wrong" impulse.

Third, Mowrer's theory allows for the "ego defenses" of Sigmund and Anna Freud, but he denies that repression, from which they spring, is central to neurosis. It is *suppression* that he thinks is important, specifically hiding one's misconduct from significant others. Like Wolpe, Mowrer gives repression no place in neurotic conflict, as Freud does. Mowrer and Wolpe are not in agreement, however, on what causes neurotic conflict. Wolpe has no more liking for *suppression* than for repression and is unconvinced that self-disclosure has much therapeutic value.

THE INTEGRITY CURE

If breakdowns occur because people have damaged their relationships with significant others in their lives, then may cures result from repairing those relationships? This is precisely Mowrer's theory. He says that cure comes through two main treatment techniques, which I shall label *publicity* and *work*. He used different terms for them at different times, but in early writing he called the former "confession" and the latter "expiation" or "restitution."

Publicity

Publicity is a prior if less important step. It stems directly from the theory of neurosis: If neurotic conflict grows from secrecy over what one has done, then publicizing one's secret will help reduce the conflict. And if part of the conflict also comes from the continued activity of the troublesome impulses, then since these impulses are socially unacceptable to begin with, they will be most active if they are kept secret. Mowrer proposes that their publication works to inhibit them, reducing their strength and thereby their contribution to the conflict.

Expiative Work

Publicity may help reduce conflict, but it is not enough to cure, mainly because people have long memories attached to their feelings and relationships. Maybe it was conflict that produced breakdown, but it was the violation of sociality that produced the conflict in the first place. By itself, publicizing secrets does not undo the results of the original transgression, and unless this happens, the neurotic person's sociality is not restored. If confession has to stand alone, in fact, with nothing else changed, it may further violate one's sociality, becoming a kind of paean of guilt that reinforces a continued separation of oneself from society.

Cure only happens when people, now relieved of conflict, recognize the source of their trouble in their overt acts and recommit themselves to the society they have foregone and foresworn. They must treat their original violations directly or, if this is impossible (as it often is), must pay in kind, that is, compensate for their bad behavior with new acts which facilitate sociality instead of violating it.

This positive commitment must be a continuous process, not an isolated event, much as physical health is a process and not a single fact. The curative work has two stages, an *expiative* one in which people address the transgressions from which their conflicts arose, and another, *involved* one where they are reinforced for expiation by other people's approval of relationships in which their participation is now visibly, and hence appreciably honest, responsible, and committed.

CRITIQUE OF MOWRER

The initial expiative act may address the violation of one's relationship with a single individual, but the ongoing involvement ambiguously implied in Mowrer's writing is a broader one. He thinks society, broadly conceived, must be taken as the main source of people's big life goals and the main means by which they can channel and control their selfish impulses. It is acceptance of sociality and immersion in it which gives most meaning to people's acts and, finally, to their lives. Whether and how our higher needs can be fully met in personal relationships alone is a question Mowrer did not confront directly in his writing. But it always niggled at him, and it explains in part his early fascination with religious language and institutions. As a practical matter, it led him to change Integrity Therapy from a two-person consulting room professional therapy into a nonprofessional group activity in its own eyes much like Alcoholics Anonymous.

FROM INTEGRITY THERAPY
TO INTEGRITY GROUPS

Early in the development of Integrity Therapy, as he then called it, Mowrer discovered that the best way for him to teach personal openness was to be a model of self-disclosure, that is, to exhibit it himself. His openness did not mean the "personal transparency" that Carl Rogers speaks of, but telling patients his past sins. This speeded up their learning that they likewise could reveal themselves to significant others. "But then," he says:

> *"it was found that this process could be still further expedited by two or more patients meeting simultaneously with the therapist and talking to each other as well as to the therapist. From this it was but a short step to the emergence of groups, ranging from six to ten participants. Thus, the phenomenon of mutual aid and interaction increased so that today Integrity Groups are self operated and function without professional intervention...." (1980, p. 314).*

If using small groups to implement the "I.G. Process," as Mowrer now called it, were a purely technical matter, then the last sentence of the above quotation would be irrelevant, for there is nothing pertinent to group psychotherapy in "professional intervention." But in fact the origin of Mowrer's group method is all but accidental and its lay character is central, just as in Alcoholics Anonymous. For the group Mowrer advocates is not a mere instrument for trying out one's reconciliation with society. It is a society! Its being nonprofessional is important because it means first, that no member has final authority for what it does, and second, that only coin of equal value is exchanged among its members. And those things in turn mean that it can dissolve or perpetuate itself on any terms its members wish.

Integrity Group members, it seems, use the group for limited time and limited problems, not as an expanded family, a worker-owned business, or a kibbutz. This is clear from the guidelines and ground rules of its 1975 "manual," so called, *Integrity Groups: The Loss and Recovery of Community* (Mowrer, Vattano, Baxley, & Mowrer, 1975). But that is beside the point, which is, to quote Mowrer again,

> *". . . that everyone needs social support systems, membership in which involves not only privileges but also commitments, contributions, and co-operation. Recovery and personal change involve the willingness and capacity to give as well as receive, to be interdependent instead of dependent" (1980, p. 315).*

The social support system of Alcoholics Anonymous, as everyone knows, goes far beyond the immediacies of the group meeting. Its ideological point of departure, routinely expressed in the confessional of the group meeting, is "I am an alcoholic," once and future too. For Integrity Group members, the equivalent would be "I am a sinner." What does this mean in Mowrer's terms? Why is it important?

COMMUNITY AS THERAPY: A–THEISM IN RELIGION

Mowrer had some personal reasons for couching the early statement of his therapy in religious language, but they are not important here. The terminology itself is important, however, even though it has been replaced in most writing about Integrity Groups by counterpart secular language less offensive to secular scientific and professional ears. It is important because its moral implications are more stark than the usual mental health terms and because it elaborates his contra-Freudian hypothesis that moral rather than biological "frustration" is the main cause of neurosis (1963). *God, religion, sin, guilt, confession, expiation,* and *salvation* are typical terms of Mowrer's early therapeutic vocabulary. A glossary of them is in order.

God means the idealization of the socialization process. Mowrer often uses a pet phrase of Anton Boisen (founder of the Mental Health movement), "that social something we call God" (1961, pp. 128, 154 and elsewhere). He emphatically lacks a theological interest in God; he uses the term only to reinforce the idea ". . . that man is pre-eminently a *social* creature—or, in theological phrase, a Child of God . . ." (1961, p. 131 and elsewhere). His references to God are really to what might be called godliness in human behavior, and even that only in the sense that "... our first obligation is to be good human beings ..." (1972, p. 11). Mowrer indicates, without saying it outright, that whether or not he believes a deity exists is beside the point of his argument (let alone that it is none of the reader's business).

Religion, it follows, does not mean what clergymen usually think it does, and Mowrer vigorously rejects the idea that he is "... trying to smuggle conservative Biblical teachings into academic and professional circles." Even the notion that religion involves belief in God is a "... really quite unfortunate misconception. Religion, in terms of its derivation from Latin sources, simply means 're-connection.' ... Thus religion in its literal sense—and that is the sense in which we use it—has no necessary relationship with theology ..." (1972, p. 11).

Sin means acts that violate sociality (transgression).

Guilt means what it means in law: responsibility for transgression or sin, as well as the subjective state of feeling bad about such behavior. Mowrer argued that guilt is always "real," by which he meant that the feeling of transgression refers to some overt transgressive act. His theory logically allows for the existence of neurotic guilt, which would mean about the same thing Freud meant by it: guilty feelings about ideas, thoughts, and impulses that have not been acted on. But where such rare feelings exist, Mowrer would say, they are not big sources of conflict. His point is that psychotherapists must not "... deny the objectivity of guilt and ... interact with patients only in terms of guilty *feelings,*" but that guilt must be taken seriously, "... particularly when kept hidden from 'significant others' ..." and dealt with "in terms of *honesty* (self-disclosure, confession), *responsibility* (making amends, restitution), and *involvement* (concern for and aid to others)" (1980, p. 314).

Confession, as you can see, means self-disclosure.

Expiation means making amends, making restitution or, in the most general sense, as above, taking responsibility.

Salvation means the achievement of mental health, which in turn means the pursuit of "man's inveterate sociality and morality." Finding it requires not merely *"restoring* the individual to his *former* self," but *"reformation"* of "a duplicitous and disgraceful life style." "... 'recovery' from such a state of affairs is *never* easy ... and it is totally unrealistic to encourage such persons, either in the context of secular psychotherapy or religious conversion, to believe that their 'salvation' can be simple and easy. Salvation is, nonetheless, *possible;* and it is our obligation to see and delineate that possibility clearly and accurately" (all quotations in this paragraph are from 1961, p. 153; quote marks and italics as in original text).

Let us leave to Mowrer's biographer the question of how he got involved with religious idiom in the first place. What we must understand of his religious talk is that it expresses two vital ideas: First, that "the fullest actualization and fulfillment of individuals" depends on their morality (1972, p. 10) and second, that morality means an integrated relationship with one's reference group, that is, one's community. Maybe he uses "God" as a metaphor for whatever power motivates this "true and ultimate nature of man" (1961, p. 153), but all his other religious terms, including "religion," are concrete aspects of the relationship of individual and community. That Mowrer grapples so blatantly with the question of human nature (which is the broadest statement of the problem of meaning) and that he binds it so relentlessly to community, is what makes his work important.

SIGNIFICANCE OF MOWRER'S WORK

Viewed in the technical spectrum of psychotherapies, Mowrer's method is an uneasy blend of insight and action. Like insight theories, his is an ego psychology in which mental balance rests on self esteem. Like Sullivan, who influenced him greatly, he treats self-esteem largely as a function of good reputation, but of merited reputation (in terms of one's own conscience), not the mere fact of popularity. For Sullivan, moreover, self-esteem is largely a product of early experience, while Mowrer's theory lacks developmental details. Mowrer denies, on the other hand, that insight is itself curative. But unlike early action theories, he only considers action curative when it is initiated by the sufferer (not conditioned) and only when it is aimed toward social integrity rather than freedom from anxiety. In his concern with life styles and goals, he is more like Alfred Adler than any other therapy theorist, at least in their shared belief in "social interest" as a main life goal. But the premises and techniques of their therapies are so different that the similarity of goals is almost coincidental.

It is the peculiarly social thrust of Mowrer's thought, in fact, which makes his melding of insight and action so uneasy. That thrust has become more clear and unequivocal over twenty odd years, through changes in language from religious to secular, in format from individual to group treatment, in therapist concept from professionalism to peerage among participants, and in ambition from a utopian hope to cure all mental illness to the modest aim of treating problems of alienation and "*identity crisis*" (1980, p. 313). It says that therapy techniques only count toward cure when they help relate people's behavior to society.

But what is society? To Mowrer, it is two things: (1) A sizable group of real-life people who enduringly need each other, and (2) an idea, a symbolic thing, a hypothetical normative moral order. Together they make "community."

Antidote to Alienation

"It used to be," he writes, "that people who lived adjacent to one another constituted a neighborhood or community." Not now. Especially "in cities, . . . anonymity and personal isolation are instead the rule." Also, ". . . urbanization, geographic and socio-economic mobility, and assorted technological changes have badly disrupted the traditional institutions of home, church, school and neighborhood, with the result that great masses of people are no longer finding the sense of personal identity, emotional intimacy, and cosmic meaning which they once knew" (1972, p. 8).

Mowrer does not say explicitly that the identity crises he treats may be functions of the times, but that is implicit in these quotations, as it is in statistics which show that depression has replaced hysteria as today's neurosis of choice. It is easy to believe that the conditions of our era have spawned an epidemic of the alienation neuroses which Integrity Groups correct. A society so fluid and diverse and educated and generous as ours in its options on space and time and opportunity can hardly not be full of lonely people. They get disconnected from one another, at first casually, even pleasurably, by lack of shared needs and shared burdens—and later, unable to claim the rights of tenure that constancy and familiarity confer, by lack of lasting loves, joint griefs and fears, shared joys and, finally, the consolation of each other's company. Where it is not common to expect or use them, the skills of social integrity go unexercised and everyone grows alien to all.

One use of Integrity Groups which Mowrer envisioned is a role he thought they could share with other parts of what he called the "small groups movement," namely that of ". . . a *new primary social group* of institutions which will compensate for these basic human losses." ". . . the Small Group . . . emerging as a new primary social institution . . . may help stabilize the nuclear family by providing a kind of substitute for the Extended Family which has become almost nonexistent in our society for great masses of persons" (1972, pp. 8-9). Mowrer did not claim to know how such groups would ". . . be related to the more traditional primary groups . . . ," and some would say it is naive to think that groups such as his could really substitute for them. It would be even more naive, however, to believe that the deterioration of traditional social structures in modern society is not happening or something not to worry about. And it is plain that one important meaning of "society" to Mowrer is concrete, conventional, and central to the meaning of neurosis and cure.

Normative Moral Order

The other meaning of society, the symbolic one, is the "normative" or moralistic aspect of the social intercourse which underlies personal wholeness. Mowrer makes no apology for his therapy's being "moralistic" because he believes that people's ability to achieve stable personal states depends on their ability to formulate viable moral systems. "Guilt" is a better term for him than "anxiety" as the center of neurosis because, as Freud observed, guilt is "moral anxiety." One need hardly ask what are the moral implications of Mowrer's therapy, for the warp and woof of it is the tie between people's behavior and their moral sense about human relationships, first individually, then severally, and finally in the abstract. The first step is interpersonal. But then, all this implies (but never says), it is only as we reinvest the integrity we practice in personal relationships in people we cannot know and value so close at hand that we ripen a technically functioning society into a morally fulfilling community.

So Mowrer's concept of community goes far beyond the idea of people simply living together in amity. The final price of mental health after that is still commitment, not only to specific "significant others" nor even to any real society as it stands. It is commitment to an ideal group, to a potential society motivated toward its members by some hypothetical good, by "norm" as an optimum, not an average state. He calls his ideal the Judeo-Christian ethic; others might call it Humanistic or something else. The point is that the therapeutic demand for commitments is calling for something more than most therapy theories, let alone theories of adjustment, have bargained for. It not only exonerates heroic virtues—courage, altruism, self-sacrifice, in people's lives. It also intimates that their encouragement may be a proper business for psychotherapy.

Broad mental health theories all make assumptions about human nature and the structure of society, regardless what specific problems they address. The theorist is not responsible to recognize all these assumptions, which is well for Mowrer, who does not always do so. His theory rejects the instinctivism and the metapsychology of Freud. Its underlying premise is biosocial. It says that human beings are biologically built as social animals, evolutionary complications of the gregariousness whose first phyletic glimmer is the sexual reproduction of species. From there, it builds on the near certainty that humans have never lived outside of organized groups, to propose that they never can but at their peril, and so they never should. Moral sensibility in individuals is the general cybernetic biocode steering their social interest, and guilt is the fever signal that their energy is misdirected. Some teleology is unspoken here, some Messianic drive, but it leads to no certain salvation. The theory only warns that we will satisfy this drive in company with each other or not at all. Unsure what goodness is, it says that people must try to be good, striving for an ideal that need not be defined to be fulfilled.

Mowrer's is the most pretentious mental health theory since Freud's, with which it most conflicts. It is also the most integrative of all the therapies we have seen, and being so, it forces us to entertain some problems that therapists find hard to flee and must be loathe to face:

First, what is wrong with people who need psychotherapy, he says, is a disease of their relationships with each other and society. It is the business of therapy to "re-connect" them, which is what "religion" means.

Second, therapeutic change, called by any name, from "feeling better" to "salvation," means enhanced "integrity." "Integrity" means "wholeness," "oneness," being all-of-a-piece.

If what he says is true, half true, or ever true, then just what business are we psychotherapists in? What are its limits, its duties, its goals? If we cannot stay within the once obvious boundaries of our craft, selling understanding or activity, what ought we do? What should we want, demand, implore, advise, contract, or negotiate with our clientele? Shall we send them to nunneries, to war, to stand for parliament, to bathe more often, or to seek such fortunes as their fantasies invent? Who should we refuse to see? And just what is our relationship to the society of which we are part and to which we must "wholesomely" relate our clients and ourselves? What are the duties of our trade, its privileges, the sanctions it can claim from law and custom, the demands for livelihood?

Everyone with much experience at psychotherapy, regardless of their views on Mowrer, has worried over questions such as these. For patients' lives are largely of a piece, no matter how fragmentary their neuroses are. And therapists, no bigger fools than are the rest of us, know that.

Just such questions, accordingly, will concern us from here on.

V

THE SAVING GUILD

THE ARGUMENT

Psychotherapists make up an informal guild. After years of battle among the mental health professions to win clientele, and among psychoanalysts, behaviorists, and others for hegemony in the academic marketplace, all psychotherapies have been lately accused of incompetence to solve the problems they address. One reason for the attack is that psychotherapy overlaps confusingly both medicine and education, the two guilds with which it has closest historical and practical connections. Another reason is that psychotherapy superficially looks so much like other social intercourse, especially like intimate conversation, that its delicate technology is obscured in casual observation. It seems like something anyone could do, or like something not worth paying for.

The accusations are invalid. Psychotherapy is not cheap imitation or poor cousin with other healing or teaching crafts. Nor are its results trivial, as research now firmly shows. And its technology can only become more and more apparent as it gets probed, now that we know it is worth probing. Those things assured, the hard-core problems of this enterprise then appear. They are, in my opinion, two:

The first problem is that the scientific or technical function of psychotherapy is the manipulation or control of behavior. Questions of fact arise in this connection which are straightforward and can be answered by diligent scientific study: What kinds of control are possible in psychotherapy and how can they be implemented? But questions of propriety also arise and are not always so clear or so answerable: What kinds of control are proper for psychotherapists to exercise, and over whom? These are moral questions. They will not yield to facile inquiry.

Psychotherapists now constitute a de facto secular priesthood for an important minority of people in the world's most democratic and open societies. They become willy nilly arbiters of morality when they help clients to resolve future courses of action and to rationalize their resolve. This role has a quasi-sacerdotal or priestly quality because modern society lacks religious moral authority. People lend moral authority to psychotherapists because of their scientific inclinations and connections. This sanctifies, so to speak, the pronouncements of psychotherapists about how people ought to live. Theirs is a secular priesthood, however, because science is only a method of critical inquiry, not a repository of eternal truths or moral codes. It can make useful factual predictions but not abiding moral prescriptions.

Psychotherapists are not well suited to this priesthood either by training or by disposition. They must accept it even so, for there is no way fully to separate their technical skills and moral inclinations from their clients' need to act upon the world and live in it, with or without the saving grace of eternal and external authority. Since their only moral recourse is to personal faith and experience and to the deductions they make from the ever-changing sciences they study, therapists should face this role with fear and trembling and awe at the responsibility historical circumstance has thrust on them and at the damage they can do their clients and the world in meeting it. But they must not shirk it by passing moral responsibility to society; its legislation is capricious. Nor can they pass it decently to their guilds, trading collective conviction for individual courage. Least of all can they saddle clients with total responsibility, once having participated in the problem, until they have shared their opinion in its solution. For no moral authority bestrides the modern world, but only power, which is transient and immoral, and science, which is insubstantial and unredemptive. The moral life, in our time, is merely personal, and the moral posture which psychotherapists therefore offer is, finally, no more nor less than the messages and models of themselves.

13

Psychotherapy as Service Guild

The Sanctions of Science and Society

Most guilds, trade unions, and professional societies, medieval or modern, spend great organizational energy protecting their turf against competitors. This serves their needs for power, money, and prestige. Insofar as their claims to expertise are right, however, it may also protect the public against rogues, charlatans, and incompetents outside the guild.

If the guildcraft really does require much training and expertise, moreover, as in medicine, or the job to be done is complex and the expertise ill defined, as in education, then general confusion ensues when the guilds try to stake out their territories and the public tries to assess their claims. Pretentious, unscrupulous, bilious, or merely foolish champions of either side use the vagaries of professional jargon to lay claims and counterclaims. All crafts have jargon terms enough: In medicine, for instance, some are true but obscure (e.g., "resistance to infection"), some false but useful (e.g., "nervous breakdown"), and some are merely masks for other ends (as when the American Medical Association railed against general health insurance as a danger to "the doctor-patient relationship"). Education jargon is aired less for money than to buttress the claim to expertise, speaking of its "foundations," "methods," and "goals" as if a vast technology lay beneath its sonorous titles. All guilds do this.

Most psychotherapists are members of the broader professional societies of their diplomas—in medicine, usually psychiatry; in psychology, commonly clinical; in education, likely counseling or rehabilitation; and in social work, the clergy, and others. This has meant, until recently, that their occupational fate as psychotherapists has been that of the broad service guild to which they belonged.

A service guild is an organization of skilled persons who certify each other's ability to perform their craft and who decide what training is needed to learn it, who can qualify for the training, and who can be colleagues after getting it. Guilds are economic creatures; they limit the number of trainees to keep the number of competing practitioners small, often successfully. But if the craft is so vague or easy that outsiders may compete with it for work, the guild may seek society's sanction for raising trade barriers against them.[1]

The bargain struck is that society gives title or function of the craft only to members or minions of the guild. They can take jobs and collect fees for their services in that craft. In return, the guild guarantees the society that it will perform its service faithfully and will see to it that its members do so. The arrangement may be formalized in licensing and certification laws. In the United States, licensing restricts the *practice* of a craft by defining its activity. Certification, a weaker sanction, restricts only the *title* of craftsmen, thereby limiting how they advertise themselves.

Since psychotherapy has always been a subtopic of some parent professional enterprise, efforts to get it sanctioned in the U.S. have been indirect. Psychiatrists, already licensed to practice medicine, want psychotherapy included in State Medical Practices Acts. Psychologists want license as a profession to do therapy independently of psychiatrists. Social workers, marriage counselors, and other psychotherapists seek other sanctions for practice. The main fight has been between psychiatrists and psychologists; the former seek monopoly control, the latter a bigger slice of the same economic pie.

Both guilds appeal to the public interest, of course. But however truly they wish to protect the public from psychic snake oil salesmen, they also want to create competitive trade barriers, much as plumbers and bicycle makers might do. It is easy to see, however, what protecting plumbers and bicycle makers means. Everyone knows what they do that they want to prevent others from doing on the same terms. But what do psychotherapists do? It is not so obvious, not even when we compare them to doctors and teachers, though it is from medicine and education that psychotherapy chiefly has sprung.

PSYCHOTHERAPY, MEDICINE, AND EDUCATION

Some psychotherapists consider their craft a branch of medicine that cures people of sickness. Psychologist therapists of this sort may not like my language because their quarrel with psychiatrists makes them avoid medical usage even

---

[1] Some crafts, like airplane or ship pilots, can be wholly controlled by restricting training, for nobody will hire a pilot not certified by someone already proved in piloting. Mark Twain, in *Life on the Mississippi,* tells how a guild of river pilots gained control over the industry in this way, without any social sanctions. Many jobs can be done well, on the other hand, by almost anyone—the closed union shop is meant precisely to prevent such free marketing of work.

when they believe it. Even so, their (reasonable) idea is that while psychotherapy may treat illness, medical training is as irrelevant to its practice as it is to optometry. Optometry is a subprofession of physics; psychotherapy, of psychology. They are "medical" crafts, but need no physician to do them.

Educationally bent psychotherapists, on the other hand, see themselves as consultants or specialized teachers, think of the troubles they treat as "problems," not "illness," and see their customers as "clients," not "patients."

Each usage makes some sense; none stands up too well to close scrutiny. Most psychotherapy patients plainly are not sick in the sense of having disease or tissue damage. Even for psychosomatic conditions, psychological treatment is not like medical treatment. The dose of talking which the doctor gives for ulcers would not be raised or lowered as they healed.

Nor are therapists too much like physicians. Physicians define their craft by the ability to diagnose specific troubles of the body and to attack them mainly by chemical or physical means like medicine or surgery. Even little children have a pretty good idea of how to play doctor. How do you play psychotherapist? Also, since medical expertise claims to depend on technical skills and scientific knowledge, the need for long training and apprenticeship prior to guild membership is easily argued. The need for similar expertise in psychotherapy, if real, is protean; there are fewer things for which all can agree on what is wrong or when it is righted, and no way to submit them to the antiseptic judgments of x-ray or microscope.

Along with common history, there is much parallel and overlap among medical and psychological ailments and treatments. But that is not the point. Psychotherapists are no more physicians now than surgeons still are barbers. The disciplines have long gone separate ways. Most medicine leans toward high technology, while psychotherapy has broadened so far beyond its medical origins that it is no more a medical specialty, not in structure, not in function, hardly in name.

Psychotherapists are not exactly teachers either, though their work is more education than medicine, and its roots are as deep in one as in the other. Much teaching is the communication of knowledge, often of information the teacher has that the student lacks. Psychotherapy does not do that much, nor by the same means. And while teaching also includes skill training, which therapy does aplenty, therapeutic skills are unusual, undoing habits more than learning them. Also, the "students" of therapy are troubled and disordered to begin with, while those of education, mostly, are empty and hungry, but not in pain.

In terms of expertise, moreover, educators say they must know a subject to teach it and have a technology to teach it well. The expertise of psychotherapists has been more vague—lacking common contents, rules for using them, and tools for measuring their effects. If the job of teachers seems complex, that of therapists seems abstruse.

Now if these doctors are not quite doctors and teachers not quite teachers because they cannot quite explain what they do in the first place, their need for guild sanctions is doubtful, at the least! Victor Raimy (1950) put it wryly at a 1948 conference on the training of clinical psychologists: *Psychotherapy is an undefined technique applied to unspecified cases with unpredictable results. For this technique, rigorous training is required!* His quip has since become a banner for a still unsettled war over therapy.

RESEARCH AND INSURANCE: BATTLEFIELDS OF THE THERAPY WAR

Skepticism about psychotherapy was not widespread in 1948. Hostile critics then, chiefly of psychoanalysis, spoke without evidence and often in voices too muted or too strident to be attractive. In 1952, however, Hans Eysenck of London University's Maudsley Hospital launched an empirical attack. He said that psychotherapy worked no better than simply waiting out one's neurosis. This was the first shot in an intellectual civil war among therapists which still goes on. During it, clinical psychologists have gotten licensed in 37 of the United States, new therapies have proliferated by the dozens, or hundreds, and professional schools of psychotherapy have grown so fast that the State of California alone, by one mid-1970s estimate, produces doctoral psychologist therapists faster than the whole United States did a few decades ago.

By the mid-1970s, insurance companies and government took arms in an American psychotherapy war. Private insurance for psychotherapy had expanded as it grew popular. Now it became a candidate for coverage in a possible national health insurance law. Since it is expensive, and since its value had been questioned both from within and by outside observers, some Congressmen thought claims for its value should be proved. No national health insurance came to pass, but clamor has continued for proof of psychotherapy's value.

[We must digress here to note that "proven value" is a rare standard for judging professional practice. No wonder. The meaning of value is so varied for most practice that it defies definition. The two standards common in medicine are "routine and established practice" and "safety." For new drugs, the U.S. Food and Drug Administration also sets standards of "efficacy," that is, evidence that the drugs work, which is fairly easy to measure. No such standards exist for surgery, which costs far more (nationwide) than psychotherapy and is far more dangerous. The Office of Technology Assessment, indeed, reports that 80% of routine medical practices in America have no scientific backing whatsoever (Office of Technology Assessment, 1980; Parloff, 1985).]

The proof, in some views, must come from "outcome" studies which show that it works faster or for longer than other treatments (such as drugs) or than no treatment. In fact, there are now enough such studies to conclude that it is valuable and ought to be insurable. What is more, the ingenious method by which those studies have lately been analyzed, for strictly *scientific* purposes, helps clarify the *moral* dilemmas of all psychotherapy.

PSYCHOTHERAPY OUTCOME RESEARCH

Until 1952, most psychotherapy research studied process, not outcome—relationships, communication between therapists and clients, the emotional distance between them, the roles they played, the behaviors of therapists of different schools and of more- and less-experienced therapists. Few scholars asked whether or not therapy "worked." Presumably it did. A 1941 study by Robert P. Knight of psychoanalytic therapy showed generally favorable outcomes. For the rest, the testimony of healing from clients and therapists and the witness of many scholars and observers seemed to do. The big research task was to reveal the subtle and delicate technology which wrought vital changes in people from what seemed to be merely intimate conversation. The "mechanisms" of the therapeutic process had to be uncovered and its technology bared (the word "technology" would not have been used at the time)—but there was little doubt about its fundamental value.

There was doubt aplenty soon after. Eysenck's 1952 review of two empirical studies concluded that psychologically troubled people improved spontaneously, without treatment, at about the same rate as psychotherapy clients did with treatment. If generally true, this meant that the net benefit of treatment, across a broad sample of cases, was zero!

Eysenck's was the first quantified attack by an eminent scientist, which made it important. Oddly, however, no one ran for evidence that he was wrong (Astin, 1961). Years later, in fact, E. Rubinstein and M. B. Parloff noted that outcome study was hardly mentioned at a 1958 conference called "Research in Psychotherapy" (1959). Outcome studies were the stepchildren of psychotherapy, one reason they became the darlings of behavior therapy.

"Psychotherapy," back then, really meant Insight therapy. Eysenck was attacking only "traditional" psychotherapy, then as in his later writings on the effects of psychotherapy (1952). He was an early advocate of "Behavior Therapy," edited the first book with that name in the title (1960), and has remained a stalwart in its camp. He is misrepresented by those who imply that his criticism is meant for all psychological therapy.[1]

Battles over psychotherapy research were always part of what Mary Lee Smith, Gene V. Glass, and Thomas I. Miller call

---

[1] Ambiguous use of the term "psychotherapy" is still confusing. As late as 1971, when J. Rachman wrote "...we do not have satisfactory evidence to support the claim that psychotherapy is effective" (p. 229), he meant, like everyone else whose literature reviews held strong negative conclusions, only Insight Therapy.

". . . an internecine war. Although there are many combatants . . . ," they write, *". . . the principals in the war are behaviorists and nonbehaviorists. These groups have called each other names and traded high-sounding insults. But the issue was not over psychotherapy versus no psychotherapy, but over brand A psychotherapy versus brand B psychotherapy.*

. . . Different forms of therapy were viewed as adversaries, competitors, or contestants, and the arena of conflict was the controlled experiment. The referee judged the performance and results and declared one therapy the winner and the other the loser" (1980, pp. 2-3).

Controlled studies of psychotherapy are many and varied. The problem is: How can they be combined and compared?

It makes a great difference, for instance, if you study psychotherapy proper or, instead, study laboratory analogs to it, that is, if you study therapy clients who have come looking for help or, instead, solicit volunteers with problems *x, y,* or *z* for a therapy experiment, or seek volunteers without problems and then provoke problem behavior in a laboratory situation. And for which problems shall we study therapy's benefits? Phobias? Depressions? Alcoholism? Psychoses? Midlife crises? Delinquency? Hysteria? Obsessions? Among real patients, shall we study clinic patients or hospital patients, from college counseling centers or medical outpatient clinics, from free public facilities or costly private offices? Shall we study men or women, children or adults, well educated or not, middle class or lower class? And shall they be seen by seasoned therapists or fresh ones, by MDs, PhDs, MSWs, nurses, graduate students, housewives who have lately been taught psychotherapy, or healing cops? And so on. Worse, every target group we sample must be studied against a group of "control" subjects who are comparable to them in all important respects, but do not receive the treatment in question!

How to judge outcomes is no less a problem. Has therapy worked if clients afterwards merely say that they feel better? And on what dimensions of feeling? Reduced anxiety? Increased self-esteem? Global adjustment? Or shall we require behavior change as well? Or the latter without the former? And if so, what behavior? Social skills? Making friends? Standing up to relatives? Doing school work? Passing exams? Performing sexually? Selling toothpaste? And should we measure physiological change? And so on. Many standards of improvement test the many troubles people bring to treatment.

And how, having solved those problems, shall we draw general conclusions about treatment versus no-treatment and treatment A versus treatment B? If college students feel less anxiety and more self-esteem after treatment, but their grades are no better, has therapy "worked" or not? What if grades and esteem both rise, but for males and not females? Or suppose both sexes improve, but only in self-esteem for males and only in grades for females? And what if the whole puzzle shows up in mirror image when treatment A is compared to treatment B? Which is better therapy? What does "better" mean?

If we were to design from scratch one grand experiment to include only the major variables of a more or less definitive outcome study program, says Morris Parloff, "At best we are contemplating a multi-billion dollar program extending over an indefinite period" (1982).

Psychotherapy outcome research, in any case, has not been one experiment, but a collage of over one thousand studies, each studying a few variables, testing treatments against whatever standards interested each scholar. They have varied hugely in quality of design and execution and, even when these are good, of subject matter and intention. Who calls what psychotherapy, how samples are selected for study, what standards are used for treatment, or for outcome, or even for defining untreated or other comparison groups, differ from one work to another.

All the possible problems, moreover, the flaws, distortions, and ineptitudes that damage individual studies, apply also to reviews that summarize and interpret them—at times worsened by the added dissonance of carping, incivility, and flaming bias. Reviewers "have reached different, even contradictory conclusions . . . despite the fact that they often read and reviewed the same collection of studies." Of course. They had to depend on their own skill to absorb more information than the unaided mind can grasp and on their own ability to avoid prejudice in choosing studies and interpreting them. They had no objective way to quantify results and compare them across many studies. Just such a statistical device was introduced by Gene V. Glass in 1976 and applied to psychotherapy by Mary Lee Smith and him in 1977. Called "meta-analysis," it is the most important tool for summarizing large arrays of complex research results since the introduction of statistical analysis to psychotherapy.

META-ANALYSIS

"Meta-analysis," as Glass defines it, is ". . . the integration of research through statistical analyses of the analyses of individual studies." It is used in what Parloff calls the "monumental survey" of psychotherapy results by Smith, Glass, and Thomas Miller called *The Benefits of Psychotherapy* (1980). In it, they first collected all the English-language studies they could find which met their minimal scientific standard of comparing a treatment group to an untreated control group or to another treatment. Such special treatments as hypnosis, drugs, and bibliotherapy were excluded, but they compared 78 different treatments, including all the conventional ones, in over 475 studies of some 25,000 patients in treatment for an average of 16 sessions.

They then took the quantitative results of each study which showed "the magnitude of the effect of therapy" and made them all mathematically comparable by a statistical device called "effect size." The standardized results were then compared with respect to types of treatment, client traits, kinds of outcome, and so forth. The main finding, as Parloff put it, was that "the average person who received therapy was better off (on some outcome measure) at the end of treatment than were 85% of the patients who did not receive treatment . . . individuals at the 50th percentile of the untreated population could expect to rise to the 85th percentile of that population after undergoing treatment." This means, he says:

"The size of the effects of psychotherapy can now be judged to be not merely modest but demonstrably great. By the standards of medicine, education, and social programs, any treatment that elevates the typical patient from the 50th to the 85th percentile on a measure of well-being is highly significant not only statistically but probably clinically.

"The typical elementary school pupil, for example, learns an amount of reading or math in one year of schooling that raises him from the 50th to about the 85th percentile on a national group norm. If a year of schooling is "significant," can the demonstrated effects of psychotherapy be considered less significant? Consider, too, the fact that the demonstrated strength of the relationship between psychotherapy and treatment outcome appears to be twice as large as the demonstrated relationship between smoking and lung cancer . . .

"These findings, which are consistent with those reported in other reviews of a more limited body of evidence, now give persuasive rebuttal to the widely held view that psychotherapy is simply the beneficiary of spontaneous remission."

Criticisms of Smith, Glass, and Miller

Smith, Glass, and Miller's work is not a final assessment of psychotherapy. A few critics argue that meta-analysis is not a very good method (Eysenck, 1978; Wilson & Rachman, 1983). Even if it is, however, they only used it on less than half the empirical work extant. Also, the studies they used do not represent most of the "real world" population of patients and therapists or of treatment settings. Fifty-six percent of them, for instance, were done in schools and colleges, only 12 percent in hospitals, and only 15 percent in outpatient facilities. Clients averaged only 23 years of age. Only 22 percent of them had sought treatment; the rest were solicited by experimenters. Only 46 percent, moreover, had complaints typical of people seeking therapy—only 3 percent were depressed, for instance, and none was alcoholic. And these are two of the commonest mental health problems in America! The therapists, finally, averaged only a little more than three years' experience; most were psychiatric residents or clinical psychology students.

Even so, their findings cannot be dismissed, as some critics wish. Firm evidence for this was found by Gavin Andrews and Robin Harvey when they examined a subsample of the original data which included "only studies of persons who would normally seek psychotherapy . . . who had neuroses, depressive disorders, or emotional-somatic disorders and . . . who had sought treatment themselves or had been referred for treatment" (1981, p. 1204). There were 81 such studies. As expected, the patients were older (average 30 years), the therapists more experienced (52 percent psychiatrists, 28 percent psychologists), and the treatment settings more typical (two-thirds were health-care facilities) of "real" psychotherapy than was true in the other studies of the survey. They analyzed the subsample by the same means Smith, Glass, and Miller had used—and got almost exactly the same result! "The average . . . effect size . . . was 0.72. This indicates that for neurosis, the average subject after treatment had scores superior to 76% of control group subjects assessed at the same time" (p. 1205). This was not significantly less than the average Effect Size of .87 obtained in the larger study. Andrews and Harvey also found, however, unlike the larger study, that behavioral and dynamic therapies both were relatively more effective than "counseling," client-centered therapy, or placebo therapy, which were all equivalent; that long treatments (more than 20 hours) were more effective than short ones; and that benefits tend to last—they "are stable for many months but decline slowly thereafter at an estimated 0.2 effect size units per annum" (p. 1206).

While *The Benefits of Psychotherapy* is far from the last word on outcome research, it is evidently definitive enough for fair critics to expect further variations on this careful work to bolster its main claim—that psychotherapy of many kinds is effective in the relief of many problems (Lambert, 1979). The studies that have followed qualify and compromise and renegotiate the details of that statement, but their effect is to refine, not to refute it (Landman & Dawes, 1982; Rosenthal & Rubin, 1982; Rosenthal, 1983; Shapiro & Shapiro, 1983).[1]

With that the case, the political-economic-professional storm over psychotherapy will end with psychotherapy technically triumphant. Despite canards and cavils and in face of honest skepticism, it will have been proved worthy by the supreme court of rational appeal, that of scientific evidence.

But the evidence leaves puzzling questions. The facts throw doubt on the special claims of psychotherapy schools—one may be about as good as another, and any of them is better than not getting treatment would be. If so, then what do the evident differences between them really mean and where do their common therapeutics really lie? Some practical lessons may be here.

---

[1] See especially the *Journal of Consulting and Clinical Psychology,* 1983 (February), *51*:1, 3–75, "Special Section: Meta-Analysis and Psychotherapy."

TRAINING, PRACTICE, AND POLICY

Considering that all the tested psychotherapies have been around for long enough to know, the finding that they all work fairly well should be no surprise. If "A" worked well and "B" did not, it would suggest that advocates of treatment "B" were victims of a common placebo or delusion. This could also be so with "A" and "B" working equally, of course, but we would rather think that placebo treatments do not work well.

Maybe they do. Indeed, if "est" and "scientology" and "laying on of hands" are slipped into a good research design next to psychodynamic and behavior therapy, they may yet cause havoc in the guilds by proving their effectiveness. But until then, it seems reasonable to believe that the major therapies all work for good reasons: They are practiced in the same set of professional groups on a similar array of clients by therapists with similar distribution of backgrounds and training. From the data so far, the best guess about different effectiveness is that some therapies work better with one kind of client than another. Also, some methods may be better suited to some therapists than to others and, therefore, sharper tools in their hands. One way to find out would be to teach many techniques to therapists.

Multimodal Training

It seems obvious from the evidence of equal outcomes that all psychotherapists should study many methods: Insight therapy, Behavior therapy, Cognitive therapies, and more. At present, despite the existence of well-constructed manuals for teaching them, this is rarely done or even permitted (Beck et al., 1978; Klerman et al., 1984; Luborsky, 1984; Strupp & Binder, 1984). Universities, hospitals, and clinics, in psychiatry, psychology, and social work training, commonly teach one set of techniques and one brand of theory, discouraging interest in "competing" methods. There are many explanations. None of them is justified by evidence. The fact is that theory still leads practice by the nose in psychotherapy training. Most therapists who wish diverse training must "bootleg" it in courses, seminars, workshops, or work outside their home bases. Some must wait until they finish at home base for fear their heterodoxy will be discovered and they will be disciplined or dismissed. It is sad comment on the enlightenment of some leaders of this scientific profession. It makes of "guild" a dirty word.

Fair Practice

By the same evidence, it is questionable whether legal sanctions against therapeutic competition are justified. Though some therapists are certainly more effective than others, there is no evidence that specific training in psychiatry, clinical psychology, or other learned professions equips people with the technical skills that make them effective psychotherapists. We have no firm knowledge yet of what those skills may be. Certification and licensing laws may be promoting the therapeutic practice of incompetents and charlatans with good credentials as much as protecting the public from incompetents and charlatans with bad ones. Efforts to find out if professional psychotherapy harms some clients have been inconclusive (Hadley & Strupp, 1976; Strupp, Hadley, & Gomes-Schwartz, 1977). Treatment by supervised nonprofessionals has been quite successful (Marks, 1983). The dangers of treatment by the untrained are unknown. The United Kingdom, in any case, does not license physicians, still less psychotherapists (but it does license dentists!). Maybe other countries should follow suit.

The ingenious way in which the facts of therapy outcome have been found raises other questions than practical ones. Some are as vital to students of morals, culture, and society as to those of science, healing, or education. The implications of meta-analysis go far beyond its technology.

THE IMPLICATIONS OF META-ANALYSIS

The empirical genius of meta-analysis is the concept of *effect size*. It is "the great equalizer" among the many ways of judging therapeutic outcomes—changes in feelings, in behaviors, in physiology and, among the many measures used, tests, questionnaires, reports of others, and more. Effect size provides a common numeric rule for all contents. It is the equivalent, for therapy, of classing apples and artichokes together as food so their nutritional value can be compared. In Smith and Glass's words, "effect size was calculated on any outcome variable the researcher chose to measure . . . : self-esteem, anxiety, work/school achievement, physiological stress, etc." (1977, p. 753).

The method lets individual investigators decide what success in treatment means, using any self-consistent method they choose, and it then assesses the treatments by statistics that disregard the meaning of each criterion. This "therapeutic relativism" treats changes in laboratory snake phobias in college sophomores after desensitization therapy in the same way it treats changes in ulcerative colitis after psychoanalysis or agitated depression after cognitive behavior therapy.

Now, is it sensible to lump trivial experimental analogs with severe clinical problems and view the result as a general assay of how well treatment works? Smith and Glass respond thoughtfully:

> *Mixing different outcomes together is defensible. First, . . . all outcome measures are . . . related to "well-being" and so at a general level are comparable. Second, it is easy to imagine a Senator conducting hearings . . . or a college president deciding whether to continue funding the counseling*

center asking, "What kind of effect does therapy produce—on anything?"
Third, each primary researcher made value judgments . . . of positive thera-
peutic effects for the particular clients . . . studied. It is reasonable to
adopt these value judgments and aggregate them in the present study.
Fourth, since all effect sizes are identified by type of outcome, the magni-
tude of effect can be compared across type of outcome to determine
whether therapy has greater effect on anxiety, for example, than it does
on self-esteem (1977, p. 353).

Indeed, the technical question is not very tough at all, for the technique of
meta-analysis will work the same way, and the comparison of effect sizes
answers the same questions, for any scheme one concocts about gravity of problems, division of patients, or distribution of psychotherapists.

The hard problem of effect size concerns the semantic, then social, cultural,
philosophic, or moral question to which it gives rise. For its equalizing calculation assumes that whatever an investigator wishes to define as cure *is* cure, as
if one cure were the same as another. For research comparisons, this standard is
indispensable. For purposes of living, let alone of supplying treatment that
changes how people live, it is absurd. The inseparability of the scientifically
necessary and the morally absurd highlights the inescapable irony of the dual
functions of psychotherapy.

14

Scientific Priesthood and Secular Salvation

"How well does psychotherapy work?" What seems answerable at first by the ingenious manipulation of meta-analysis becomes a shrewd and disquieting inquiry when we couple the calculation to the questions, "What ought "work" to mean, and who decides its meaning?" In psychotherapy, blurred answers must often do, and often by common consent of patients and therapists.

Now this is a far cry from most of medicine because the press on doctors of obvious illness leaves them little time for dealing with much else or room for doubt over what to call treatment. But it is a far cry too from the origins of psychotherapy itself, where the symptoms of disorder fairly screamed at everyone, regardless of what they signified or how they could be fixed.

Psychotherapy has spilled over, by tacit mutual agreement of the participants, from medicine, psychology, and mental health to almost anything for which counsel is asked or can be offered, for which feelings of well-being can stand alone as standards of value, and for which no formal expertise, such as in accounting, law, or plumbing is visibly required.

This spillage is what demands the meta-analytic strategy of taking all outcome measures as acceptable standards for therapy's effects. "Acceptable" is meant here only technically, of course, not ethically. But for psychotherapy results, even technical criteria imply a measure of social acceptability because changes much beyond the pale of social convention are unlikely to be listed as technical triumphs in the first place. Sexual frigidity, for instance, an "emotional-somatic disorder" in Smith, Glass, and Miller's catalog, is not treated by psychotherapists in order to promote "incest improvement." Nor are job supervisor ratings, an outcome measure of "work/school achievement," meant to record the improved marksmanship of paid assassins.

The breadth of psychotherapy's scope has always lurked implicit in this craft. It began gestating on the day Freud and, separately, Pierre Janet, observed that neuroses were *functional disorders,* not physical ailments. For once they severed neurotic illness from the body, contending that it could arise without tissue damage and heal with no cell repair, they broke the boundaries which contained psychiatry, inviting hordes of foreign notions and professions onto the terrain of mental ills and treatments. So it is description, not deprecation, to say that psychotherapists are not quite doctors and not quite teachers. They never were quite either, but always had more complex functions, most plainly so in recent years. Outcome research studies show us that they largely succeed at what they try to do even without defining fully what those functions are. Understanding them should hone their skills still more.

Psychotherapists have, I think, two functions, one *scientific* and one *moralistic.* The scientific function is more or less explicit, the moralistic one is often just implied. Neither function is wholly independent. In practice, they can be corollary to each other, confounded, or competing.

The scientific function of psychotherapists is that of *manipulators of behavior.*

Their moralistic function is that of a *secular priesthood.*

Some psychotherapists will reject this terminology. Insight advocates especially may take offense at the idea that their scientific job is to manipulate. And therapists of every stripe may not like to hear that they have a moralistic role at all, still less that it is sacerdotal. But I think both claims are true and that these ideas encompass what psychotherapy is and does in all its variants.

THE MANIPULATION OF BEHAVIOR

In their early days, the Action therapies looked better than the Insight therapies as scientific schemes, but more limited in scope. They seemed less suited to address large issues in people's lives, while Insight therapies, on the other hand, seemed to lack good answers to them. Mowrer's was a compromise. It promoted insight, but into people's social needs, not their selfish or unconscious motives, and it fostered action, but to restore sociality, not to fix habits or impulses.

Without much discussing it, early Action therapies more or less readily accepted the manipulative or control function of psychotherapy more than other systems did. But neither questions of fact—how much control of what kind *can* therapists have, nor questions of propriety—how much control of what kind *should* they exercise, was aired much in the schools.

In general, Insight therapists tend to exert a minimum of control, and only over the client's thoughts and feelings in the consulting room. There are many rationales for this, but it is common to all Insight therapies to be interested in the control of insight only, not of action. Control is sometimes indirect, as in interpretation or reflection, but it is real.

All psychotherapists wish to control some aspects of behavior, and only innocence, caprice, or orthodoxy lets them deny it. The issue is sometimes clouded by ambiguous language. Terms like "permissiveness," "warmth," "spontaneity," and "transparency," popular in experiential therapies, may suggest an aura of laissez-faire encounter in which psychotherapists are totally at the disposal of their clients' whims. This is never the case, as every therapist and patient knows. Wise Insight therapists use these terms as guides to therapist conduct which creates the conditions for client growth, not because they adjure all control. Even when Carl Rogers says that "The politics of the client-centered approach is a conscious renunciation ... by the therapist of all control over ... the client," he is talking about control as domination or seduction. He is wholly in favor of "... the facilitation of self-ownership by the client and the strategies by which this can be achieved" (1977, p. 14). The very word "manipulation" has a double meaning. It means, on the one hand, any activity aimed to get someone to do what you want; but it also connotes misleading, seductive efforts to get compliance. Behavior therapists have used the term ambiguously, as in Krasner's otherwise incisive analysis:

"... apparent spontaneity on the therapist's part may very well be the most effective means of manipulating behavior. The therapist is an individual programmed by his training into a fairly effective behavior control machine. Most likely the machine is most effective when it least appears like a machine" (Krasner, 1961).

Some Insight therapists, like Rogers, rightly wanting therapy to be a conscientious and honest interaction that interferes as little as necessary in people's lives, refuse to use words like "control" and "manipulation" even in their innocent sense.

With ambiguity done, it should be plain that therapists' scientific task, from any vantage, starts with producing the situation needed to direct, manipulate, channel, and control behavior, whether to discover hidden motives, elicit feelings, change habits, or reconcile people with society (Bandura, 1969).

THE PROPRIETY OF CONTROL

The possibilities, limits, and economics of control are technical problems. They are questions of fact that can be addressed by scientific means. What can *not* be decided by recourse to science is the propriety of control, the ends it serves, the values it addresses. For this is finally a moral question against which the techniques of treatment must be justified. It poses a dilemma to psychotherapists—seeking partial control of behavior for limited purposes, they cannot honestly escape the question of how people *ought* to live. Nor can they easily confront it without waffling.

Some Insight therapists have tried to dodge by offering understanding as their only coin, disclaiming all authority for telling patients how to live. Were this wholly true, their counsel would be sterile. It would be mere information a computer could deliver just as well, and they would paralyze themselves and heal no wounds, just as Action therapists used to claim. If "understanding" can be understood as more than merely intellectual, as indeed it must, then they do more than just inform clients who then go "find themselves."

At the other end, Behaviorists may retreat to the too demonstrable, gaining a polemical and sometimes statistical advantage over Insight therapies, but at some cost of breadth and depth. To turn down existential troubles as unfit for therapy would much curtail their business. To analyze them (no pun meant) into functional events puts Actionists into the same box as Insight therapists. Quietly accepting the reality of patients' needs, they have broadened their work to include the whole range of psychotherapy problems, increased their clinical tools to handle them, and relaxed their theoretical purism to permit it. This may be one reason that some *current* research shows equal outcomes from Insight and Action therapies.

Much of psychotherapy must confront this moral problem. To cope with it, it must offer an action system which is justified in a network of meaning which can be tested, revised, and satisfied by its consequences in behavior. Such a treatment would integrate a pattern of behavior, indeed a life style, and a moral code which rationalizes it.

THE FUNCTION OF AN INTEGRATIVE PSYCHOTHERAPY

Such a therapy may not be possible, may not be desirable, and is not always needed. It does not take an integrative treatment to heal simple phobias and anxiety attacks. Pure Action therapy may do for these, and the control the therapist exerts in it need not be tempered much by reservations about its ultimate intrusion on the patient's life.

There may likewise be no need for such a therapy to salve much unhappiness, ennui, and the whole class of miseries which can be taken as pure cases of flawed meaning. Insight therapy ought to do for it. This is less certain because maybe the need for meaning cannot be met outside the context of some action system. Then, pure Insight treatment would be as inadequate to such events as pure Action would be irrelevant.

But much psychological pain is not pure symptomatic nor existential woes. Much falls between them, in lives full of faulty action and values too weak to make a clear pattern of behavior meaningful. So-called psychopaths or character disorders reflect the extremes of such conditions. But millions of secular moderns represent most of them. An integrative therapy might help them all.

Human beings are creatures of action and meaning both. Deliberate action always has some end, which is its meaning. And meanings have intentions, which are the basis for our acts and which make action the index of intent. Our acts signify some meanings, some evaluations, to us—and our meanings take their meaning from the action they create.

For purely symptomatic problems, people need a doctor. For problems of existence, at the other pole, they need a priest, or someone who can fill the role for which, in other times or places, they would seek a priest. In between, where most of us may fit, they need both, for people in that group suffer from moral problems of the plainest kind—they do not know how they ought to live. They need to be told, in some way, ends to help make their lives meaningful, and to learn, by some means, how to pursue such ends.

At that point, where therapists assume this capacity, they add a grand strategy to their manipulative tactics. At the juncture where a doctor is not competent and a priest is not credible, the psychotherapist becomes an arbiter of morality.

THE SECULAR PRIESTHOOD

Life would be easier for psychotherapists if they could contain their work entirely within the boundaries of "breakdown" as they did a century ago. Then they could see themselves as "fixers" and their standard of repair as that of helping people function better. Theirs would be a reconstruction job, and they could dodge the question of how people ought to live just as physicians do huge service to humanity without facing it. But people's behavior is so varied, complex, and differentiated that their problems do not fit neat categories. Those suited to psychotherapy are often less prone to merely symptomatic problems than to existential ones. Repairing damage takes a retrospective view, which allows clear description and concrete plans. But how to live is a prospective problem; it concerns a future that is always vague and hard to address wisely. Problems from the past, which were once the whole subject matter of psychotherapy, need rehabilitation, remedy, or cure. But those that speak to the future are entangled with what, in short, are problems of *salvation,* even when the future of concern may be immediate. The acts which solve or complicate those problems will win or lose that salvation, insofar as it is subject to personal control. And the arguments which explain and justify those acts, taken together, total to a moral code. Once psychotherapists address such behavior, they cannot help but arbitrate and mediate those codes. How? By what schemes? According to what values?

THE MORAL SCHEMES OF PSYCHOTHERAPIES

Each of the three systems of therapy we have discussed implies a different principle of valuation, intrinsic to its healing schemes: Insight therapy implies a moral code that is essentially the patient's own and that may, in the extreme, oppose that of the therapist. Action therapy implies a code that is the therapist's, which may oppose that of the patient. Mowrer's combination of insight and action lets neither party judge the proper end of treatment—the good life is only possible in society, so a normative system is the value standard.

Each position poses problems, vagaries, and dilemmas to puzzle conscientious therapists and lead them to borrow from each other's schemata.

The trouble with letting clients identify all their own goals, however good in most respects, is like the trouble with letting children learn everything by experience: they cannot judge the stability of some aspirations or the consequences of some experiments. No one can, but children are additionally disabled by childhood from judging. Troubled people, likewise, may be disabled by the trouble itself from making the kind of judgments that its absence would permit.

Therapists who are scrupulous about clients' free choice of goals support a morality of total personal liberty. Wholly devoted to serving patients' ends, their ministry is tested by patients who threaten to destroy themselves; it would demand that the therapist loyally attend this destruction. They must also overlook the fact that people's troubles are themselves motivators which sap some good goals and pervert others. Acting on the fact might mean challenging the patient's goals with the therapist's, maybe rationalizing that they are the patient's latent goals. (Some critics think libertarian therapists do this anyway.) The position demands also that therapists let patients violate the social order if they wish. Some critics contend that therapists are only entitled to seek social sanction for their practice in order to restore people to society.

The trouble with a normative system of morals which looks to society for its norms, on the other hand, is that a free society is always ambiguous, lacking clear norms for important things. In that case, does it make sense to say that one's actions must be rationalized in society's moral currency? Saying so makes the legitimacy of the behavior a function of patients' skill at rationalizing. Well, maybe it is. At least it gives them some integrity. Also, maybe it is more realistic to base a system of goals on the idea of a social code more than on an individual one. But doing so may mean promoting a culture of conformity which could stifle the growth of that society. Is stifling constrictiveness better than wild libertarianism?

Suppose the third alternative, that the therapist frankly decides what is good for the patient. This may seem an arrogant and ill-considered idea, but can it not be said that therapists do this anyway? Are not therapeutic relationships always structured by therapists, even when they seek to justify them in patients' personal needs, or in their social ones? Suppose they make virtue of necessity and ask themselves how, since their technical capacities imply a moral role anyway, they could exercise that role most wisely.

Then they would fill a role more like that of a priest than of any other profession. But unless they are already operating from a normative creedal stand, as Bergin's "theistic realism" suggests (1980), they would be secular priests, whose justifications are not a theodicy revealed from heaven, but in a code discovered or inspired in clinic, laboratory, and other earthly premises. The genesis of their consideration would be human nature, and their gospel the fulfillment of that nature, its decalogue the medium of behavior—all preached from the altar of science.

For secular psychotherapists must finally appeal to science to justify their work, just as clergy appeal to revelaton. Their scientific connection is what gives them technical credibility in the first place. But science cannot justify a moral order, as religion can. It does not speak to the point of morality, as religion does. Science is only a method of systematically cumulating information and testing its accuracy, not a code on how to live. It reveals only facts, not prescriptions for how to act on them. To arrive at moral conclusions from scientific facts requires a leap of inferential faith which, finally, has no facts to rest upon. Science has great potential for ever more sharply defining human nature, but not for spelling out the goals toward which that nature should be steered (Haan, 1982).

This problem has no firm solution. Psychotherapists cannot take their function wholly from the social order, as educators or lawyers perhaps can, nor from the physical norms or optima that medicine often can use. Still less can they parallel the certainty of clergy that their keys to salvation will unlock its vaults. If there is a natural law of behavior on whose foundation moral codes can rest, as scholastic theologians claim, it renders no easy judgment psychotherapists can use. Yet without such backing, they must confront people whose troubles need moral solutions that will help them live decently and well. How can our science make us wise?

A NEW SCHOLASTICISM

In this age of competing mores and diminished belief, psychotherapists are assigned by circumstance to posts of moral counselor like that of religious authorities, but without the backing of a scientific philosophy. They lack a doctrine to parallel or compete with or substitute for the revealed word of religious doctrine. If they want one, they must build their own. How can this be done? Or should it be? Maybe there is some instruction from religious thought.

The moral codes which come from most religions assume that there is a cosmic order in which we fit teleologically, a divine purpose for existence which includes the individual lives and purposes of human beings. Human nature, meaning the common attributes of humans from which individual traits derive, is part of that lawful scheme. The moral order of religion corresponds to natural law so that, by acting according to its prescription, we fulfill the destiny we were created to serve.

Religious thinkers, believing this, use knowledge of the moral order as a means of discovering human nature. They assume, sensibly enough, that God would not demand of people what they could not supply. Since the revelation at hand says with certainty how people ought to act, it gives us some certainty about what they are. Knowing what ought to be, we may deduce what is; the potential of one depends on the reality of the other. Not everything about human nature can be deduced, but that is not necessary. As long as we know that it is within human capacity to follow the moral law, we can use the knowledge to promote the growth of that capacity. Thus religious thought, certain what are right morals, borrows science from the moral order, for human nature, like all questions of fact, is a scientific problem.

The problem of secular moralists like psychotherapists is the obverse. Perhaps it calls for an obverse approach. Just as the theologian uses moral certainty for axioms from which to deduce scientific views, may secular psychotherapists use the certainties of science to study hints or clues to plausible morality? Can they not look to empirical inquiry about human nature and use that information to help calculate how people ought to live? They could not do so confidently, to be sure, unless idolatrous arrogance made them think they understood the meaning of life in an ultimate and universal way. But without such hubris, perhaps they can probe the parameters of human nature well enough to lend a thoughtful voice to moral dialogue in areas where it is pertinent to people's lives—at work, at home, at school, at play, in love, law, education, medicine, and, not least, in psychotherapy. People should not be told to live in ways that trespass on their natural limits, for doing so pollutes their lives—it mocks ambition, dishonors aspiration, blinds hope, makes pleasure meaningless, and sows confusion and despair. But without some credible concepts for envisioning human nature, trying to guide them is like pushing on a dangling string.

Learning what people are like, in short, tells what we may help them be like. For that, the moral posture of therapists must depend on their willingness to ponder the questions and study the findings of the life and human sciences. And since those change greatly as knowledge grows, the morals psychotherapists draw from them may change as well with time.

CHANGED SCIENTIFIC VIEWS OF HUMAN NATURE

Science makes assumptions and axioms as firm and fundamental as religious doctrines do. Like them too, it needs interpreters to learn practical lessons from. In revealed religions, as in constitutional law, moral rules are commonly referred to history. In science, the basic assumption about facts is that they exist in some quantity (which is theoretically measurable) and that they cannot contradict. It is a long distance from those assumptions to scientific theory and an even longer one, in the life and social sciences, to conclusions about human morality.

This has not stopped theorists from theorizing or moralists from moralizing, but it has made of such speculation an art form whose products change with scientific fashion, not a logically robust offspring of fact or theory. Freudian theory, for instance, once argued that the final goal of living creatures is entropy or quiescence. From this came the idea that we have a "death instinct" and (later) an "aggression instinct." Another assumption, that sexuality is a prepotent force in children, gave rise to the theory of the Oedipal complex. A third was the notion that repression, mainly of Id impulses, is the basis of neuroses. This led to the idea of the compelling power of unconscious mental processes.

These ideas were parts of a biological orientation that was relatively inattentive to the relationship of individuals and society. This gave psychoanalytic treatment a distinct moral cast in some eyes. If neuroses came from thwarted sexual and aggressive needs central to human nature, then would not sexual and aggressive libertarianism be their cure? If human acts and motives are compelled by things we know not of, then can we be responsible for them? From this scientific position, a moralistic one comes easily that says: Human nature aims our lives toward selfishness and irresponsibility, meeting our needs and choosing our acts only for the impulse satisfactions they afford.

Whether psychoanalysts actually preached this code or not (some did, some did not), the personality theory that informed it was public property, and the moral was self-evident, if not inevitable, from the theory. It was founded in science even though the propositions supporting it are undemonstrated.

The early Action therapies made fewer leaps of faith only because their scientific pretensions were humbler. They aimed for less than a whole theory of human nature and were therefore less prone to getting hoisted on broad moral petards. Even without such theories, however, saying that the therapist, not the client, is responsible for the therapy's goals, they (naively or bravely) made themselves practical judges of morality.

Most scientists have been reluctant to paint broad pictures of human nature, not from fear of their moral connotations, but from awe at the size of the task and the certainty that, whatever their answers, progress in science would later show the error of their speculations. Some have speculated, even so, about aspects of human nature with important implications for the morals of psychotherapy.

The ideas of the late Gardner Murphy, for instance, offer an interesting scientific rationale for the therapy of O. H. Mowrer. Murphy argued that all simian species inherit strong social needs, and that "simian sociality" is therefore basic in human nature and so, presumably, important to mental health (1958). If so, it stands to reason that psychotherapy should aim to restore the relation of individual to society and the balance between what C. Wright Mills called "individual troubles" and "social issues."

Murphy also argued that "aspiration" is another basic trait of human nature. Research on human development and experimental studies of the so-called "curiosity drive" convinced him that human nature impels people to seek novelty. Science and art, in his view, are inevitable products of human biology. If so, promoting such creativity, as in Jungian analysis, might be a moral goal of psychotherapy, just as restoring "social interest" (Alfred Adler's term) would be.

The problem of "free will" and "determinism" is another big issue in the morals of psychotherapy because it speaks to people's responsibility for their acts. Philosophers and theologians have pondered it forever. The great physician physiologist Charles Sherrington (1940) and experimental psychologist Edwin G. Boring (1957) addressed it as scientists in this century. They said that the subjective experience of free will is intrinsic to humans. ". . . if he have it not," said Sherrington, "he is a biological failure and will die out."

Scientific study of this problem concerns the senses of control or self-efficacy, of hope and, contrarily, of helplessness. People vitally need to feel control of their lives. Personality theories have said so for decades, and much scientific work is exploring this area. It shows that the need to feel control over events is so great that people will delude themselves that chance situations can be controlled (Langer, 1983; Lefcourt, 1973). The sense of being able to act effectively, on the other hand, mobilizes people to do so and feel free (Bandura, 1977b, 1978). When they feel victimized and helpless, however, human beings, like other animals, suffer physically, emotionally, intellectually, and socially (Richter, 1957; Seligman, 1975).

Such notions are not formal parts of any therapy scheme, just as entropy was never a formal part of psychoanalysis. But stated as scientific, not moralistic propositions, they are potentially useful guides for the moral conduct of secular people, because most of the same moral problems beleaguer everyone with moral sensibilities. "Should I change wives, consorts, careers, friends, sex habits, gender, schools? Should I seek fulfillment in pleasure, in duty, in family, in religion, in physical fitness, in money, in power, in polymorphous perversion? Shall I pay taxes, ransom, bribery, lip service, the piper?"—these are moral, not medical questions, not related to the efficacy of psychotherapy, not covered by health insurance and, to most people who put them to therapists in the first place, not answerable by appeals to holy script, common custom, or civil law. But they are just as legitimate as so-called clinical questions, and people who can ask one, can ask another—cure my phobia, fix my premature ejaculation, calm my anxiety, and tell me whether adultery is "really" a sin?

Science cannot, of course, answer these questions any better for secular people than religion can. But science, in this age of disillusion, dread, and boredom, has a kind of moral authority—it inspires awe because it sponsors the great power of technology; and it earns respect because its claims to truth are so impersonal. So, since everyone with a sense of right and wrong seeks credible answers to moral questions in their own life, they will borrow comfort and courage from the best moral source intelligence and experience can find. Science lacks wisdom, but it has authority.

The more scientific theory, fact, and speculation speak to moral problems, therefore, the more they may be seen as guides to moral conduct. Donald T. Campbell (1975) speaks to the scientific foundation of morals, and to its connection to psychotherapy, in an essay called: "On the conflicts between biological and social evolution and between psychology and moral tradition." He makes a strong case for the scientific validity of the traditional morals of self restraint and social interest which classical (i.e., not antinomian or libertarian) religious and philosophic traditions have preached throughout civilization. This opposes the moral thrust of much of modern psychotherapy.

THE BIOSOCIAL BASIS OF MORALITY

Campbell's essay is adapted from his 1975 presidential address to the American Psychological Association. A renowned scientist, he warns that his essay ". . . is not hardheaded science but an exercise in quasi-scientific speculation. Here are no facts to depend on, but at best provocations about new areas of scientific concern to which psychology should attend."

Those areas, he says, are the evolutionary basis of human morality. The current state of knowledge in evolutionary genetics supports:

> . . . a thesis about basic biological human nature that is in agreement with traditional religious teachings. The religions of all ancient urban civilizations (as independently developed in China, India, Mesopotamia, Egypt, Mexico, and Peru) taught that many aspects of human nature need to be curbed if optimal social coordination is to be achieved, for example, selfishness, pride, greed, dishonesty, covetousness, cowardice, lust, wrath (pp. 1103-1104).

The evidence of the human sciences, of genetics, and of sociobiology, says Campbell, testifies that social and biological evolution are independent events in human history. The same principles (selection and adaptation) govern both evolutions, but the ". . . cumulation of skills, technologies, recipes, beliefs, customs, organizational structures, and the like" is "retained through purely social modes of transmission, rather than in the genes" (p. 1104). There are some biological foundations for morality in genetic tendencies to altruism and cooperation in many species, but Campbell concludes that social and biological evolution are largely competing processes: *"Human urban social complexity,"* he says, *"has been made possible by social evolution rather than biological evolution. This social evolution has had to counter individual selfish tendencies which biological evolution has continued to select as a result of the genetic competition among the cooperators"* (p. 1115; his italics).

The selfish biological tendencies social evolution had to counter include what are major sins everywhere: Murder, theft, violence, incest, greed, pride, cowardice, and such. But they also include smaller vices: stinginess, gluttony, envy, promiscuity, gossip, backbiting, and scolding. The list of positive precepts which have evolved is just as long, starting with honoring one's parents.

Campbell believes that the permissive moral posture which dominates the mental health professions, promoting self-indulgence, is scientifically unjustified and, considering the facts of human nature, may be damaging to our welfare:

> ... *present-day psychology and psychiatry in all their major forms are more hostile to the inhibitory messages of traditional religious moralizing than is scientifically justified. (p. 1103)*

> *The epistemic arrogance of behavioral and social scientists is perhaps as much an obstacle to understanding these matters as is the epistemic arrogance which traditional religionists exhibit in their claims of revelation and absolute certainty. (p. 1120)*

> *It is certainly my impression, after 40 years of reading psychology, that psychologists almost invariably side with self-gratification over traditional restraint. . . .*

> *If, as I assert, there is in psychology today a general background assumption that the human impulses provided by biological evolution are right and optimal, both individually and socially, and that repressive or inhibitory moral traditions are wrong, then in my judgment this assumption may now be regarded as scientifically wrong from the enlarged scientific perspective that comes from the joint consideration of population genetics and social system evolution. (p. 1120)*

Campbell applies his argument to psychotherapy:

> *I am indeed asserting a social functionality and psychological validity to concepts such as temptation and original sin due to human carnal, animal nature. This orientation makes me sympathetic to psychotherapists such as Mowrer . . . and Menninger . . . who have come to regard much human sin with an almost traditional disapproval, and who are recommending that guilt feelings often should be cured by confession, expiation, restitution, and cessation of guilt-producing behavior, rather than by always removing the demands of conscience, interpreting away feelings of guilt as neurotic symptoms. I can only hope that by raising this conclusion in the context of modern scientific concerns about the problems of complex social co-ordination and the population genetics of altruistic traits, I can make the*

*point more convincing to psychologists and psychiatrists than Mowrer and
Menninger have been able to do. (p. 1116)*

THE SECULAR MORAL ORDER

If Campbell is right, then a psychotherapeutic morality much favoring hedonism will harm its clients, and therapists must learn to teach a healing syntax of
control, responsibility, and self restraint, as well as the releases they have long
known how to trigger. Its common denominator, perhaps, is what one might
fancy as the civilized, socialized behavior of educated, well-functioning people
everywhere, an ecumenical, secular expression of traditional religious and moral
codes.

There is remarkable agreement among saints, scholars, and historians on the
nature of virtue. The distillation of the moral codes that have most captured the
human heart throughout history—in Confucius, Buddha, Lao-Tze, Classical
philosophy, the Biblical prophets and Talmudic Rabbis; in the Gospels and
Koran, in Church Fathers and Scholastics; in the visions of Dante, the *Ethics* of
Spinoza, the fantasies of utopian novelists and the meditations of philosophic
essayists; in modern thought as disparate as Walter Lippman's *A Preface to
Morals* and B. F. Skinner's *Walden Two*—the messages are much the same. Virtue
is a compound of selfishness and social interest. It is born of some learned
knowledge of one's inner self and of the outer world. It is expressed in a learned
capacity for self-restraint and measured self-expression. It is reinforced by the
love of others and the sense of self which knows it merits that. It is the standard
which, beyond survival and material success, makes life precious. Campbell has
brought no new contents to this almost universal thesis, but a new partner to
the consensus—modern science. He has offered an intellectual foundation for
morality which suits scientific fancy better than the older wisdom can.

For those who need it, psychotherapists might be able to argue this ethic
from their secular scientific position better than could clergymen from their
traditional one. But have they the right to arbitrate morality, any morality?

In important ways, as I have argued from the first, they have little choice as
they are faced with moral problems. Even the differences between Insight and
Action therapies, however great, do not imply different moral postures or possibilities for taking one, only different sources of suggested answers. Whether the
client is the source or the therapist, and whether the answers lean toward libertarian or toward classical morality, the therapist is party to them.

In being so, it can be said, therapists fill a moral vacuum in modern life, acting as a third force in an area once dominated by philosophy and religion. Who
else should? Philosophy, after all, commonly demands more intellectual interest,
if not ability, than most people are wont to give it. And religion, in some institutional forms, is so disspirited in goals or primitive or threadbare in ideals as
to make poor claim on the loyalties of many good minds. Science is our sacred

cow today. Psychotherapists, with their apparent roots in it, may be right to preach what moral codes they do, not only on their claims of truth, but also because so much of modern clergy abdicates its claim to moral competence in favor of psychology and so many modern congregants forsake their clergy.

Were this a religious era, many of the problems raised here would rise less, and psychotherapists would be faced less with moral problems than with technical ones. For they would know, or their patients would, or their patients' ministers would, how people ought to live, and their main problem then would be to ease the pain preventing them from living so. But the secular character of our time fosters moral doubts. It divorces Christians from simple faith, hope, and charity, and Jews from the functional simplicity of their commandments, in both traditions knowing what the meanings of their lives are, or knowing where to find out or that they do not need to know.

People's ultimate reference for morals once was God. For many, this is no longer true, for it does not easily translate to concrete propositions for the righteous conduct of one's business, or career, or love affairs. The absence of compelling religious belief does not leave people indifferent to salvation, but only more aware of lacking clear ideas of what it is and how to get it. These are not offered by society. They perhaps cannot be by a free society, which may serve us best by its aloofness from such intimate concerns. Psychotherapists, offering only a secular morality, leading to a secular salvation, which puts meaning and pain in delicate balance, with no promise of final resolution or lasting reward, may seem in so doing to have recast God as Science. This should not be their intent but must not be their concern. The forms of religion are not their problem, and the moral contents they must come to from their own grounds.

In much of their work, psychotherapists are finally like priests and rabbis, wonder workers and gurus and their like. But those counselors have words rooted in revealed truths and confident prophecies of how to live the good life and the rewards it brings. Therapists do not. They must speak less certainly on how to live and have less to say.

Even so, their words and work have value, and they do it well. Knowing their moral agency should help them do it better, as understanding their technology should also do. As their ability grows, some moral quandaries of their enterprise will be more visible. But as their knowledge of human nature also grows, they may feel more competent with the responsibility of handling moral discourse which they can neither master fully nor dismiss. Their moral title to guild status then will be free and clear, and their counsel, to individuals and society, will be dear.

References

Adler, N. *The underground stream: New life styles and the antinomian personality.* New York: Harper & Row, 1972.

Alexander, F. *The scope of psychoanalysis: 1921-1961.* New York: Basic Books, 1962.

Alexander, I. E. The Freud-Jung relationship—the other side of Oedipus and countertransference: Some implications for psychoanalytic theory and psychotherapy. *American Psychologist,* 1982, *37,* 1009–1018.

American Psychiatric Association. *Diagnostic and statistical manual of mental disorders,* 3rd Ed. Washington, D.C.: American Psychiatric Association, 1980.

Andrews, G., & Harvey, R. Does psychotherapy benefit neurotic patients? A reanalysis of the Smith, Glass, and Miller data. *Archives of General Psychiatry,* 1981, *38,* 1203–1208.

Appelbaum, S. A. Challenges to traditional psychotherapy from the "new therapies." *American Psychologist,* 1982, *37,* 1002–1008.

Astin, A. W. The functional autonomy of psychotherapy. *American Psychologist,* 1961, *16,* 75–78.

Azrin, N. H., & Foxx, R. M. *Toilet training in less than a day.* New York: Simon & Schuster, 1974.

Bachrach, A. J., Erwin, W. J., & Mohr, J. P. The control of eating behavior in an anorexic by operant conditioning techniques. In Ullman, L. P., & Krasner, L. (Eds.), *Case studies in behavior modification.* New York: Holt, Rinehart & Winston, 1965.

Back, K. W. *Beyond words: The story of sensitivity training and the encounter movement.* New York: Russell Sage Foundation, 1972.

Baer, D. M. Applied behavior analysis. In Wilson, G. T., & Franks, C. M. *Contemporary behavior therapy.* New York: Guilford, 1982.

Balakian, A. Asocial act of mercy. A review of *The executioner,* by Pierre Boulle. *Saturday Review,* December 23, 1961, 24.

Bandura, A. Punishment revisited. *Journal of Consulting Psychology,* 1962, *26,* 298–301.

Bandura, A. *Principles of behavior modification.* New York: Holt, Rinehart & Winston, 1969.

Bandura, A. *Social learning theory.* Englewood Cliffs, N.J.: Prentice-Hall, 1977a.

Bandura, A. Self-efficacy: Toward a unifying theory of behavioral change. *Psychological Review,* 1977b, *84,* 191–215.

Bandura, A. The self system in reciprocal determinism. *American Psychologist,* 1978, *33,* 344–358.

Bandura, A. Model of causality in social learning theory. In Sukemune, E. (Ed.), *Advances in social learning theory.* Tokyo: Kaneko-shoho, 1983.

Bandura, A., & Walters, R. H. *Social learning and personality development.* New York: Holt, Rinehart & Winston, 1963.

Barlow, D. H., & Wolfe, B. E. Behavioral approaches to anxiety disorders: A report on the NIMH–SUNY, Albany Research Conference. *Journal of Consulting and Clinical Psychology,* 1981, *49,* 448–454.

Beck, A. T. *Cognitive therapy and the emotional disorders.* New York: International Universities Press, 1976.

Beck, A. T., & Mahoney, M. J. Schools of "thought." *American Psychologist,* 1979, *34,* 93–98.

Beck, A. T., Rush, A. J., Shaw, B. F., & Emery, G. *Cognitive therapy of depression: A treatment manual.* Philadelphia: Beck, 1978.

Bellak, L. Psychoanalysis as therapy: The need for new conceptualizations. In Klebanow, S. (Ed.), *Changing concepts in psychoanalysis.* New York: Gardner, 1981.

Bergin, A. E. Psychotherapy and religious values. *Journal of Consulting and Clinical Psychology,* 1980, *48,* 95–105.

Bieber, I. Psychoanalysis, 1938–78: A personal history. In Klebanow, S. (Ed.), *Changing concepts in psychoanalysis.* New York: Gardner, 1981.

Beverly Hills High School. *1983 Training manual for counseling skills.* Adapted by the Counselor Training: Short-term Client Systems Task Force, Jacobs, B., Buschman, R., Schaeffer, D., & Dendy, R. F., from Hinds, W., James, M., Gieszer, M., & Jacobs, B., *A survival manual for the drug center volunteer.* East Lansing, Michigan: National Drug Abuse Center, 1973.

Boring, E. G. When is human behavior predetermined? *Scientific Monthly,* April 1957, 189–196.

Bromberg, W. *The mind of man: A history of psychotherapy and psychoanalysis* (2nd ed.). (Originally published 1936). New York: Harper & Row, 1959.

Campbell, D. T. On the conflicts between biological and social evolution and between psychology and moral tradition. *American Psychologist,* 1975, *30,* 1103–1126.

Cohen, S. I., & Ross, R. N. *Handbook of clinical psychobiology and pathology.* (Volume 2). Washington, D.C.: Hemisphere, 1983.

Davison, G. C. Politics, ethics, and therapy for homosexuality. *American Behavioral Scientist,* 1982, *25,* 423–434.

Dollard, J., & Miller, N. E. *Personality and psychotherapy: An analysis in terms of learning, thinking and culture.* New York: McGraw-Hill, 1950.

Ellis, A. Rational-emotive therapy. In Herink, R., *The psychotherapy handbook.* New York: New American Library, 1980.

Ellis, A. On Joseph Wolpe's espousal of cognitive-behavior therapy. *American Psychologist,* 1979, *34,* 98–99.

Emmelkamp, P. M. G. The behavioral study of clinical phobias. In Hersen, M., Eisler, R. M., & Miller, P. M. (eds.), *Progress in behavior modification.* Vol. 8. New York: Academic Press, 1979.

Engelhardt, T. H., Jr. Psychotherapy as meta-ethics. *Psychiatry,* 1973, *36,* 440–445.

Evans, R. I. *Carl Rogers: The man and his ideas.* New York: Dutton, 1975.

Eysenck, H. J. The effects of psychotherapy: An evaluation. *Journal of Consulting Psychology,* 1952, *16,* 319–324.

Eysenck, H. J. (Ed.). *Behavior Therapy and the Neuroses.* New York: Pergamon Press, 1960.

Eysenck, H. J. An exercise in mega-silliness. *American Psychologist,* 1978, *33,* 517.

Fiedler, F. E. A comparison of therapeutic relationships in psychoanalytic, nondirective and Adlerian therapy. *Journal of Consulting Psychology,* 1950, *14,* 436–445.

Foa, E., & Emmelkamp, P. M. G. *Failures in behavior therapy.* New York: Guilford Press, 1983.

Frank, J. D. *Persuasion and healing: A comparative study of psychotherapy* (Rev. Ed.). Baltimore, Md.: Johns Hopkins, 1974.

Frank, J. D. The present status of outcome studies. *Journal of Consulting and Clinical Psychology,* 1979, *47,* 310.

Frank, J. D. Therapeutic components shared by all psychotherapies. In Harvey, J. H., & Parks, M. M. (Eds.), *Psychotherapy research and behavior change.* Washington, D.C.: American Psychological Association, 1982.

Franks, C. M. On conceptual and technical integrity in psychoanalytic and behavior therapy, two fundamentally incompatible systems. In Arkowitz, H., & Messer, S. (Eds.), *Psychoanalytic and behavior therapy.* New York: Plenum, 1984.

Frankl, V. E. *Man's search for meaning: An introduction to logotherapy* [Original title: *From death camp to existentialism.*] New York: Pocket Books, 1963.

Friedman, P. H. Integrative psychotherapy. In Herink, R., *The psychotherapy handbook.* New York: New American Library, 1980.

Fromm, E. *Escape from freedom.* New York: Holt, Rinehart & Winston, 1941.

Fromm, E. *Man for himself: An inquiry into the psychology of ethics.* New York: Holt, 1947.

Fromm, E. *The sane society.* New York: Holt, 1955.

Galbraith, J. K. *The affluent society.* Boston: Houghton-Mifflin, 1958.

Galbraith, J. K. *The new industrial state.* Boston: Houghton-Mifflin, 1967.

Galbraith, J. K. *The age of uncertainty.* Boston: Houghton-Mifflin, 1978.

Garfield, S. L. Special section: Meta-analysis and psychotherapy. *Journal of Consulting and Clinical Psychology,* 1983 (February), *51*(1), 3–75.

Garfield, S. L., & Kurtz, R. Clinical psychologists in the 1970's. *American Psychologist,* 1976, *31,* 1–9.

Gitelson, M. Communication from the president about the neoanalytic movement. *Journal of the American Psychoanalytical Association,* 1962 (January), 373–375.

Glass, G. V. Primary, secondary, and meta-analysis research. *Educational Researcher,* 1976, *5,* 3–8.

Goffman, E. *Asylums.* New York: Anchor Doubleday, 1961.

Goldfried, M. R. (Ed.). *Converging themes in psychotherapy: Trends in psychodynamic, humanistic, and behavioral practice.* New York: Springer, 1982.

Goldfried, M. R., & Davison, G. C. *Clinical behavior therapy.* New York: Holt, Rinehart & Winston, 1976.

Goldfried, M. R., & Wachtel, P. L. (Eds.). *Society for the exploration of psychotherapy integration newsletter.* 1983, *1*(1), 16 pp.

Grings, W. W. Verbal-perceptual factors in the conditioning of autonomic responses. In W. F. Prokasy (Ed.), *Classical conditioning: A symposium.* New York: Appleton-Century-Crofts, 1965.

Haan, N. Can research on morality be "scientific"? *American Psychologist,* 1982, *37,* 1096–1104.

Hadley, S. W., & Strupp, H. H. Contemporary views of negative effects in psychotherapy. *Archives of General Psychiatry,* 1976, *33,* 1291–1302.

Halleck, S. L. *The politics of therapy.* New York: Science House, 1971.

Hare-Mustin, R. T., Maracek, J., Kaplan, A. G., & Liss-Levinson, N. Rights of clients, responsibilities of therapists. *American Psychologist,* 1979, *34,* 3–16.

Harper, R. A. *Psychoanalysis and psychotherapy: 36 systems.* Englewood Cliffs, N.J.: Prentice-Hall, 1959.

Harris, B. Whatever happened to Little Albert? *American Psychologist,* 1979, *34*(2), 151–160.

Hendin, H. *The age of sensation: A psychoanalytic exploration.* New York: Norton, 1975.

Herink, R. *The psychotherapy handbook: The A to Z guide to more than 250 different therapies in use today.* New York: New American Library, 1980.

Jahoda, M. *Current concepts of positive mental health.* New York: Basic Books, 1958.

Josephs, G. S., & Khalsa, G. S. Burn-out prevention. In Herink, R., *The psychotherapy handbook.* New York: New American Library, 1980.

Kazdin, A. E. *History of behavior modification: Experimental foundations of contemporary research.* Baltimore: University Park, 1978a.

Kazdin, A. E. The application of operant techniques in treatment, rehabilitation and education. In Garfield, S. L., & Bergin, A. E. (Eds.), *Handbook of psychotherapy and behavior change: An empirical analysis* (2nd Ed.). New York: Wiley, 1978b.

Klerman, G. L., Weissman, M. M., Rounseville, B., & Chevron, E. *Interpersonal therapy of depression.* New York: Basic Books, 1984.

Knight, R. P. Evaluation of the results of psychoanalytic therapy. *American Journal of Psychiatry,* 1941, *98,* 434–446.

Koch, S. The image of man implicit in encounter group theory. *Journal of Humanistic Psychology,* 1971, *11,* 109–128.

Korchin, S. J. *Modern clinical psychology: Principles of intervention in the clinic and community.* New York: Basic Books, 1976.

Krasner, L. The therapist as a social reinforcement machine. In Strupp, H. H., & Luborsky, L. (Eds.), *Research in psychotherapy, Volume II.* Proceedings of the 2nd Conference on Research in Psychotherapy. Chapel Hill, N.C.: University of North Carolina, 1961.

Lambert, M. J. Psychotherapy outcome research. *American Psychologist,* 1979, *34,* 91.

Landman, J. T., & Dawes, R. M. Psychotherapy outcome: Smith and Glass' conclusions stand up under scrutiny. *American Psychologist,* 1982, *37,* 504–516.

Langer, E. *The psychology of control.* Beverly Hills, Calif.: Sage, 1983.

Lasch, C. *The culture of narcissism.* New York: Norton, 1978.

Lazarus, A. A. Broad spectrum behavior therapy and the treatment of agoraphobics. *Behaviour research and therapy,* 1966, *4,* 95–97.

Lazarus, A. A. *Behavior therapy and beyond.* New York: McGraw-Hill, 1971.

Lazarus, A. A. Multimodal behavior therapy: Treating the BASIC ID. *Journal of nervous and mental disease,* 1973, *156,* 404–411.

Lazarus, A. A. *Multimodal behavior therapy.* New York: Springer, 1976.

Lazarus, A. A. A matter of emphasis. *American Psychologist,* 1979, *34,* 100.

Lazarus, A. A. *The practice of multimodal therapy: Systematic, comprehensive and effective psychotherapy.* New York: McGraw-Hill, 1981.

Leedy, J. J., & Reiter, S. Poetry therapy. In Herink, R., *The psychotherapy handbook.* New York: New American Library, 1980.

Lefcourt, H. The illusion of freedom and control. *American Psychologist,* 1973, *28,* 417–425.

Levis, D., & Malloy, P. F. Research in infrahuman and human conditioning. In Wilson, G. T., & Franks, C. M. (Eds.), *Contemporary behavior therapy.* New York: Guilford, 1982.

Lieberman, M. A., & Gardner, J. R. Institutional alternatives to psychotherapy: A study of growth center users. *Archives of General Psychiatry,* 1976, *33,* 157–162.

Lindsley, O. R., Skinner, B. F., & Solomon, H. C. *Studies in behavior therapy.* Status report 1. Waltham, Mass.: Metropolitan State Hospital (as reported by Rachman & Wilson), 1980.

Lippman, W. *A preface to morals.* New York: Macmillan, 1929.

London, P. *The modes and morals of psychotherapy* (1st Ed.). New York: Holt, Rinehart & Winston, 1964.

London, P. The end of ideology in behavior modification. *American Psychologist,* 1972, *27,* 913–920.

London, P. The future of psychotherapy. *Hastings Center Report,* 1973, *3*(6) (December).

London, P. The psychotherapy boom. *Psychology Today,* 1974, *8,* 62–68.

London, P. *Behavior control* (Rev. Ed.). New York: New American Library, 1977.

London, P. The moral dilemma of military psychology. *Hastings Center Report,* December 1979, 42–44.

London, P. Review of *The powers of psychiatry* by J. Robitscher. *Psychiatry,* 1981, *44,* 377–379.

London, P. Science, culture and psychotherapy: The state of the art. In Rosenbaum, M., Franks, C. M., & Jaffe, Y. (Eds.), *Perspectives on behavior therapy in the eighties.* New York: Springer, 1983a.

London, P. Ecumenism in psychotherapy. Review of Goldfried, M. R. (Ed.), *Converging themes in psychotherapy. Contemporary Psychology,* 1983b, *28,* 507–508.

London, P. Behavior therapy grows a belly. *Contemporary Psychology,* 1984, *29,* 376–378.

London, P., Englehardt, H. T., Jr., & Newman, R. G. Fear of flying: The psychiatrist's role in war. In Levine, C., & Veatch, R. M. (Eds.), *Cases in bioethics from the Hastings Center Report.* Hastings-on-Hudson, N.Y.: Institute of Society, Ethics and the Life Sciences, 1982.

London, P., & Engstrom, D. R. Mind over pain. *American Health,* September/ October 1982, *4,* 62–67.

London, P., & Klerman, G. L. Evaluating psychotherapy. *American Journal of Psychiatry,* 1982, *139,* 709–717.

Lovaas, O. I. *The autistic child.* New York: Irvington, 1977.

Lovaas, O. I. Parents as therapists. In M. Rutter & E. Schopler (Eds.), *Autism: A reappraisal of concepts and treatment.* New York: Plenum, 1978.

Lovaas, O. I., Ackerman, A. B., & Taubman, M. T. An overview of behavioral treatment of autistic persons. In Rosenbaum, M., Franks, C. M., & Jaffe, Y. (Eds.), *Perspectives on behavior therapy in the eighties.* New York: Springer, 1983.

Lowen, A. *The betrayal of the body.* New York: Collier Books, 1969.

Luborsky, L. *Principles of psychoanalytic psychotherapy: A manual for supportive-expressive treatment.* New York: Basic Books, 1984.

Mahoney, M. J. Cognitive-behavioral therapies. In Herink, R., *The psychotherapy handbook.* New York: New American Library, 1980.

Maliver, B. *The encounter game.* New York: Stein & Day, 1973.

Marcuse, H. *Eros and civilization: A philosophical inquiry into Freud.* Boston: Beacon, 1962.

Marcuse, H. *One-dimensional man: Studies in the ideology of advanced industrial society.* Boston: Beacon, 1966.

Marin, P. The new narcissism: The trouble with the human potential movement. *Harper's,* 1975, *251,* 45–56.

Marks, I. Behavioral psychotherapy of adult neurosis. In Garfield, S. L., & Bergin, A. E. (Eds.), *Handbook of psychotherapy and behavior change: An empirical analysis* (2nd ed.). New York: Wiley, 1978.

Marks, I. Behavioral concepts and treatment of neuroses. In Rosenbaum, M., Franks, C. M., & Jaffe, Y. (Eds.), *Perspectives on behavior therapy in the eighties.* New York: Springer, 1983.

Marmor, J., & Woods, S. M. (Eds.). *The interface between the psychodynamic and behavioral therapies.* New York: Plenum, 1980.

Maslow, A. *Motivation and personality.* New York: Harper, 1954.

May, R. *Man's search for himself.* New York: Norton, 1953.

May, R. (Ed.). *Existential psychology.* New York: Random House, 1961.

McGlashan, T. H., & Miller, G. H. The goals of psychoanalysis and psychoanalytic psychotherapy. *Archives of General Psychiatry,* 1982, *39,* 377–388.

Mead, G. H. Language and the development of the self. In C. W. Morris (Ed.), *Mind, self and society.* Chicago: University of Chicago, 1934.

Meador, B. D., & Rogers, C. R. Person-centered therapy. In Corsini, R. J. (Ed.), *Current psychotherapies* (2nd Ed.). Itasca, Ill.: Peacock, 1979.

Meichenbaum, D. *Cognitive behavior modification: An integrative approach.* New York: Plenum, 1977.

Meichenbaum, D., & Cameron, R. Cognitive-behavior therapy. In Wilson, G. T., & Franks, C. M. (Eds.), *Contemporary behavior therapy: Conceptual and empirical foundations.* New York: Guilford, 1982.

Mellinger, G. R., Balter, M. B., Uhlenhuth, E. H., Cisin, I. H., Manheimer, D. I., & Rickels, K. Evaluating a household survey measure of psychic distress. *Psychological Medicine,* 1983, *13,* 607–621.

Menninger, K. *Theory of psychoanalytic technique.* Menninger Clinic Monograph Series No. 12. New York: Basic Books, 1958.

Messer, S. B., & Winokur, M. Some limits to the integration of psychoanalytic and behavior therapy. *American Psychologist,* 1980 (September), *35*(9), 818–827.

Mowrer, O. H. *Learning theory and personality dynamics.* New York: Ronald, 1950.

Mowrer, O. H. *The crisis in psychiatry and religion.* Princeton, N.J.: Van Nostrand, 1961.

Mowrer, O. H. Payment or repayment? The problem of private practice. *American Psychologist,* 1963, *18,* 577–580.

Mowrer, O. H. *The new group therapy.* Princeton, N.J.: Van Nostrand Reinhold, 1964.

Mowrer, O. H. Integrity groups: Basic principles and procedures. *The Counselling Psychologist,* 1972, *3,* 7–32.

Mowrer, O. H. Integrity groups. In Herink, R. (Ed.), *The psychotherapy handbook.* New York: New American Library, 1980.

Mowrer, O. H., Vattano, A. J., Baxley, G., & Mowrer, M. *Integrity groups: The loss and recovery of community.* Urbana, Ill.: Integrity Groups, 1975.

Mullahy, P. *Oedipus myth and complex: A review of psychoanalytic theory.* New York: Hermitage, 1948.

Munroe, R. L. *Schools of psychoanalytic thought.* New York: Holt, 1955.

Murphy, G. *Human potentialities.* New York: Basic Books, 1958.

Murray, E. J. A content-analysis method for studying psychotherapy. *Psychological Monographs,* 1956, *70.*

Norcross, J. C., & Prochaska, J. O. A national survey of clinical psychologists: Characteristics and activities. *Clinical Psychologist,* 1982, *35,* 1–9.

O'Connell, W. E. Natural high therapy. In Herink, R., *The psychotherapy handbook.* New York: New American Library, 1980.

Office of Technology Assessment. *The implications of cost-effectiveness analysis of medical technology.* Background paper No. 3, *The efficacy and cost effectiveness of psychotherapy.* Washington, D.C.: U.S. Government Printing Office, 1980. (Stock No. 052-003-00783-5)

Parloff, M. B. Shopping for the right therapy. *Saturday Review,* February 1976, pp. 14–20.

Parloff, M. B. Can psychotherapy research guide the policymaker? A little knowledge may be a dangerous thing. *American Psychologist,* 1979, *34,* 296–306.

Parloff, M. B. Psychotherapy research evidence and reimbursement decisions: Bambi meets Godzilla. *American Journal of Psychiatry,* 1982, *139,* 718–727.

Parloff, M. B. Psychotherapy: It works, but why? Invited address to the American Association for the Advancement of Science, May, 1983.

Parloff, M. B. Psychotherapy outcome research. In Cavenar, O. J., & Michels, R. (Eds.), *Psychiatry: A loose-leaf text.* Philadelphia: Lippincott, 1985.

Parloff, M. B., Goldstein, N., & Iflund, B. Communication of values and therapeutic change. *Archives of General Psychiatry,* 1960, *2,* 300–304.

Parloff, M. B., Iflund, B., & Goldstein, N. Communications of "therapy values" between therapist and schizophrenic patients. Paper read at the American Psychiatric Association annual meeting. Chicago, Ill., May 13–17, 1957.

Parrish, L. Cooking as therapy. In Herink, R., *The psychotherapy handbook.* New York: New American Library, 1980.

Paul, G. L., & Lentz, R. J. *Psychosocial treatment of chronic mental patients: Milieu versus social learning programs.* Cambridge, Mass.: Harvard University, 1977.

Paul, W., Weinrich, J. D., Gonsoriek, J. C., & Hotvedt, M. E. *Homosexuality: Social, psychological and biological issues.* Beverly Hills, Calif.: Sage, 1982.

Perls, F. S. *Gestalt therapy verbatim.* New York: Bantam, 1969.

Perls, F. S., Hefferline, R. F., & Goodman, P. *Gestalt therapy: Excitement and growth in the human personality.* (2d ed.). New York: Dell, 1951, 1965.

Rachman, S. J. *The effects of psychotherapy.* Oxford, U.K.: Pergamon, 1971.

Rachman, S., & Wilson, G. T. *The effects of psychological therapy.* Oxford: Pergamon, 1980.

Raimy, V. C. (Ed.). *Training in clinical psychology.* Englewood Cliffs, N.J.: Prentice-Hall, 1950.

Reich, W. *Character analysis* (3rd ed.). New York: Farrar, Straus, 1961.

Relf, P. D. Horticultural therapy. In Herink, R., *The psychotherapy handbook.* New York: New American Library, 1980.

Rice, L. N. The evocative function of the therapist. In Wexler, D. A., & Rice, L. N. (Eds.), *Innovations in client-centered therapy.* New York: Wiley, 1974.

Rice, L. N., & Greenberg, L. S. (Eds.). *Patterns of change: Intensive analysis of psychotherapy process.* New York: Guilford, 1983.

Richter, C. On the phenomenon of sudden death in animals and men. *Psychosomatic Medicine,* 1957, *19,* 193–198.

Rieff, P. *Freud: The mind of the moralist* (Rev. Ed.). New York: Anchor Doubleday, 1961a.

Rieff, P. A schema of therapeutic types. Unpublished paper delivered at a symposium of the American Psychological Association, N.Y., September 1961b.

Rieff, P. *The triumph of the therapeutic: Uses of faith after Freud.* New York: Harper & Row, 1966.

Rieff, P. *Fellow teachers.* New York: Harper & Row, 1973.

Riesman, D., Glazer, N., & Denney, R. *The lonely crowd: A study of the changing American character.* New Haven: Yale University, 1950.

Robitscher, J. *The powers of psychiatry.* Boston: Houghton-Mifflin, 1980.

Rogers, C. R. *Counseling and psychotherapy.* Boston: Houghton-Mifflin, 1942.

Rogers, C. R. *Client-centered therapy: Its current practice, implications, and theory.* Boston: Houghton-Mifflin, 1951.

Rogers, C. R. *On encounter groups.* New York: Harper & Row, 1970.

Rogers, C. R. Remarks on the future of client-centered therapy. In Wexler, D. A., & Rice, L. N. (Eds.), *Innovations in client-centered therapy.* New York: Wiley, 1974.

Rogers, C. *Carl Rogers on personal power.* New York: Delacorte, 1977.

Rosenthal, R. Assessing the statistical and social importance of the effects of psychotherapy. *Journal of Consulting and Social Psychology,* 1983, *51,* 4–13.

Rosenthal, R., & Rubin, D. B. A simple, general purpose display of magnitude of experimental effect. *Journal of Educational Psychology,* 1982, *74,* 166–169.

Rosenthal, T. L. Social learning theory. In Wilson, T. G., & Franks, C. M. (Eds.), *Contemporary behavior therapy: Conceptual and empirical foundations.* New York: Guilford Press, 1982.

Rosenzweig, S. Some implicit common factors in diverse methods of psychotherapy. *American Journal of Orthopsychiatry,* 1936, *6,* 412–415.

Rotter, J. B. Analysis of trends in clinical psychology. In Koch, S. (Ed.), *Psychology: A study of a science.* Vol. 5. New York: McGraw-Hill, 1963.

Rubinstein, E., & Parloff, M. B. (Eds.), *Research in psychotherapy,* Volume I. Washington, D.C.: American Psychological Association, 1959.

Ruitenbeek, H. M. *The new group therapies.* New York: Avon, 1970.

Rush, A. J. Cognitive therapy. In Herink, R. (Ed.), *The psychotherapy handbook.* New York: New American Library, 1980.

Seligman, M. E. P. *Learned helplessness.* San Francisco, Calif.: Freeman, 1975.

Shapiro, D. A., & Shapiro, D. Comparative therapy outcome research: Methodological implications of meta-analysis. *Journal of Consulting and Clinical Psychology,* 1983, *51,* 42–53.

Sherrington, C. *Man on his nature.* Baltimore, Md.: Penguin, 1940.

Shipler, D. K. The other Israeli casualties: The mentally scarred. *New York Times,* January 8, 1983.

Skinner, B. F. *Walden Two.* New York: Macmillan, 1948.

Skinner, B. F. Behaviorism at fifty. *Science,* 1983, *140,* 951–958.

Skinner, B. F. *Beyond freedom and dignity.* New York: Knopf, 1971.

Skinner, B. F. *About behaviorism.* New York: Random House, 1974.

Smith, M. L., & Glass, G. V. Meta-analysis of psychotherapy outcome studies. *American Psychologist,* 1977, *32,* 752–760.

Smith, M. L., Glass, G. V., & Miller, T. I. *The benefits of psychotherapy.* Baltimore, Md.: Johns Hopkins, 1980.

Snow, C. P. *The two cultures and the scientific revolution.* New York: Cambridge University, 1959.

Solomon, R. L., Kamin, L. J., & Wynne, L. C. Traumatic avoidance learning: The outcomes of several extinction procedures with dogs. *Journal of Abnormal and Social Psychology*, 1953, *48*, 291–302.

Stampfl, T. G., & Levis, D. J. Essentials of implosive therapy: A learning-theory-based psychodynamic behavioral therapy. *Journal of Abnormal Psychology*, 1967, *92*, 496–503.

Stolz, S. B., & Associates. *Ethical issues in behavior modification*. San Francisco: Jossey-Bass, 1978.

Strupp, H. Patient-doctor relationships: The psychotherapist in the therapeutic process. In Bachrach, A. J. (Ed.), *Experimental foundations of clinical psychology*. New York: Basic Books, 1962.

Strupp, H. H., & Binder, J. L. *Psychotherapy in a new key: A guide to time-limited dynamic psychotherapy*. New York: Basic Books, 1984.

Strupp, H. H., Hadley, S. W., & Gomes-Schwartz, B. *Psychotherapy for better or worse: The problem of negative effects*. New York: Jason Aronson, 1977.

Sundland, D. M., & Barker, E. N. The orientations of psychotherapists. *Journal of Consulting Psychology*, 1962, *26*, 201–212.

Tolman, E. C. *Purposive behavior in animals and men*. New York: Century, 1932.

Truax, C. B. Reinforcement and nonreinforcement in Rogerian psychotherapy. *Journal of Abnormal Psychology*, 1966, *71*, 1–9.

Vattano, A. J. Integrity groups. In Corsini, R. J., *Handbook of innovative psychotherapies*. New York: Wiley Interscience, 1981.

Wachtel, P. L. *Psychoanalysis and behavior therapy: Toward an integration*. New York: Basic Books, 1977.

Watson, P. *War on the mind: The military uses and abuses of psychology*. New York: Basic Books, 1978.

Weinstock, H. I. Summary and final report of the central factgathering committee of the American Psychoanalytic Association (mimeo). January 1958.

Wexler, D. A. A cognitive theory of experiencing, self-actualization, and therapeutic process. In Wexler, D. A., & Rice, L. N. (Eds.), *Innovations in client-centered therapy*. New York: Wiley, 1974.

Wexler, D. A., & Rice, L. N. (Eds.). *Innovations in client-centered therapy*. New York: Wiley, 1974.

White, T. H. *The once and future king*. New York: Putnam, 1958.

Wilson, T. G. Adult disorders. In T. G. Wilson & C. M. Franks, (Eds.). *Contemporary behavior therapy: Conceptual and empirical foundations*. New York: Guilford, 1982.

Wilson, T. G., & Rachman, S. J. Meta-analysis and the evaluation of psychotherapy outcome: Limitations and liabilities. *Journal of Consulting and Clinical Psychology*, 1983, *51*, 54–64.

Wolfe, B. E. Moral transformations in psychotherapy. In R. Stern, L. S. Horowitz, & J. Lynes (Eds.), *Science and psychotherapy*. New York: Raven, 1977, 177–189.

Wolfe, B. The cultural context of psychotherapy. Unpublished manuscript, 1977. (Available from the National Institute of Mental Health, Parklawn Building, 5600 Fishers Lane, Rockville Md. 20857.)

Wolpe, J. Reciprocal inhibition as the main basis of psychotherapeutic effects. *A.M.A. Archives of Neurology and Psychiatry,* 1954, *72,* 205–226.

Wolpe, J. *Psychotherapy by reciprocal inhibition.* Stanford, Calif.: Stanford University, 1958.

Wolpe, J. Unpublished paper delivered at a symposium of the American Psychological Association, New York, September 1961.

Wolpe, J. Cognition and causation in human behavior and its therapy. *American Psychologist,* 1978, *33,* 437–446.

Wolpe, J. *The practice of behavior therapy* (3rd Ed.). New York: Pergamon, 1982.

Wolpe, J., & Rachman, S. Psychoanalytic "evidence": A critique based on Freud's case of Little Hans. *Journal of Nervous and Mental Disease,* 1960, *131,* 135–148.

Yalom, I. D. *Existential psychotherapy.* New York: Basic Books, 1980.

Index